Understanding
Liberal Democracy

Understanding Liberal Democracy

BARRY HOLDEN
University of Reading

Philip Allan

OXFORD AND NEW JERSEY

First published 1988 by

PHILIP ALLAN PUBLISHERS LIMITED
MARKET PLACE
DEDDINGTON
OXFORD OX5 4SE (UK)
and
171 FIRST AVENUE
ATLANTIC HIGHLANDS
NEW JERSEY 07716 (USA)

© Barry Holden, 1988
All rights reserved

British Library Cataloguing in Publication Data

Holden, Barry
  Understanding liberal democracy.
  1. Political ideologies: Liberation. Theories
  I. Title
  320.5′1

Library of Congress Cataloging in Publication Data

Holden, Barry.
  Understanding liberal democracy.
  Bibliography: p.
  Includes index.
  1. Democracy. I. Title.
JC423.H7444 1988 321.8 88-10511

ISBN 0-86003-405-4
ISBN 0-86003-705-3 (pbk)

Typeset in 10/12 Baskerville by The Alden Press, London.
Printed and bound in Great Britain by The Alden Press, Oxford.

To Barbara

Contents

Preface

Liberal democracy and its associated ideas are central to thought about politics, at least in the West. Up to a point these ideas are reasonably clear and we operate with them readily enough. However, difficulties lurk only just beneath the surface and they frequently cause trouble for the unwary. This may happen under the pressure of criticism, but even without it trouble is bound to be encountered at some point. It is hoped this book will be of help in such cases. It is written with the conviction that liberal democracy is insufficiently understood and its importance not widely enough realised. Indeed, the two are related; a prime reason for the failure to appreciate properly the importance of liberal democracy is a lack of understanding of its nature.

Insufficient understanding can be harmful in several ways. It can lead to lack of concern with liberal democracy because it is taken for granted by those who benefit from it. Conversely, attempts to understand it might breed confusion and withdrawal of interest. Inadequate understanding of liberal democracy can also foster or allow attacks upon it by those who mistake its nature.

One of the most potent sources of confusion is the matter of definition. What *does* 'liberal democracy' mean? This is the subject of the first chapter, where it is argued, among other things, that although there are some complexities, finding an answer to this question is not nearly as difficult as is often supposed.

More substantial as a source of confusion has been the existence of different interpretations, ideas and principles connected with the general notion of liberal democracy. There are differing traditional theories, and there are modern theories. There are theories which may or may not be counted as being about liberal democracy; and there are allegedly democratic theories which clearly challenge it. We hope to bring some order and clarity to these matters in Chapter 2.

In Chapter 3 we turn to the 'radical critique' of liberal democracy.

It is important to grasp what this is about not least because understanding it further enhances our understanding of liberal democracy itself. Basic conceptions of liberal democratic theory are sometimes attacked in this sort of critique. But an important theme – even, to a considerable extent, in Marxist criticism – is one that involves acceptance of some of these ideas. What is then attacked is the failure of systems that claim to be liberal democracies to embody them. We shall be concerned to appraise this sort of attack critically, in both Chapters 3 and 4.

In Chapter 4 we focus on the justification of liberal democracy. Is it a good – indeed, the best – system of government; and, if so, why? We look at the main sorts of argument advanced on its behalf and ask whether they are applicable generally, or only to the 'developed' world.

In the Conclusion we shall again highlight the importance of our subject. And it is, indeed, hoped that this book contributes to the understanding necessary for a proper appreciation of the importance of liberal democracy and a commitment to it.

I should like to thank those without whom this book would not have been possible. Mrs Pam Tyler first put some draft chapters on the word processor for me. Mrs Margaret Bensley coped incredibly with processing the whole book – typing, re-typing and checking – under very great pressure; I am profoundly grateful. I am also extremely grateful to Dr Christine Howell for preparing the indexes. Finally, I should like to thank my wife, Barbara, who had to put up with the disruption of our normal life whilst this book was being written.

On another note I should like to honour the memory of my sister, Mrs Jean Merriton, who was notable in the practice of liberal democracy and to whom I owe a great deal.

1
What is Liberal Democracy?

This chapter discusses the general nature of liberal democracy. We begin with the question of definition, first of 'democracy' and then of 'liberal democracy'. This paves the way for an analysis of the relationships among the three central ideas of democracy, liberty and equality. There follows an Appendix on 'majority rule', a subject central to the consideration of the nature of liberal democracy. But it is a large one; moreover, it leads into associated topics which become quite complex. Space forbids a full analysis but the Appendix emphasises the main issues and gives guidance on further reading.

1.1 Defining 'Democracy'

It is usually helpful to begin an analysis by defining that which is to be analysed. However, in the case of democracy (and, indeed, of liberal democracy), definition presents key difficulties that we should consider first before a definition is offered. There will then be a brief discussion of problems which arise out of that definition.

The definition of 'democracy' is frequently held to be controversial. We shall argue in a moment that the problems are not as great as is often supposed; but some undoubtedly do exist.

To begin with, it is difficult to define any word used, often casually, in widely varying circumstances. This is particularly true of words, such as 'democracy', which are applied to political systems – entities that are themselves complex and about which thinking is often vague and confused.

There are also problems specific to 'democracy'. Let us begin with one that can be disposed of quickly. It arises from a historical change of meaning. At least until the end of the eighteenth century the use of the term 'democracy' was restricted to forms that would now be called 'direct democracy'. Today, however, both direct and indirect representative forms are clearly included in the meaning (direct and indirect democracy are considered in the next chapter).

Another difficulty arises from the fact that democracy is now approved of almost universally. This was not so prior to the end of the First World War, but today few people would admit to thinking that democracy is a bad thing. There is thus a tendency to call a system 'democratic' simply because we approve of it. When we do this, however, we convey information only about our views, not about the system itself. When this happens, it has been said, 'democracy' becomes merely a 'hurrah! word' (meaning 'hurrah! for this political system'), emptied of all descriptive meaning. Now, it can be maintained that this happens less than is often supposed, and that when it does, the word 'democracy' is being *mis*used (it will be argued below that 'democracy' does have a correct use and an identifiable meaning). In this way, such difficulties are not with the meaning of the word itself but with its misuses. Misuse, though, can breed confusion. Moreover, this kind of confusion is associated with another, to which we shall now turn.

It is fairly commonly held that 'democracy' is a term applied so widely that it has become vague to the point of meaninglessness. Nearly every form of organisation in the political (and not only the political) sphere has been called 'a democracy' or 'democratic'. Most notoriously, political systems as different as those of the United Kingdom and the United States on the one hand, and the Soviet Union on the other, are spoken of as democracies.

Now, some of the issues raised here constitute genuine difficulties. Nonetheless the difficulties do not have the character or seriousness that is often supposed, and there is a good deal of misunderstanding of them. The fundamental point is that the disagreement involved in – and the difference in meaning implied by – the 'indiscriminate use' of the word 'democracy' is far less than at first appears. Disagreement about the *application* of the word need not involve disagreement about its *meaning*: it usually reflects disagreement about the things to which it is applied. When both the USA and the USSR are called 'democracies' this usually implies differing judgements about the nature of their respective political systems. An American and a Russian could agree that 'democracy' meant, say, 'government by the people'; but they might well disagree about whether government by the people actually existed in one or other (or either) of the political systems.[1] To put the point another way, Western liberal democrats will vehemently disagree with anyone who calls the USSR a democracy precisely because they do know what such a person means: they know that it is being asserted that in the USSR there is government by the people, and they maintain that this assertion is false. If the word 'democracy' were meaningless they would not know what the assertion was and therefore could not maintain that it was false.

Sources of Confusion

The meaning of 'democracy', then, is much less vague than is often supposed. The failure to realise this is usually due to a failure to recognise the distinction between *defining characteristics* and *necessary conditions*. A defining characteristic of an object, we can say, is one by virtue of which a word is correctly applied to that object; a necessary condition, on the other hand, is something that must be present in order for the object to exist or to continue to exist. For example, the presence of wings is a defining characteristic of butterflies – the meaning of the word 'butterfly' is such that it could not be correctly applied to a creature without wings. The presence of a certain degree of warmth, however, is a necessary condition for the existence of butterflies. The difference here is clear; and disagreement about necessary conditions (alleged observations of butterflies in polar regions or the possible evolution of a new cold-climate species might be cited) implies no disagreement about the definition of the term 'butterfly'. In the case of 'democracy', however, confusion can become rife: disputes about necessary conditions can *seem* as if they are disputes about defining characteristics. But once the true nature of such disputes is recognised, no disagreement about definition remains. For example, disagreement about whether democracy requires a certain degree of popular participation might appear to be disagreement about defining characteristics. But this need not be so: such disagreement may well be about whether democracy can exist – or continue to exist – in the absence of such a degree of participation (where there is in fact agreement on what democracy *is* when it *does* exist).[2]

Many so-called disputes about the definition of 'democracy' turn out, then, to be disputes about something else. There is in fact almost universal agreement about the definition – and hence the meaning – of the term, although there is a great deal of disagreement about many other things to do with democracy.

Finally, one last potent source of confusion should be highlighted. This is what can be called the 'definitional fallacy'. In essence it is the fallacy of believing that the meaning of 'democracy' is to be found simply by examining the systems usually called democracies. A common example of this is the idea that if you want to know what democracy is, you simply have a look at the political systems of Britain and America. There are some deep-rooted misconceptions involved here (Holden 1974). Apart from anything else, though, such an idea involves the absurdity of being unable to ask whether Britain and America *are* democracies: if 'democracy' *means*, say, 'like the British political system' we cannot ask if Britain is a democracy. (It is one thing to answer a firm 'yes' to such a question, but it is quite another to imply that such a question does not even make sense.) Unfortunately, this definitional fallacy occurs fairly widely, and breeds further confusion about the meaning of 'democracy'. Besides being an example of sloppy thinking it misleads people into thinking that the definition of 'democracy' requires little reflection, at the same time as providing the wrong answer to the question.

One way of avoiding the definitional fallacy is to view the definition of 'democracy' as the specification of an ideal system. The extent to which actual political systems approach the ideal can then be assessed. Dahl coined the term 'polyarchy' to mean a political system which was democratic to a relatively high degree. No systems could be expected to meet the ideal perfectly, so only polyarchies – and not democracies – exist in the real world (Dahl 1956). Arguably, though, only some *conceptions* (see note 1) are such that democracy is only an ideal. According to the *general concept*, as defined below, there is no special reason to believe that democracy cannot exist (whether, or where, it does so is a matter for separate analysis).

There are, then, various difficulties in the way of defining 'democracy'. Nonetheless, once the nature of these difficulties is properly appreciated they can be avoided and definition becomes relatively straightforward. Despite appearances to the contrary, 'democracy' *does* have one settled primary meaning (although there are also secondary meanings, as will be seen below). Evidence for this is provided, for example, by an exhaustive semantic survey (Christophersen 1966). There is broad agreement about the general area of meaning covered by the term and it can be fairly readily summed up in a definition.

The Definition

The word 'democracy' was first used in the fifth century BC by the Greek historian Herodotus; it combined the Greek words *demos*, meaning 'the people', and *kratein*, meaning 'to rule'. Abraham Lincoln's famous definition of 'democracy' was 'government of the people, by the people, for the people'. Phrases such as 'government by the people' and 'rule by the people' occur very commonly as definitions of 'democracy'. The definition can be made more precise – or more illuminating – by elaborating on the relevant notion of government or rule and assuming that a crucial element in such a notion is the idea of making and implementing decisions. One can also 'cover' certain ambiguities and difficulties by 'escape clauses'. In this way the following definition can be proposed: a democracy is a political system in which the whole people, positively or negatively, make, and are entitled to make, the basic determining decisions on important matters of public policy. We shall end this section by commenting on this definition and on some of the issues it raises (for a fuller discussion see Holden (1974)).

The first comment concerns the specification of 'entitlement' ('the people . . . make, *and are entitled to make*, the basic . . . decisions . . .'). It is this entitlement to, as well as the actuality of, decision making by the people that distinguishes a democracy from, say, a weak or ailing dictatorship. A system in which the ruler gives way to the people's wishes, because of the threat of riot, insurrection or whatever, is one in which the people are making the basic determining decisions. But such a system is not a democracy because the people are not *entitled* to make these decisions. The entitlement referred to comes from a constitution, or other system of basic norms, which *authorises* the making of the basic determining decision by the people. It may not always be obvious what the constitution lays down. It might be argued that in Britain the 'constitution' – if such it can be called – does not of itself authorise decision making by the people. Nonetheless such authorisation is given by widely and strongly held beliefs about the proper functioning of the political system, and these are sustained by, and reflected in, key conventions of the constitution – such as the convention that a government resigns if its party is beaten at a general election.

The converse is equally important. Entitlement alone is not enough: in order to qualify as a democracy the people must *actually* make, as well as being entitled to make, the basic political decisions. It must be recognised that it is possible to ask whether the people actually do make the basic decisions in political systems, such as the British and American, in which there is no doubt that they are entitled to do so, and hence whether they really are democracies. Systems with the forms of democracy are not necessarily democracies.

A second comment concerns the notion of 'basic determining decisions on important matters of public policy'. The phrase 'basic determining decisions' is more or less self-explanatory. The reference is to basic decisions which actually determine courses of events and from which subsidiary decisions and actions flow. To take an example from personal life, a decision to go on holiday which results in a holiday – that is, which results in the actual occurrence of the complex of decisions, actions and events that make up a holiday – could be referred to as a basic determining decision. 'Basic determining decisions on important matters of public policy' are basic political decisions; the significance of the term 'important' will be taken up in a moment. A body which makes such decisions holds supreme political power. Such bodies are often referred to as being sovereign, or as possessing sovereignty. Democracy, indeed, is often characterised as a political system in which the people are sovereign, or in which there is popular sovereignty. There are difficulties with the concept of sovereignty.[3] Not the least of these are the distinctions and overlaps between the ideas of supreme *power* and supreme *authority*[4] which concern the relationship, just discussed, between actually making, and being entitled to make, basic political decisions. Because of these difficulties some have suggested doing away with the concept of sovereignty. But its use is surely too widespread for this to be feasible; certainly the notion of popular sovereignty is very deeply embedded in democratic thought.

The third comment to be made about the proposed definition of 'democracy' relates to the 'escape clauses' used to 'cover' variations of meaning. Thus the phrase 'decisions on *important* matters of public policy' covers a gradation of views about the proper role of popular decision making. At one extreme are conceptions of democracy in which the people make the basic determining decisions on a few salient matters only – essentially on the appointment of governors and the broadest, and only the broadest, of outlines of the policies they are to follow. At the other extreme are conceptions in which – with the aid, perhaps, of devices such as referenda – the people make the basic decisions on all but the most routine of matters. Similarly the phrase 'whether positively or negatively' is used to cover differing notions about the origination of policy. On the one hand there is the 'positive' conception that policy should originate with the people: the notion that the people initiate policy proposals. On the other hand the 'negative' conception sees the people merely responding to policy proposals. Here the idea is that they choose among proposals that are put to them by those who would be their governors: the people then do not initiate policy, they consent to policies that are initiated elsewhere.

The Meaning of 'The People'

The final comment to be made about our proposed definition of 'democracy' concerns 'the people'. This is, of course, a crucial concept. But it is also one which incorporates notions that co-exist only uneasily and which sometimes are in opposition to one another. This gives rise to differing ideas, loosely, though significantly, related together within the concept of the people. We must later look at important contrasts between individualist and corporate conceptions of the people. Here we need to indicate another difference of interpretation, which gives rise to differences of conception which cut across the individualist–corporate distinction. This difference concerns the proportion of a relevant society that is held to be included within the meaning of 'the people', the 'relevant society' in any particular case being the one which is subject to, and delimited by, the state whose democratic nature is being assessed.[5] It might be assumed that all the current members of the relevant society must be included within the people. But straight away the qualification 'all *adult* members' would usually be agreed. In fact the meaning of 'the people' has varied quite widely, and has not always included all adult members.

In ancient Athens, often regarded as the original and archetypal democracy, only a minority of the society was included: aliens, slaves and women were excluded. Women – constituting a good 50 per cent of any relevant society – were given the vote only relatively recently in modern democracies: in 1920 in America, in 1918 (but only in 1928 with the same age qualification as men) in Britain, and as recently as 1971 in Swiss national elections. Again, from Aristotle onwards the term 'the people' has had a sense in which it means 'the poor' or 'the poor people' (in Aristotle's case 'those of the poor who are not aliens, slaves or women'!) This meaning is echoed in those Marxist-Leninist notions where democracy is equated with the dictatorship of the proletariat. (See Chapter 2 below.) It is also reflected in anti-democratic thought, where the people have often been characterised as the mob. By way of contrast, 'the people' sometimes meant the middle classes rather than the poor – the term then being used to refer to those who had a stake in society and were thereby properly members of it, i.e. property owners.[6]

What is the upshot of this variation in meaning? Are political systems with widely differing proportions of society having a share in political power all to be counted as democracies, because different meanings are given to 'the people'? According to Schumpeter, for example, it would seem that more or less any kind of political system in which governmental power depends on winning competitive elections could be counted as a democracy (Schumpeter 1976). Even where there is clearly rule by a minority Schumpeter maintains that is a democracy provided those who hold political power *consider themselves* to constitute 'the people': even South Africa could count as a democracy! This sort of view is surely unacceptable. And yet it would appear difficult to deny that the meaning of 'the people' is an arbitrary matter if one accepts any exclusions. We have already mentioned that the exclusion of non-adults is very commonly accepted. Is this not as arbitrary as counting out any other category – be it women, the rich, the poor, slaves, those with a certain colour of skin, or whatever? The answer to this, it can be argued, is provided by three considerations.

First, there has been a historical change of meaning. The development of democratic theory was tied in with the growth of the demand for universal suffrage. Whatever used to be the case, in democratic thought today 'the people' almost invariably means virtually the whole adult population (and even the democratic status of ancient

Athens itself tends to be queried because of its 'undemocratic' conception of 'the people').

Second, there are good reasons for this change – for this enlargement – of meaning. They are reasons which overlap with the arguments for democracy itself. In essence they are the grounds for the view that as large a proportion as possible of the members of a society should take part in the making of basic political decisions. Essentially, democrats hold that all those who are not obviously unfit to do so should take part in political decision making. Now although Schumpeter, for example, argues that such fitness 'is a matter of opinion and degree' (Schumpeter 1976), the point is that democrats can and do reach some kind of objectively based agreement on this matter. This is reflected in those limits to membership of the people that *are* commonly prescribed, even by democrats: it is generally accepted that there are compelling reasons for not giving the vote to children, the insane and – less certainly – criminals. There are two points to note. The first is that these exclusions reflect very general agreement about what makes some people unfit for political decision making: that they are incapable of the relevant thought processes (criminals are sometimes held to have excluded themselves from the community, but here the agreement is less widespread). Moreover – and this is the crucial point – although there might be some individuals whom all would agree are unfit for political decision making, children and the insane (and possibly criminals) are the only *categories* of individuals about which there is this type of agreement. The second point to note is that a dispute about the precise *location* of the boundary of a category does not imply dispute about it as a category of individuals to be excluded. Disagreement about how much 'irrationality' constitutes insanity, and what age marks the beginning of adulthood – 18, 21 or whatever – does not call into question agreement about the exclusion of the insane and children from political decision making. No one would give the vote to three-year-olds.

The third consideration behind the view that the democratic conception of 'the people' is non-arbitrary and legitimate is more complex. But let us put the matter as simply as possible. In liberal democratic theory conceptions of 'the people' are generally 'individualist'. We shall be discussing this later, but the key point is that according to such conceptions 'the people' means simply a collection of individuals, and this is all it can mean. The question then arises: which individuals? And some are excluded – as we have just seen.

However, 'corporate' conceptions of the people also exist. Here the people is a corporate entity equivalent to, having the same 'boundaries' as, the relevant society. As such the people is a body consisting not only of the individual members of a society at a particular moment in time, but also of the past and future members; as well as the institutions, structures and culture within which such individuals find themselves. Just as, say, a regiment consists of more than the individuals who happen to be serving in it at any particular time: its past and future membership and its history, traditions, customs and so on are crucial features of its existence. Indeed, how else could you distinguish it *as* a regiment or as a particular regiment? Now, since such corporate conceptions of the people embrace the whole of society, all individuals within a society at any particular time tend automatically to be included. These conceptions occur outside liberal democratic theory. Non-liberal democratic theory contains such conceptions – see Chapter 2 – and they also occur within non- or anti-democratic theory. But the point is that they can be combined with the idea that supreme authority resides in the people. In contrast to the liberal democratic idea, however, it is not then held that this supreme authority entitles the people to make policy decisions. Rather the people's authority confers legitimacy on those who do make decisions. Decision-makers symbolically represent[7] the people perhaps – as in some medieval conceptions of kingship. Since there is no question of decisions being made by the people, the question of fitness for decision making does not arise and all individuals can quite happily be included within the conception of 'the people'. Here, then, is a concept of 'the people' as possessing supreme authority and quite clearly including all individuals within its meaning. True, this concept is not part of democratic or, at any rate, liberal democratic theory; but, because of the shared idea of supreme authority, it influences concepts within democratic theory. And it tends to legitimise the most inclusive notions of the proportion of individuals that are to be counted as an integral part of 'the people'.

The dominant meaning of 'the people', then, in the definition of 'democracy' includes all – or virtually all – the adult population. But we should recognise that there is also a secondary meaning. The notion of 'the people' meaning 'the poor people' has been referred to already. It has been so persistent, however, that this idea of 'the common people' must be regarded as a meaning – albeit a subsidiary one – in its own right, as in the expression 'a man of the people'.

The Subsidiary Meaning of 'Democracy'

Before we leave the definition of 'democracy' we should note that, as in the case of 'the people', the term 'democracy' has a subsidiary meaning, as well as the dominant meaning with which we have so far been concerned. We shall see shortly that there are close connections between democracy, in the dominant sense, and equality. But apart from this – or rather, as a development of it – there is a subsidiary meaning of 'democracy' according to which a democracy is necessarily a society in which there is equality. In the dominant sense there is, arguably, the *implication* that equality will exist in a democracy; but in the subsidiary sense the word 'democracy' actually *means* a society in which equality exists. Moreover it is social and economic, and not just political, equality that is meant.

1.2 Defining 'Liberal Democracy'

We have now looked at the definition of 'democracy' and it is time to return to our original concern with the definition of *'liberal* democracy'. We shall be looking at the relationships between liberty, democracy and equality shortly, and the contrasts between liberal and non-liberal forms of democracy will be the subject of a section of the next chapter, so only a brief word is necessary here. We shall focus on two main points.

The first is that defining 'liberal democracy' is complicated by the effects of differing political viewpoints. This is over and above any analogous difficulties affecting the definition of 'democracy' itself. Thus liberal democrats – those who think liberal democracy to be the best kind of political system – tend to the view that a liberal democracy is the *only* kind of democracy possible. Other types of political system that might claim to be democracies are viewed as bogus, the contention being that they are not democracies at all. For the liberal democrats' critics, on the other hand, it is liberal democracy that is bogus: 'liberal democratic' regimes are dismissed as shams which disguise the existence of undemocratic social and political forms. Aspects of the important issues raised here will be discussed later, but it can already be seen how the existence of these differing viewpoints complicates the relationship between the meanings of 'democracy' and 'liberal democracy'.

The second point is that in so far as the term 'liberal democracy' is seen as a qualification of – rather than as a synonym for – 'democracy', it can refer to democracy of a limited kind. However this is not always too clear, since, as we have seen, many liberal democrats for much of the time treat liberal democracy as the same thing as democracy. In their more reflective moments, though, or when issues arise involving individual liberties and the need to limit the power of government, most liberal democrats will acknowledge that the two components of 'liberal democracy' can modify each other.

The nub of this point is that the adjective 'liberal' as applied to systems of government classically implies a concern with individual freedoms that centres on the need to limit the power and authority of government. Liberals,[8] from this classical viewpoint, are those who think it desirable that the power and authority of the government should be limited, typically by subjecting the government to regulation by such devices as a written constitution and/or a bill of rights. Viewed in this way, a liberal democrat is therefore one who holds democracy to be the best form of government but believes that even a democratic government should be limited. In a democracy the government expresses the will of the people; but even so, says the liberal democrat, the power of the government should be limited. We shall see that there is also another way of viewing the idea of liberal democracy, where democracy is seen as *necessary* for the realisation of liberal ideals. However, it remains implicit in this view, too, that government in liberal democracy is limited in some important sense; only here the idea is that such limitation is a necessary part of, rather than a restriction placed upon, democracy.

In the classical view 'democracy' refers to the *location* of a state's power,[9] i.e. in the hands of people, whereas 'liberal' refers to the *limitation* of a state's power. From this viewpoint, then, a democracy is a political system in which the people make the basic political decisions, but in which there are limitations on what decisions they can make. More precisely, and referring back to our previous definition of 'democracy', this conception would be that a liberal democracy is a political system in which (a) the whole people positively or negatively, make, and are entitled to make, the basic determining decisions on important matters of public policy; and (b) they make, and are only entitled to make, such decisions in a restricted sphere since the legitimate sphere of public authority is limited. This definition captures the classical notion of liberal democracy but it will need to be modified later when we look more fully at the relationships between liberty and democracy.

There are different theories within liberal political thought about why public authority should be limited. Historically, the two most important have been theories about individual rights and John Stuart Mill's defence of individual liberty (see also Chapter 4 below). Theories of individual rights maintain that individuals have basic rights or entitlements: it is contended that every individual has a fundamental moral right to do as he or she wishes in certain areas of life. The grounds or basis for these rights, following John Locke (1632–1704), were originally seen as being provided by natural law – a universal moral code binding on all men and ultimately ordained by God (see, for example, D'Entreves (1967), Sigmund (1971) and Finnis (1980)). Individuals' rights were therefore called 'natural rights'. This idea has recently had something of a revival, but the term 'human rights' now tends to be used because of doubts about the validity of the idea of natural law. There is still the insistence that *all* individuals, whatever their social or cultural differences, have essential basic human qualities in common by virtue of which they have certain basic rights. (On individual rights see, for example, Raphael (1967), Kamenka and Tay (1978), Tuck (1979), Pennock and Chapman (1981), Campbell (1986) and Lomasky (1987).) The precise extent of the area of individuals' lives that rights theorists maintain should be protected from public authority is subject to some controversy. It is roughly the same as that outlined by John Stuart Mill (1806–73) from a different, utilitarian, theoretical stance, which stresses the fundamental value of individuality. Mill is not apparently a rights theorist,[10] but in his famous essay *On Liberty* (Mill 1982) he proposes a practical principle to define an area of individual liberty: the individual should be left free to do as he wishes in those areas where he does not harm others (on Mill's principle of liberty see, for example, Ten (1980) and Gray (1983)). In modern times John Rawls has based a defence of a similar area of protected individual liberty on a theory of justice (Rawls 1972); see also Chapter 4 below.

Within liberal democratic theory and practice there are different accounts of the ways in which the sphere of public policy should be limited, and of the linkage between these and the types of entitlement by the people to public policy decision making. We cannot go into

these here but a key point to note is that, classically, in a properly
functioning liberal democracy (a) the people do not make decisions in
certain areas, and (b) this is because they are not entitled to make
such decisions. Another important point is that this restriction of
entitlement can be manifested in different forms. Restrictions in the
form of a written constitution and of a bill of rights have already been
mentioned. These are important in the United States, but such
mechanisms reflect basic underlying ideas which can be effective in
themselves if they are widely held. This is arguably the case in the
United Kingdom where there is no written constitution or bill of
rights. Whether restriction is as effective in the United Kingdom, or
whether, on the contrary, the American system is effective only
because the constitutional mechanisms reflect widely held underlying
ideas, raises further matters of controversy.

We have outlined what the notion of liberal democracy amounts to.
However, in order to understand its nature and significance more
fully we need now to look at some of the conceptual issues it generates,
and which can be quite troublesome.

1.3 Three Key Concepts

When we use, or think about, the notion of liberal democracy, tricky
and important questions arise – and need to be answered. We have
already remarked that the notion has component parts which can
differ to a significant extent; and it is from a consideration of this that
the questions arise. They will be discussed in the next three sections.

Our discussion will be limited to the most important of these
questions – those that concern the relationships among the three key
concepts of democracy, liberty and equality. By definition, of course,
the concepts of democracy and liberty have a key role in the notion
of liberal democracy; and we have already said something about their
relationships. Less clear is the part played by the concept of equality.
Nonetheless it, too, is of central importance, not least because of its
role in the tensions between the other two. Equality is closely associated with democracy; and when it is held that there are tensions
between liberty and democracy these are often seen as tensions
between liberty and equality. Let us now look at these matters a little
more closely.

Democracy and Equality

First, how is equality associated with democracy? Determining the meaning of 'equality' is itself a difficult matter, but the basic feature of the concept is clear enough. (On equality see, for example, Williams (1962), Tawney (1964), Pennock and Chapman (1967), Rees (1971), Rae (1981), Norman (1987).) Equality has to do with 'sameness' and its proper recognition: things (persons, groups or whatever) are equal if they are the same in important respects and the principle of equality demands that things which are the same in relevant important respects ought to be treated equally, i.e. in relation to those respects in which they are the same, they ought to be treated in the same way. Of course the terms 'important' and 'relevant respects' highlight the points which give rise to difficulties and controversies. This is not the place to go into such issues, although a consideration of some of their aspects must be included in a discussion of democracy and equality.

The principle of equality has played a central role in the democratic credo. That all men are created equal was the first of the 'self-evident' truths of the American Declaration of Independence. There is in fact a 'double strength' to democrats' typical belief in equality. First, most democrats hold that the principle of equality – in this case the principle that all people should be treated equally – is intrinsically valid. They also hold that the principle is best maintained or promoted in a democracy. A commitment to equality is therefore closely linked with a commitment to democracy (see also Chapter 4 below).

This link is usually tied in with the second element of the bond between equality and democracy: the assumption or contention that equality is implied by the notion of a decision by the people. This flows from liberal democratic theory's 'individualist conception' of the people, already mentioned and further discussed in Chapter 3 below. In this conception the people consist simply of a certain number of individuals. Now, if the people – the *whole* people (i.e. all the people rather than just some of them) – are to make decisions then all the constituent individuals must be involved. This means that each individual must to a crucial extent have an equal say. Anything else would mean, in effect, that decisions were made by a group within – i.e. smaller than – the whole people, namely those individuals with a disproportionately large say. The idea of one person one vote, widely accepted as a distinctive feature of democracy, is a direct reflection of this. (There are two important issues associated with this idea of political equality which will not be taken up for the moment. First, there are the questions that arise from the fact that in liberal democracies there are almost always differences in the way people vote. In what sense, for example, does a person voting with the minority – i.e. voting *against* the decision that prevails – have an equal say? Aspects of the key issues here are discussed in the Appendix to this chapter. Second, apart from these issues there are questions concerning the degree and genuineness of this political equality. For example, does the possession merely of equal voting rights imply or guarantee full equality of political power in any meaningful sense? Questions of this sort are taken up particularly in Chapter 3.)

There is, then, a very strong connection between democracy and equality. So strong is this connection that 'democracy' is sometimes *defined* in terms of political equality. Arguably, though, it is more accurate, and certainly less confusing, to regard political equality as a feature – a desirable feature – that is associated with democracy but one which does not actually form part of the definition. Indeed, the existence of political equality may often be regarded as necessary if a system is to qualify as a democracy – a 'logically necessary condition' (Holden, 1974). But, again, it is helpful to distinguish this from actually regarding political equality as a defining feature. In other words 'democracy' should be *defined* as, say, 'government by the people', or the elaboration of this that has already been suggested, whilst leaving as a separate issue the question of whether, or to what extent, political equality must exist before it can be said that government by the people exists.

Having said this, however, it must be acknowledged (as we have already seen) that there are some instances where equality does feature in the very definition of 'democracy'. Again this is a case of a primary or dominant meaning and secondary or subsidiary ones. 'Government by the people', or an elaboration of this, is the primary meaning, but there are also others. It is true that there is often confusion, and what appear to be other senses of 'democracy' turn out not to be different meanings after all. Nonetheless there are certain usages of 'democracy' persistent and consistent enough for us to say that there are subsidiary meanings, connected though they are with the dominant meaning. There is a sense, then, in which 'democracy' *means* a system in which there is political equality: Tocqueville, for example, often used it in this way.[11] There are also meanings in which other kinds of equality figure. These are sometimes indicated by the terms 'economic democracy' and 'social democracy'. Although sometimes hard to pin down, they mean, roughly speaking, systems or states of affairs in which there is economic and/or social equality, though a distinction is often not drawn between these forms of equality and the two meanings tend to merge.

A matter of considerable importance is the existence of a certain kind of view about the relationship between political and these other kinds of equality. It is quite often held that political equality without economic and/or social equality is a facade, and hence that democracy in the sense defined by or associated with political equality is also a facade. It is contended either that political equality by itself is 'not really' equality, or else that political equality cannot in fact *exist* in the absence of economic and/or social equality. Views of this kind, and the issues raised by them, will be discussed in Chapter 3, and different kinds of equality are further discussed in later sections of this chapter.

The use of the term 'social democracy' – where it is distinguishable from 'economic democracy' – implies the existence of social equality: roughly speaking a classless society, or something approaching it, in which there are few differences in status and/or 'social advantages'. 'Social democracy' can also be used in conjunction with 'democratic socialism'. Here there can be additional elements in its meaning: besides social equality as the desired state of affairs, the term may also refer to ideas concerning the proper means for bringing this about – that is to say, by democratic means rather than by revolution or by imposition from above.

'Economic democracy' is sometimes used to refer to the economic aspects of social equality, i.e. where social equality is held to imply an equality of economic resources. However, it is also frequently used in another sense; a sense in which there are additional connections with the primary meaning of 'democracy'. Used in this way economic equality is taken to imply equality of control over the economy; or at least over those aspects of the economy that most directly affect an individual – such as the conditions of work and the running of the workplace. Such 'equality of control' can be held to imply anything from social mechanisms which do not affect the general framework of the state – primarily increased worker participation or 'industrial democracy' – to anarcho-syndicalism, in which the state is superseded by autonomous units of production under the control of the workers.

Indeed, 'economic democracy' may here be viewed as a special case of the primary meaning of 'democracy': in this case the 'basic determining decisions' are those concerning the running of the economy, and 'the people' are the workers (here we see again the secondary meaning of 'the people'). Economic democracy of this kind may be thought to operate within the state – itself preferably democratic – or, as in anarcho-syndicalism, to supersede the state and its activities. These and related ideas will recur when the Marxist critique of liberal democracy is discussed in Chapter 3.

Democracy and Liberty

Let us now turn to the concept of liberty. The notion of liberal democracy seeks to lock together the two concepts of liberty and democracy. Indeed, they do fit together and reinforce each other to a considerable extent. Nonetheless, we have already seen that liberty and democracy can conflict. We shall now look at this relationship in detail; this will clear the ground for a look at some questions raised by another, although often overlapping relationship, that between liberty and equality.

The matter of definition again raises important issues and controversies. There will be no attempt to cover these here,[12] though some key points will come up in the discussion that follows. To simplify the matter we can say that 'liberty' means freedom in a social context. The term 'individual liberty' then refers to the freedom of individuals with respect to their social – and particularly their political – environment. 'Freedom' we can say means self-determination: the free individual is the one who determines his or her own actions. Differing accounts of freedom arise from differing accounts of the nature of self-determination, the environment of the individual and the ways in which this environment does or does not interfere with individual self-determination.

We have seen that the notion of liberal democracy involves an 'individualist' conception of the people and the point at issue here is the relationship between democracy and individual liberty. Where the 'liberty of the people' as a collective entity is at issue then democracy and liberty largely overlap: the self-determination of the people consists in making its own determining decisions. We shall now turn to a brief examination of the former relationship.

It should be noted that initially we make the key assumption that there is a very close connection between individual liberty and limited government. This assumption will come under fire at various points later on, but for many liberal democrats it appears self-evident. We shall go along with this for the moment and assume that threats to individual liberty come only or mainly from the state or government,[13] and hence that individual liberty exists or is most likely to exist where, and to the extent that, the power of government is limited. Looked at in this way the relationship between individual liberty and democracy is the same as the relationship between limited government and democracy.

Let us turn first to the affinities between liberty and democracy. It is clear that they intermesh in some, important, ways; and we shall now look at some of these. What is not so clear is when, and the extent to which, this is or is not just a matter of the necessary, conceptual links between the two ideas.

One of the most important of these links is central to the distinction, discussed in the next chapter, between liberal and non-liberal ideas of democracy. It concerns fundamental ideas about the way in which the people can make a decision. The central point is that a liberal democrat can make sense of the notion of the people making a decision only where there is freedom to present different viewpoints to the people and where the people are free to make whatever decision they wish. In this way, freedom of speech, organisation and assembly, and so on, are seen as essential if democracy is to exist at all. In other words key individual liberties must necessarily be present in a democracy; whether or not wider individual liberty is safeguard in a democracy will be discussed below.

Another link between liberty and democracy – though not *conceptually* one of the tightest – arises from a tendency to view 'the people' and 'the government' as separate and potentially hostile bodies. This tendency is particularly marked in Anglo-American, as distinct from 'Continental', democratic theory (see Chapter 2 for the nature of this distinction). It can be best understood by contrasting it with the view, more common in Continental democratic theory, which sees the government as the *agent of* the people. In this second view the government is simply the agency through which the people act. It is therefore an integral part of the people; rather as, for example, a pianist's hands are an integral part of the pianist. According to the first view, however, the government is a body separate from the people and one

which governs – 'governs over' – them. Despite the greater importance of one or the other in any particular form of democratic theory,
these different views tend to co-exist – somewhat uneasily – and there
is a tendency to shift back and forth between them, without always
realising that this is being done. The idea of separateness is illustrated
when conceiving the people as being able to act independently of the
government, as when a government is overthrown by the people. This
is an idea which is important in the political philosophy of John
Locke, who holds that the power of the people lies in their right to
revolt against the government if and when it acts improperly by
attacking individuals' fundamental, or natural, rights. Locke is a key
figure in liberal democratic theory (see Chapter 2). However he is a
forerunner rather than a democratic theorist proper; in true democratic theory the sanction of the right to revolt is unnecessary since the
people exercise their power through the ballot box.

Where the government is viewed in this way as a body separate
from, and potentially hostile to, the people, there is a close connection
between liberty and democracy. If the government is 'above' the
people and rules over them, the people themselves have power only
in so far as they limit this other power exerted over them. In the last
resort the people have more power than the government: they are
able to make the *basic* determining decisions. Here the ideas of limiting the power of government, and of the people making the basic
decisions, coalesce; and limited government exists *by virtue of* popular
power. Democratic government *is* limited government and liberty is
necessarily maintained by democracy. It should be realised, though,
that this view rests upon two, related, questionable assumptions both
of which have already been briefly mentioned.

The first assumption is our initial one, that the only really significant threat to liberty comes from the government. A key idea in
classical liberal theory is that although government is necessary – to
protect individuals from invading each other's liberty – it is also itself
a dangerous threat to individual liberty; it is a necessary evil. It is set
up to protect individual liberty; and this it does, so long as it sticks to
its proper limited function. But once set up it has tremendous hostile
potential; the potential to use – to abuse – its power in ways that
invade individual liberty.

The second assumption is that the question of whose liberty is
subject to threat admits to a single, unambiguous, answer: it is simply
the liberty of people. Or, to put the essential point another way, the

assumption is that since the liberty of the people and of the individual are the same thing, then threats to the liberty of the people are necessarily also threats, and are the only threats, to the liberty of the individual. But this is an assumption incompatible with an individualist conception of the people, and what it overlooks is that the individual can also be oppressed by the people. This point will be taken up in a moment.

What of the other view of the relationship between the government and the people? This notion of the government as the agent of, rather than as governing over, the people involves a different conception of the connections between liberty and democracy. This conception, although more typical of Continental theory, is nonetheless of some importance in Anglo-American ideas about democracy. The 'agency' notion is involved to an important extent in the very ideas of state and government and as such is one that everyone tends to use at some time, although they often slip in and out of using it without always realising it.

When this idea is used in democratic theory there is a link between liberty and democracy through the connection between self-government and self-determination: the self-determined – the free – individual is the self-governing individual. Here individual liberty is seen to involve participation in, rather than the absence of, government activity. Individuals are free not just when they are unsubjected to the processes of government but also when they participate in, and thereby help to take charge of, those processes. This idea can also link up with other conceptions of the way in which self-government enhances liberty, which we shall consider when we come to look at liberty and equality.

As noted, 'the self-determination view' can be found in Anglo-American democratic theory. However it is also closely related to, and shades off into, ideas largely alien to this sort of democratic theory – ideas which centre on the 'positive' conception of liberty. This conception is important in Continental democratic theory and is further discussed below. We should note one point here however. This concerns the role of the positive conception in coming to grips with an issue that baffles Anglo-American theory, since 'Anglo-American conceptions' of the link between individual liberty and self-government cannot properly digest and cope with the liberty of the individual being different from the liberty of the people. The positive conception of liberty involves ideas that transcend, and thereby 'solve', what becomes a problem issue in Anglo-American theory, not least because it is often ignored. Where (as in individualist conceptions of the people it must be) the liberty of the individual is something other than the liberty of the people, so the self-government (the self-determination) of the individual is something other than the self-government of the people. It is true, of course, that there are important connections between them. Nonetheless, in the absence of the ideas and theory centred on the positive conception of liberty it cannot be said that each individual determines himself just because the people determine themselves: in a real sense the individual is then governed *by the people*. This point is not properly appreciated – indeed it is often overlooked or not understood at all – when in Anglo-American liberal democratic theory[14] a link is postulated between liberty and democracy via the notion of self-government.

As this example suggests, there are significant tensions within liberal democratic theory. These are the tensions which exist, alongside the close connections, between liberty and democracy. Their basis is to be found in the liberal conception of the opposition between state power and individual liberty, where liberty exists in the silence of the law and to the extent that governmental power is limited. As we have seen, the thought is that state power is necessary to protect individuals from one another, but should be limited to this protective function. Individual liberty consists in the absence of state power: it exists, and exist only, in those areas of life in which the individual is not subject to the power of government.

Now, democracy is a *form of state* – and this is the key point. The basic tension between individual liberty and the state is incorporated even into democracy. We have remarked that the definition of 'democracy' refers to the *location* of power within the state, namely in the hands of the people; but the definition of 'democracy' itself, as distinct from 'liberal democracy', says nothing about the *limitation* of the state's power. It may be assumed that the people would wish to limit the power of government; and if so they would necessarily have the power in a democracy to translate that wish into reality. Such an assumption would, indeed, seem to be inherent in the link between liberty and democracy associated with the first conception of government and people we discussed – where the goverment was seen as separate from and potentially hostile to the people. It is in fact very probable that the people will have a wish to limit the power of government, but it is a mistake to assume that they will not also or at other times have other and incompatible wishes. For example, much of the modern welfare function of government derives from the wish of the people for governments to do things to help them, to provide social security, combat unemployment, etc., rather than to refrain from doing things.

Let us not go too fast, though. Might it not be mistaken to assume the wish for the government to do things implies a decrease in individual liberty or that the people wish for such a decrease? Might not the idea of a government as a separate and potentially hostile body, rather than as an agent, be a mistake? If the government is viewed as the agency through which the people act – and if, in the way already indicated, individual liberty is seen in terms of participation in the governmental process – then positive, interventionist, governmental activity can be seen in a different light. Action by government to do what the people wish can be seen as a component of, not a threat to, liberty.

The Individual and The People

There is, indeed, much in this argument. However, we have already seen how liberal democratic theory typically does not follow it through properly: how it fails to cope with the relationship between the individual and the people. It is true that action by the government to secure benefits desired by the people may be seen as enlarging rather than as restricting their liberty. This, though, is the liberty of *the people*, and it might still involve interfering with the liberty of particular *individuals*, as when the building of motorways which are wanted by the people involves disregarding the wishes of individuals who live near them. Within liberal democratic theory there is so often the tendency to assume that an issue is simply one concerning the relationship between the individual and the government when in fact it may be the relationship between the individual and the people that is crucial.[15]

We can now see that there are two different, but intertwined, threads in the twisting argument about the ways in which liberty can be threatened by democracy. One thread concerns the threat to individual liberty inherent in the institution of the state. Democracy, as a form of state, merely fails to modify the threat: this is not so much a case of democracy being a threat to individual liberty as failing to remove a pre-existing one. The second thread, however, involves a central element of democracy itself. This concerns the way the individual may be oppressed by the mass of the people. Here democracy can amount to an especial threat to individual liberty over and above that already constituted by the state. More accurately, the threat 'already constituted by the state' is made more severe, since it is a case of the state being used by the people: i.e. the people act *through* – their action takes the form of action by – the government.

Let us look just a little more closely at this notion of the individual being subject to oppression by the people (see also the excellent discussion in Dahl (1985)). The key point is that within Anglo-American democratic theory it is not really possible to equate the 'will of the people' with the will of every individual; there are immense problems here – see the discussion of majority rule in the Appendix to this chapter. Within the terms of this type of theory it has to be accepted that it is usual for the wishes, and therefore the wills, of some individuals to clash with those of others. It follows that the 'will of the people' cannot, except in the unlikely case of unanimous agreement, comprehend the will of every individual. Therefore action that implements the people's will must conflict with the wills – and thereby threaten the freedom – of some individuals. This source of conflict between the individual and the people has given rise to three sorts of view of democracy as a threat, actual or potential, to liberty.

First of all there is the majority tyranny argument. Here the focus is on the threat to the liberties of minorities constituted by what is seen as the existence in democracies of rule by the majority. A central feature of much democratic thought has been the idea that since unanimity does not exist the 'will of the people' is in fact the will of the majority of the people (see the Appendix to this chapter). Some have held that this involves actual or potential tyranny by the majority – the minority being ruled despotically by the majority. Madison, Tocqueville and John Stuart Mill feared this; and in recent times Hayek.[16]

Second, there is the idea that the tyranny, actual or potential, is by the many over the single individual, rather than over some particular minority group or groups of individuals. As John Stuart Mill put it, 'the "self-government" spoken of is not the government of each by himself, but of each by all the rest' (Mill 1982). Although it involves conceptions that are alien to individualist liberal democratic theory, there is often a slide from this idea into one which sees the individual as being subject to the corporate people or the society or the community. This involves a move from the notion of one or a few *particular* individual(s) being subject to many other individuals, to the notion of *any* or, indeed, *all* individual(s) being subject to the people or the society or the community. This clearly involves a move to non-individualist ideas and, once again, it is in Continental rather than Anglo-American democratic theory that the adequate conceptions exist. Be that as it may, however, we should also note here that pressure on the individual is seen by some theorists as being exerted directly by the people, as well as via the government. The contention is that public opinion, social convention and so on, as well as laws and other governmental actions, can restrict an individual's liberty. Both John Stuart Mill and, before him, Tocqueville were concerned about this. Tocqueville also argued that the 'atomising' of society into isolated and vulnerable individuals was characteristic of democracy and that this exposed the individuals to oppression.

The third view of how democracy is a threat to liberty arises from a consideration of the special power of popular government. A government whose function is to implement the will of the people can be extremely powerful. This is a development of the point already made about democracy posing an especial threat to individual liberty by making more severe the threat constituted by the state. The focus is on the fact that a democratic government is more threatening, because it is more powerful, than an autocratic government. An autocratic government has only 'its own' power and does not also embody the power of the whole people. Also, although public opinion may shelter dissidents in an autocracy, who is to shelter the dissidents from public opinion itself? An additional, and rather different, argument sometimes creeps in. This relates not so much to democracy as to systems which *purport* to be democracies, but where government may 'get away' with tyranny because people are lulled into a false sense of security by the thought that their government is democratic. 'Every man allows himself to be put in leading strings, because he sees that it is not a person or a class of persons, but the people at large, that holds the end of his chain. By this system the people shake off their state of dependence just long enough to select their master, and then relapse into it again.' (Tocqueville 1968)

In the face of these various arguments and ideas suggesting a hostility between liberty and democracy one cannot simply be content with the notion that there are some inherent or 'natural' connections between the two conceptions. It would, indeed, seem more satisfactory to maintain that for a democracy to be a liberal democracy there should exist at least some of the traditional liberal limitations upon government. If this is seen as a limitation of democracy – since it is a limitation of the instrument of the people's will – then so be it. This simply shows that liberal democracy is an amalgam of different, to some extent conflicting, ideas. As long as this is realised, the ideas can be allowed to modify each other in harmony rather than fundamental discord. Yet not all theorists or supporters of Western democracy would support this view. Some – including those who focus on the ideas, to be discussed below, about democracy being necessary for the realisation of liberal ideals – would discern sufficient 'inherent' connections between liberty and democracy; whilst others tend to stress the importance of what they see as the democratic aspects at the expense if necessary, of the traditional liberal limitations on government.[17]

If liberal democracy is subject to illiberal tendencies, how much more might this be true of a type of democracy that is discussed in the next chapter – whether this is seen as a tendency within non-communist 'Continental' theories of democracy, or as a part of the theory of 'people's democracy'. This is the type of democracy, inspired by the famous French philosopher Jean-Jacques Rousseau (1712–78), in which a government implementing the single all-powerful will of the people seems to leave no room at all for a limitation on government control of minorities or individuals. The view that this kind of democracy is illiberal and totalitarian is common, as implied by the title of J. L. Talmon's well-known book, *The Origins of Totalitarian Democracy* (Talmon 1952). It must, however, be realised that the Rousseauist notion of democracy is tied in with Rousseau's idea of freedom according to which individuals are perfectly free in a democracy of this kind. Those who see it as illiberal are viewing it in terms of the liberal's 'negative' – rather than Rousseau's 'positive' – concept of freedom.

Negative and Positive Liberty

The difference between negative and positive liberty can be considered only briefly here, but in outline is as follows. The negative concept of freedom sees individual self-determination as consisting in the individual doing what he or she wishes. Doing what one wishes is conceived to include simply acting to fulfil one's desires. The positive concept, on the other hand, sees individual self-determination as rational autonomy. The individual is self-determined when his or her actions embody reasoned decisions and are more than reactions to the desire of the moment. The difference between the two conceptions is best illustrated by an example – albeit one that over-simplifies in order to bring out the contrast. Consider the position of a person who has decided to give up smoking but who finds himself with a cigarette in front of him. The advocate of the positive concept of freedom would say that the self-determined individual is the one who would resist the desire for the cigarette and refrain from smoking it. But, such an advocate would argue, according to the negative concept self-determination would consist in fulfilling the desire to smoke the cigarette: smoking the cigarette is, in an important sense, what he wishes to do and he is free to do so if not prevented. In terms of the positive concept, however, 'giving in' to desires in this way is not so much freedom as slavery – being a slave to one's desires.

This difference between positive and negative freedom translates itself into a political context. The negative concept implies, as we have seen, absence of governmental restraints: the absence of restraints upon individuals carrying out their various desires. A liberal, it might be said, is one who values individual freedom in this sense. A crucial part of the positive concept, however, is the idea that the individuals' pursuit of their desires might give way to the rational guidance of the state. The state is the organisation for the promotion of the common good. The promotion of the common good is the rational objective of all individuals, and therefore the state is seen as the manifestation of all individuals' 'rational will'. Hence the guidance of an individual by the state is, according to this view, not a limitation of freedom but a vital part of it. Rousseau's conception of the general will, which we shall look at in the next chapter, incorporates these ideas and also contains the notion that the common good is actually, even if not apparently, willed by every individual. It is not merely that the common good is what would be the objective of those who thought about it – rather it is actually willed by everyone.

Seen in its own terms, then, the Rousseauist conception of democracy contains no negation of individual liberty. Indeed the opposite is the case – in such a democracy perfect freedom exists. Individuals are free because they are acting in accordance with their own rational wills. There is a great deal in such a conception. This can be illustrated by a down-to-earth example. Although some British motorists carp about interference with the liberty of the individual, most would not regard the drinking and driving law in this light. Many a motorist in a pub will drink less than he would have done had the law not existed, but rather than seeing this as oppression, he will feel that he has acted in accordance with his true intentions. As to whether or not the Rousseauist conception of freedom, and its relationship to democracy, is adequate – or even superior to the liberal democratic view – the essential point is one that will be taken up later in the discussion of 'people's democracy'. This is that a crucial failing in the use of the conception is its association *in practice* with tyrannical government. It would seem, therefore, that the traditional liberal democratic view of Rousseauist democracy has in the end much to commend it – even if the issue is not nearly so simple as it is often made to appear, and even if in many ways Rousseau's thinking is far more profound than much of liberal democratic thinking, and elements of it have to be accepted.

Liberty and Equality

We have looked at some of the important ways in which democracy is related to equality and to liberty; because each is related to democracy, they have important relationships with each other, but these are not just indirect, via the concept of democracy. Equality and liberty are also directly linked. Democracy, equality and liberty form, as it were, the three points or angles of a triangle so that lines of relationship go not only from equality and liberty to connect with each other at the third point, democracy, but one also forms the final side of the triangle connecting equality directly with liberty. By the same token one could focus on democracy and talk of both direct and indirect links with the other two concepts.

Let us turn, then, to the direct relationship between liberty and equality. We do so in recognition that both are of fundamental importance in liberal democratic thought – an importance that amounts to more than the fact that each is conceptually connected with democracy.

The first thing to notice is that although they have affinities with each other, since both are important in liberal democratic thought, they are in tension as well. As J. Roland Pennock says, '"Liberty" and "equality" comprise the basic elements of the democratic creed. Yet these twin ideals . . . are not easily reconciled. Between them, at best, a considerable tension exists' (Pennock 1979). We shall consider some of the tensions first. These include differing social analyses as well as conceptual inconsistencies, and can be conveniently summarised in two sections.

On the one hand, there is the idea that equality suffers at the hands of liberty. Here we have arguments to the effect that the existence of extensive 'formal' liberty[18] allows, creates or maintains an unacceptable degree of inequality. The essence of such arguments is that undesirable economic inequalities flourish where the state does not intervene to prevent them: where individuals are free from governmental regulation they are also free to amass wealth at the expense of, and to exploit, other individuals. As we shall see later, it is also usually held that the social structure – until and unless it is changed by state action – gives immense advantages to some individuals in the pursuit of economic interests. Under such conditions of freedom there are great inequalities in the distribution of material resources and, more generally, of the means to a good life. We shall be looking further at arguments of this sort in Chapter 3, but we should notice now some of the important viewpoints with which they are associated. The basic view is that such inequalities are undesirable. Then it is also held that economic inequality involves economic power: those with the most material resources have power over those with the least. This in turn is considered undesirable – not least because it is undemocratic. It is often further argued that economic power goes hand in hand with political power so that the existence of economic inequality means that both economic and political power is concentrated in just a few hands. This is even more clearly undemocratic.

On the other hand, there are the arguments that it is liberty that is endangered by equality. Where social equality exists and/or is pursued as an ideal, individual liberty is threatened. This was argued most notably, perhaps, by Tocqueville, and J. S. Mill was much impressed by it. It has two main elements. First, the pursuit of equality – or rather the governmental action necessary to bring it about – involves the invasion of individual liberty by the state. Second, social equality destroys the varied social structures which not only create inequalities but also check the state by providing bulwarks against governmental power. Social uniformity also involves 'atomisation', whereby society is reduced to a mass of uniform individuals bereft of the varied relationships provided by complex social structures. Such individuals are vulnerable both to government and to the social pressures of 'mass opinion' and so on.

Fears about the connection between equality and the exercise of state power are deepened when libertarians address the arguments, just outlined, of those who think it is equality that is endangered by liberty. The basic fear, that the pursuit of equality threatens liberty, is strengthened when the focus shifts to contemplation of the suggested remedies for inequality. Attention centres on the state intervention needed to correct inequalities and, again, the fundamental argument is that such intervention threatens individual liberty. The importance of the idea of liberty as the protection of the individual from the state is re-affirmed. Extreme forms of the argument maintain the overriding importance of individual liberty and maintain that there should be *no* state action to 'remedy' inequality. An argument of this type has been developed relatively recently by Robert Nozick in his well-known – not to say notorious – book *Anarchy, State and Utopia* (Nozick 1974; see also Paul 1982). Nozick argues that individual rights are sacrosanct, that the state has only the minimal function of protecting these rights and that action by the state to promote welfare or remove inequalities cannot be justified.

Other ripostes to the idea that the price of liberty is too high because it involves an undesirable degree of inequality focus on two main themes: the extent to which economic inequality is justifiable or desirable; and the question of just what inequalities are at issue in the first place.

The focus in the first theme is on the notion that individuals ought to be allowed the fruits of their labour and if this means that some obtain more material goods than others so be it. This is often supported by the argument that economic inequalities are permissible since it is only other kinds of equality that are really important. Equal treatment by, and equal political participation in the control of, the state – in other words equality before the law and equal political participation – are the important things. This is because the state with its immense power over us – including matters of life and death – plays so important a part of our lives that it is only fair that this should be an equal part. There is usually an amalgamation of arguments. The overall libertarian case against economic egalitarianism then combines the contention that it is only political equality that is important with the notion that individuals ought to be free to keep the fruits of their labour and that attempts by the state to remedy economic inequalities involve unjustified coercive interference with this freedom.

The argument that economic inequality is permissible – indeed, perhaps desirable – merges into more general considerations about what is to count as inequality in the first place. Instead of saying that it is justifiable one might make much the same point by denying that what some people call economic inequality really is inequality. The argument here is that individuals are not all the same and that equality merely demands that individuals should be treated equally with regard only to those important respects in which they are the same (see p. 15 above). This opens up two large questions. First, in what 'important respects' are individuals the same? Second, with regard to these respects, what does 'treating them equally' amount to? Considered in these terms the argument that economic inequality does not offend against the general principle of equality would become one or both of the following. First, that since individuals are not the same in their desire for – or, indeed, their capacity to obtain – material goods, the principle of equality does not require that they be treated equally in the distribution of these goods. Second, that even if individuals are – or to the extent that they are – the same in their desire for, and capacity to obtain, material goods, treating them equally in the distribution of goods implies something other than 'allocating' the same, or the same quantity of, goods to each individual. The point is that treating individuals equally does not involve arranging things so that they are all 'given' the same, or the same quantity[19] of, material goods so much as ensuring that they have a place in society from or within which they have an equal opportunity to obtain these goods. There is a more general argument lying behind this, which brings us back to the underlying libertarian point: the idea of 'opportunity to obtain' ties in with the idea of individuals deciding what they want to obtain; and – referring back to the first contention above – individuals may not all want to obtain, or obtain the same amount of, material goods. Equality of opportunity means all individuals having an equal opportunity to live their own lives in the way they wish. This sort of argument is often put by saying that the principle of equality does not assert that individuals *are* equal but that they should be *treated* equally.

The rendering of the principle of equality as equality of opportunity is well supported but also controversial. This is not the place to discuss all the issues raised but we should note two points. The first is that much of the controversy turns on differing interpretations of what equal opportunities *are*, and whether they can actually exist. Do individuals with differing abilities really have equal *opportunities* where they merely have *places* in society that are in some sense equal? At the extreme, for example, mentally and/or physically handicapped people need to be *un*equally treated – positively helped – if they are to have anything approaching equal opportunities. Other issues concern the sorts of social arrangement that are necessary for 'equal places in society' to exist – if, indeed, they can exist at all. A key question involves the extent to which social structures such as class so shape the lives of individuals as to make equality of opportunity extremely difficult if not impossible to achieve. Another concerns the extent to which (if this is not impossible) equalising opportunities may in some cases involve *un*equal treatment or prospects for some people. Two examples of this are: 'positive discrimination' where (in its best-known exemplification) whites must be discriminated *against* in order to give blacks, with all the disadvantages they suffer in a white society, 'equal' opportunities; and the way in which the provision of equal opportunities for all young people to obtain places at universities results in inequalities of opportunities thereafter, most notably career opportunities, between those who get to university and those who do not.

The second point about the issues raised by the notion of equality of opportunity concerns the implications for the relationship between equality and liberty. In fact these implications cut both ways. On the one hand, the pursuit of equality of opportunity can be viewed as threatening to liberty. Here the focus is on the action, typically action by the state, necessary to create equality of opportunity. In the more extreme cases it is argued that coercion (of some individuals) is necessary in order to create equality of opportunity. An example is the argument that parents who wish to give their children a private education should be prevented from doing so in order that all children should have the equal opportunities provided by their all being educated in the same, the state, education system. On the other hand, attachment to the idea of equality in the form of equality of opportunity has clear libertarian implications. The basic point is the contrast between two ideas. The idea that society should be arranged, i.e. organised by the state, so that all individuals are given the same, which it is commonly held can lead off into totalitarian directions, is compared unfavourably with the idea that individuals should have the equal opportunity to live their lives as *they* wish.

This brings us back from the tensions between liberty and equality to their affinities. There are three main types of argument suggesting that it is the affinities which are important. The first is the sort just indicated – showing the libertarian implications of equality of opportunity. There is, however, no hard and fast line between this and the second type. Here we find it argued that liberty and equality are both important, that both should be promoted and that to a considerable extent they can be harmonised despite the tensions. In one of the best-known examples of this sort of argument John Rawls in *A Theory of Justice* (Rawls 1972) combines the ideas of individual liberty, that all individuals should have equal basic liberties, equality of opportunity and equality in the distribution of goods – since inequalities demand special justification[20] – into a theory of justice. This theory in turn underpins a justification of liberal democracy (see Chapter 4).

Rawls maintains the importance of basic liberties and holds that where there is a conflict between liberty and the remedies for inequalities not justified by his 'difference principle', liberty must take precedence. Nonetheless, he does not maintain that these liberties always forbid state action to promote welfare and to remedy inequalities. He is in fact subjected to a thorough-going criticism by Nozick for allowing that justice can require the invasion by the state of (what Nozick holds to be) the rights of individuals. Arguably, even in Rawls' theory a tension remains between liberty and equality.

Rawls, however, makes use of a notion in which liberty and equality are fused together, and this brings us to the third argument concerning the important affinities between liberty and equality. This focuses on the idea that all individuals should have *equal liberty*: 'each person is to have an equal right to the most extensive basic liberty compatible with a similar liberty for others' (Rawls 1972). This idea of equal liberty is very important in liberal democratic theory. Whether or not it incorporates enough of a central notion of the principle of equality – equality in the distribution of, or the opportunity to obtain, material goods – to satisfy egalitarians is another matter. The relevant considerations are largely those that we have just been discussing. Be that as it may, it can be argued that liberty and equality are both of fundamental importance in democracy and that they are partners rather than enemies. For example, another important modern theorist argues that liberty and equality are fused together in liberal democratic ideas. Ronald Dworkin in *Taking Rights Seriously* (Dworkin 1978a), puts forward the 'fundamental thesis . . . that *both* the various aspects of economic equality that Rawls tries to salvage *and* the various specific liberties that Nozick champions flow from a single and insufficiently recognised source, namely the basic conception in liberal democracy that each individual is to be treated equally and with due regard to his actual personal preferences. Dworkin's attempts to discover a single primal or pivotal source for rights may be taken as an example of a very important movement towards synthesising (if possible) the divergent polarities of equality vs. liberty, welfare vs. rights, that has come to a head in the Rawls–Nozick debate' (Kainz 1984).[21] This third argument involves rather a different way of looking at the relationships between liberty and equality, and between each of these and democracy. Indeed it has important implications for the whole notion of liberal democracy and it is further discussed in the next section.

Democracy, Liberty and Equality

We have now looked at the relationships between democracy and equality, democracy and liberty, and liberty and equality. These represent the direct connections between the three points of the triangle (see p.28 above). But, as we remarked before, there are also the indirect connections. For example, the view that equality threatens liberty often involves the idea that democracy threatens liberty *because* democracy is linked with equality. Similarly democracy can be seen as threatening equality because of democracy's involvement with liberty. Other permutations are, of course, conceivable, but these are the ones on which theorists have tended to focus.

Among theorists who focus on tensions of this sort it is those broadly sympathetic to liberal democracy who hold that it is liberty that is threatened. We have already seen how Tocqueville viewed democracy as a threat to liberty; and this was because he saw democracy as involving equality.[22] According to Tocqueville 'though democratic nations did not despise liberty, unfortunately it was not liberty but equality which was their idol. To them liberty was a secondary aim, but equality a primary one' (Bramsted and Melhuish 1978).

On the other hand the idea that it is equality that suffers – suffers at the hands of liberty and democracy – is typically developed by theorists who are critical of liberal democracy. We have already seen that 'left-wing critics' argue that equality will not be brought about where 'formal liberty' is given priority; but such arguments are usually part and parcel of a critique which sees such liberty as a necessary feature of liberal democracy. Not that these arguments are necessarily wedded to a full-scale critique of liberal democracy, though this is where they might be developed most coherently. We can in fact draw a broad distinction between Marxist and non-Marxist left-wing critiques. Marxists argue that equality cannot be achieved in those systems which go under the label of liberal democracy but which are in fact shams. In these systems there is formal liberty and no real democracy (see Chapter 3). Non-Marxist left-wing critics agree that in a liberal democracy, liberty – much (but not all) of it purely formal – is promoted at the expense of equality. But there is no absolute necessity for this to happen: to the extent that it *is* a democracy there is a chance for the people to elect a government that will put this right. This sort of argument is not put forward with much confidence, however, for two main reasons. First, even the non-Marxist left are much impressed by what they see as the difficulties in the way of a left-wing party being elected to government. Second, if such a party is elected there is a limit to what can be done: this is precisely because in a *liberal* democracy there are limits on what the state can do.

As we have already noticed, though, not everyone sees tensions. We have already looked at some affinities between liberty and equality. However, there is also a viewpoint – let us call it the liberal–egalitarian viewpoint – according to which these affinities are so close that liberty and equality in effect form one basic value. We have in fact already referred to this viewpoint, and noted also that it includes the important idea that liberal democracy is required for the realisation of this value. The key notions are (a) that a belief in the importance of individual liberty involves focusing on crucial features – such as autonomy and the capacity for self-development – which are characteristic of all human beings, thereby establishing that in crucial ways all individuals are the same, i.e. equal; and (b) that these features imply that individuals should be treated with equal concern and respect (see, for example, Lukes (1973)). It is then argued that only a political system in which all have an equal say in determining the conditions of their life, i.e. a liberal democracy, can realise these ideals.

Theories embodying the liberal–egalitarian view have already been referred to, and aspects of it are also important in neo-Idealist and participatory theories of democracy. Two related points about it should particularly be noticed. First, the connections it embodies are very tight. Liberty and equality are defined in terms of each other;

and liberal democracy rather than being found, upon investigation, to be necessary for their realisation, is deduced from them. Second, from the liberal–egalitarian viewpoint, being a *liberal* democracy is simply an aspect of being a democracy. The liberal element is not a limitation on, so much as an aspect of, the democratic element: government by the people necessarily involves all individuals freely contributing to the decision-making process. In a properly functioning democracy[23] 'negative liberty' is necessarily maintained as an integral part of the governing process and does not, as in the classical view, need protection from (even, or especially, a democratic) government.

Conclusions

How can we sum up the relationships among democracy, liberty and equality; or, rather, what conclusions can we now come to?

Let us first dispose of any idea that there is nothing that matters much here. Some readers might feel that all this discussion of the relationships is merely playing with words. But this is not so – for two reasons. First, the various issues we have just been discussing have not been concerned solely with relationships among concepts. Empirical questions about the ways in which social and political processes do or do not work have equally been involved. Secondly, where it is conceptual relationships that have been at issue this has not been a matter of a superficial concern with linguistic analysis ('playing around with words') *rather than* social and political analysis. The point is that the logic of concepts works itself out in the social and political world, and conceptual tensions become real-world tensions. Fundamental issues are involved but one straightforward point is that ideas can move people, who will then be moved by the logic of those ideas. One has only to reflect, say, on the way actions are generated by the idea of nationhood, as involved, for example, in the ideology of nationalism, to see how true this is.

To return to the relationships themselves. The preceding discussion has demonstrated some of the complexity and the differences of view that have become involved. My own view can be summarised somewhat as follows. I bring together many of the points already raised, but the focus is on democracy and liberty and on democracy and equality, where all the relationships tend to come together.

Let us take democracy and liberty first. The two concepts are combined together in the one notion of liberal democracy. The existence and the importance of this single notion may obscure tensions between liberty and democracy. To an important extent a liberal democracy is a democracy of a limited sort, a system in which there are limitations on the scope of the people's decision making. Nonetheless there are also important ties between liberty and democracy. These are of two main kinds.

First, there is a contingent connection. It is in fact, although not as a matter of logic, true that people wish to have a considerable degree of liberty in the sense of protection from governmental power. This is not to say that they *only* want restrictions on government, many people also want governments to do a great deal, but that most people do want *certain* restrictions on government. It follows that where the government is finally controlled by the people, as it is in a democracy, governmental power will be restricted in the way desired. As evidence of this kind of connection between liberty and democracy one has only to consider the way in which people vote with their feet: people living in other systems flee to the liberal democracies precisely because of the liberty that exists there but not in their own country.

Second, there are what liberal democrats see as necessary connections. They regard the existence of certain liberties as necessary conditions for the existence of democracy. The basic contention, with which I agree, is that unless there is freedom of choice – such as that provided by free elections – it cannot be said that the people are making decisions (see the next chapter). Furthermore, there cannot be freedom of choice in the absence of freedom of speech, organisation and assembly. These points are important whether or not one goes so far as to embrace the liberal–egalitarian view with its integral connections between liberty and democracy.

A key part of the case for liberal democracy, then, is that there are very important ties between liberty and democracy. We will focus on this at various points later in the book.

Let us now turn to democracy and equality. It is the relationship between *liberal* democracy and equality that is of particular interest; and consideration of this relationship will rehearse for us many of the points concerning liberty and equality as well as those concerning democracy and equality.

The key consideration is the close link between democracy and equality. But this is a link with *political* equality – and it is essentially political equality that is crucial in the liberal–egalitarian view. This involves two points. First, there is the tightness of the connection between the concept of democracy and the idea of political equality.

So tight is this connection that 'democracy' is sometimes even defined in terms of political equality. Second, there are not the same conflicts between liberty and political equality as between liberty and other ideas of equality. This is because these other ideas imply or require output by the state – state action to establish or maintain the equality; and state action of this kind threatens individual liberty. Political equality, on the other hand, primarily involves an equal share in the input (the decision-making process with regard) to any state action there may be; and such action could still be limited to that which is compatible with individual liberty. Political equality, being compatible with liberty, can thus be seen, even in the classical view, as tightly linked not just with democracy but with liberal democracy.

It should also be remembered that other kinds of equality *can* be furthered by liberal democracy. The people may wish for state action to promote more equality, even though this might involve some diminution of individual liberty. And in a democracy the people get what they wish. Provided the diminution of liberty stays within bounds the democracy can be regarded as remaining a liberal democracy. It should be further remembered, though, that problems of individual liberty will emerge when it is a case of not all of the people wanting more equality: state action desired by the majority might well be seen as involving the unjustifiable invasion of the liberty of those individuals in the minority. In part these are problems involved in the very notion of a collective decision; and it is the nature of such problems that is briefly indicated in the Appendix that follows.

Appendix
Democracy and Majority Rule

We have defined democracy in terms of decisions made by the people. It follows that some account is necessary of *how* such collective decisions can be made.

There is a central difficulty: how can many and different individual decisions be combined into a single collective decision? We shall return in Chapter 3 to the point that decision making can only be done by individuals. A collective decision must then, in some sense, be a combination of individual decisions – even though, as we shall argue, a *purely* individualist account is not possible.

The difficulty is usually conceived and stated in terms of preferences, although, as we shall see shortly, this involves a *mis*conception, which in fact largely creates the difficulty in the first place. If all individuals' preferences were the same, the decision of the people would simply be a register of what all individuals preferred. But such unanimity is so rare that we must assume its non-existence. How, then, can it be said that there is *a* (collective) decision, rather than a diversity of (individual) decisions?

A very common response to this problem is to say that the will of the majority should prevail. Usually this is based on a simple line of reasoning: where unanimity is lacking, i.e. where preferences are divided, it is the greater rather than the lesser number of preferences which should prevail, since the greater number is nearer to being the whole number – and it is certainly nearer to being the whole number than is the minority. The decision of the majority of the people is accepted because *it is counted as* the decision of all the people. This is sometimes buttressed by another argument, found in Locke, to the effect that since the majority is the greater number it is the greater force. Apart from anything else this means it will in any case eventually get its way; so it might as well have it now and avoid conflict: 'we count heads in order to avoid breaking them'. More respectably it might be said that it is 'natural' for a body to move in the direction it is propelled by the greater force within it.[24] These responses are complemented by another, to the effect that for the democrat there is no alternative to majority decision making. Abraham Lincoln expressed this well: 'unanimity is impossible; the rule of a minority, as a permanent arrangement is wholly inadmissible; so that, rejecting

the majority principle, anarchy or despotism in some form is all that is left'
(First Inaugural Address, 4 March 1861).

Whatever their plausibility as arguments for majority decision making *per
se*, the 'greater force' and the Lincoln arguments do not establish that a
majority decision can be equated with a decision of the whole people; indeed
the Lincoln argument might be said to establish the impossibility of democracy. The majority-is-nearer-to-being-all argument rapidly loses its plausibility as soon as the majority ceases to be overwhelming: 999 people out of a
group of 1,000 is indeed very nearly the whole group, but there is no sense in
which 501 people can be counted as the whole.

There are a number of possible responses to the failure of these arguments
for majority rule. We have not the space to go into them and we shall simply
mention some. For further discussion see Kendall (1941), Dahl (1956), Berg
(1965), Holden (1974) Chapter 4, and Spitz (1984). (One point to be noticed
here is that the 'justification of majority rule' tends to become absorbed into
the larger question of the justification of democracy. This is true, for example,
of Spitz (1984). However, we are here primarily concerned with whether
majority rule achieves, or is to be equated with, democracy. The question of
whether democracy itself is desirable we discuss in Chapter 4. Similarly, other
questions are only tangentially related to our concern – such as the desirability of majority rule as against the existence or protection of minority rights.)

One of the responses is to argue that majority decision making is normally
the *fairest* decision-making procedure (Rawls 1972), or that it is likely to
arrive at the correct or most reasonable decision (Black 1963). Again, though,
these may be arguments for the majority decision-making rule but they do not
in themselves show that it is a democratic decision-making rule, i.e. that a
majority decision can be conceived as a decision of the whole people. And it
should be noticed here that there is an ambiguity in the whole discussion.
There is in fact an important distinction to be drawn between (a) statements
of a rule or *method* for making decisions: 'when a decision on policy alternatives
is to be taken, that alternative which secures the greatest number of votes
should be chosen'; and (b) statements about there being rule by a certain
group of people, who constitute a majority. The use of the majority decision-
making rule only implies rule by a majority group in certain kinds of polarised
society. Otherwise 'the majority' is a mathematical expression and does not
imply that it is the same individuals who are in the majority on every issue.
Focusing on this distinction clarifies the issues and puts the majority principle
in a better light (Holden 1974). It opens the way for arguments about there
being a logical connection between the decision-making rule and equality
and popular sovereignty (Spitz 1984). But Spitz further argues that the
majority decision-making rule only achieves democracy when set in a wider
context which modifies the purely individualist analysis of most discussions.
In fact it would seem that the majority principle cannot itself give sense to the
notion of a collective decision by the people. And it is the narrow individualism with which the majority principle is associated that is the basic problem
here. But before we take this further there is a different set of problems that
must be considered.

These demonstrate that the difficulties involved go even deeper when one attempts to show that there can be collective decisions despite the existence of differing individual preferences. Even if the idea of a majority decision were acceptable, these difficulties would still be there because, in essence, it is arguable that majority decisions *cannot exist* in crucial cases. There is now a large and complex literature on this wide subject. The basic argument is that the logical and mathematical problems of aggregating preferences are such that neither the majority decision-making rule, nor any computational procedure, can guarantee that what is preferred by a majority will be the outcome.

These problems become visible when the focus shifts from the notion of voters having only one preference, or account being taken of only their first preference, on each issue. Once *orders of preferences* (for example a voter who prefers policy (a) to policy (b) might still prefer policy (b) to policy (c), and so on) are taken into account, it can be shown that in crucial cases there is no policy which can be said to be preferred by a majority. Another aspect of, or another way of stating, the problem is to focus on the different ways of putting the issues to be decided by the majority decision-making rule – for example, in taking amendments in committee – and then to point out that these can produce contrary results. 'Cyclical majorities' and the 'voter's paradox' are terms used to describe problems of this kind. Kenneth Arrow stated the problem generally in *Social Choice and Individual Values* (Arrow 1963). And it is a problem that can be viewed as very serious: 'put crudely, what Arrow has done is to show that strict democracy is impossible' (Runciman 1969). (Of course such a view assumes that there would be no problem in the first place in saying that a majority decision, if it could be had, was a democratic decision.) Not everyone agrees that the position is that serious, but the problem *is* seen as important and a whole new branch of theory – 'social choice' or 'public choice' theory – has grown up with this as one of its main subjects. (Another is the analysis of how and why, on the same individualist assumptions, governments come to provide 'public goods' in cases of 'market failure' – protection of the environment, for example.) As indicated, the literature is large, but useful recent surveys or discussions are: Mueller (1979), Elster and Hylland (1986), and McLean (1987); McLean (1986) contains a vigorous short discussion of some of the key issues; for a more extended analysis, which concerns itself with the 'confrontation between the theory of democracy and theory of social choice' see Riker (1982).

Not surprisingly, analysts differ over many of the issues, but the predominant view does seem to be that the 'Arrow problem' is insoluble within its own terms of reference. But are these terms of reference valid? There are two main lines of counter-argument here.

First, it has been argued that there is no need to try and rescue the majority principle since it is in any case defective, as we have seen. One of its faults is that it takes no account of *intensities* of preference – on the problems this raises: see Dahl (1956) Chapter 4, and Kendall and Carey (1968); see also Jones (1988). (Another fault is that it assumes that divergencies of preferences can be neatly categorised into majorities and minorities. In fact, of course, there is usually a *great diversity* of preferences rather than a split into just two categories. The 'bargaining approach' mentioned immediately below also brings in this very important point.) But if the assumption that preferences are *fixed* is challenged one can take on board differing intensities *and* moreover one can build on the notion of bargaining and reconciliation, and alteration of preferences in the face of divergencies, to arrive at the idea of unanimity. This avoids all the difficulties associated with trying to aggregate diverse fixed preferences. This line of argument was elaborated by Buchanan and Tullock (1962). Their argument does not succeed (see the critical analysis in Barry (1970)); but two, interrelated, ideas they utilise are important in the second type of counter-argument, which is surely the decisive one.

This moves on from the ideas of preferences being modified, and of a decision emerging from a process of interaction rather than being calculated from data about fixed preferences. If we push these ideas further we get to the crucial point of recognising that people have (sometimes complex) views rather than mere 'preferences'; and the process of interaction involves *discussion* and the bringing together of views. These ideas tie up with the kind of valid critique of the excessive individualism of much Anglo-American liberal democratic theory, recognised by the 'neo-Idealist' theory mentioned in the next chapter. And in fact it is neo-Idealist theory which gives us the notion of 'decisions by the people' emerging out of a process of discussion (Barker 1942, Lindsay 1935 and 1943, Thompson 1970; see also Berg 1965, pp. 48–57, and Holden 1974, Chapter 4).

It should be noted that an important aspect of this line of argument is that views can, more easily than 'preferences', relate to something beyond the individual. People can and should ask themselves 'the right question', as Rousseau would put it: they should ask not what is in my interest (what is my 'preference') but what is in the public interest? This crucially modifies the problem of majority decision making since a majority's view of that which is in the public interest is very different from – and can prove crucially less difficult for a minority than – that which is in the majority's interest, i.e. the 'preference of the majority'.

In conclusion, then, we can say that bargaining, compromise and discussion are central to the notion of a decision by the people. At some point a vote is necessary, when the majority view should prevail. However, this should be not the majority's preference, but its view of what is in the public interest. Moreover, this must be set – and arguments for majority decision making only make sense – in the context of the interactive and discursive process. (Spitz (1984) develops a similar viewpoint.) In short, what is a central problem in narrowly individualist liberal democratic theory is insoluble in its own terms. To make sense of the notion of a decision by the people it is necessary to move away from narrowly individualist assumptions and recognise the ways in which common views can arise which are not necessarily attributable to any particular individuals as such.

Notes

1. The full story is a little more complex. Besides the differing judgements about the nature of the political systems to which the term 'democracy' is applied, there are also different notions of how a political system can embody rule by the people – as we shall see when we come to discuss the idea of 'people's democracy' in the next chapter. As Graham points out, Rawls and Dworkin, for instance, distinguish between 'one overarching *concept* of democracy [and] several different rival *conceptions* of it' (Graham (1986), referring to Rawls (1972) and Dworkin (1978a)). A similar idea is expressed when it is said that democracy is an 'essentially contested concept' (Gallie 1955; Connolly 1983).

2. The position is actually rather more complicated than this as there is a further important distinction between what might be called empirically and logically necessary conditions. See Holden (1974) for a discussion of this distinction (p. 4), and an analysis of the role of this distinction in discussions of participation as a necessary condition for democracy (pp. 185–6).

3. On the notion of sovereignty see, for example, Stankiewicz (1969) and Hinsley (1986).

4. See, for example, Holden (1974), pp. 10–11.

5. This statement, in fact, brushes over some quite troublesome difficulties – see for example Dahl and Tuft (1973) and Whelan (1983) – quite apart from the question of whether democracy is necessarily a form of state (this issue is commented upon in Chapter 3 below).

6. See, for example, Spearman (1957).

7. On 'symbolic representation' see, for example, Birch (1972). We shall be discussing 'representation' in the next chapter.

8. On the nature of liberalism see, for example, Gray (1986b).

9. More accurately we should say 'the location of the control of a state's power'. The point is that the power we are concerned with is an attribute of the state; in a democracy the people control the state – and thereby have power.

10. The point being made is that Mill explicitly appeals to considerations – based on utility – other than natural rights to delimit an area of individual liberty. It is arguable, though, that in fact his political theory is not consistently utilitarian, as opposed to rights based: see, for example, Ten (1980) and Ryan (1983).

11. Tocqueville (1805–59) is a very important theorist in the context of the relationships between democracy, equality and liberty. His most important work (Tocqueville 1968) has been extremely influential. It is analysed in Dahl (1985).

12. On the concept of liberty or freedom see, for example, Cranston (1967) and Ryan (1979). The distinction between the 'negative' and 'positive' conceptions of liberty, which is referred to in the text below, was made famous by Berlin (1969). For a critique of this distinction see MacCullum (1972); see also Baldwin (1984).

13. 'State' and 'government' tend to be used interchangeably in contexts of this kind; and, where the context makes it natural, we shall fall in with this. There are important conceptual differences as well as overlaps, but there is no need to go into them here.

14. No proper distinction is being made here between 'Anglo-American liberal democratic theory' and 'liberal democratic theory'. This is because it is arguable that 'Continental' democratic theory is not really *liberal* democratic theory. However this is a controversial and complex point and discussion of it will be deferred till the next chapter.

15. In fact, of course, there are three relationships here: those between (a) the individual and the government, (b) the individual and the people, and (c) the people and the government. Liberal democratic theory tends to mix them all up. In particular it often assumes that an instance of (a) is one of (c) and thereby overlooks the possibility of its being one of (b). The converse of this, as it were, is the frequent inability to see how, in many cases, (a) involves (b): to the extent that the people act through government an action of the government *is* an action by the people. In other words, here the government versus the individual *is also* the people versus the individual (see also the main text below).

16. Hayek (1978); see the helpful discussion in Held (1987), Chapter 8.

17. See, for example, Ranney and Kendall (1956). Willmoore Kendall has even interpreted Locke in this light, in Kendall (1941). Continental views of democracy are more likely to be of this kind than are Anglo-Saxon views – see Sartori on 'Empirical Democracies and Rational Democracies' (Sartori 1965 and 1986); but see also the paragraph which follows in the main text.

18. The use of terms such as 'formal liberty' shows how these arguments link up with different ideas regarding liberty itself. The point is that those who use such arguments tend to the view that liberty involves having power over the conditions of one's life (including economic conditions), something that is not realised simply by the absence of governmental restriction. The mere absence of such restriction then amounts to 'formal' and not real liberty. See the discussion of liberty in the main text above.

19. There is of course a further dimension of variation here. Arranging an equal distribution of material goods does not necessarily mean giving everyone the same goods since people's tastes differ. So perhaps it is the same *amount* that we should focus on. But how do you quantify amounts of, say, camping equipment as against audio goods? Monetary value provides the standard answer, so that the principle becomes one of equal distribution of money (equality of income, for example). See also Dworkin (1978b) who focuses on the importance of differences in individuals' conceptions of the good life rather than the more superficial 'tastes'. He also sees the free market and representative democracy as the institutions necessary to give effect to the principle of equality of treatment (this connects up with the 'liberal–egalitarian' viewpoint discussed in the main text below).

20. According to Rawls' famous 'difference principle' inequalities are only

justified in so far as they are to the benefit of the worst off – as when the overall prosperity is raised by allowing some of the inequalities of income that are inherent in a system that specially rewards hard work.

21. See also the report of an interview with Dworkin in Magee (1979). The notion that, for the democrat, liberty and equality are inextricably linked goes back to Aristotle. For a modern analysis see Lukes (1973); but for the view that the 'necessary combination of equality and freedom cannot be elaborated into a coherent system of ethical thought' see Charvet (1981).

22. Tocqueville held that a democracy (in the primary sense of the term) was a system in which equality necessarily existed to some extent, and in which further equality was vigorously pursued as an ideal. But half the time he goes further than this and treats 'democracy' and 'equality' as synonymous – i.e. he moves to the secondary meaning of 'democracy' we identified earlier.

23. This is an important qualification. It might be argued that a weakness of the liberal–egalitarian, and a strength of the classical, view is precisely the failure to focus on the potential, *in practice*, of all – including, and perhaps especially, elected – governments to become oppressive of at least some individuals.

24. We have here an example of a common feature in discussions of majority rule: a shifting between individualist conceptions of the people, as simply a collection of individuals, and 'communalist' conceptions of the people as a corporate entity – a conception implied by the notion of the people being 'a body'.

2
The Nature
of Liberal
Democracy

In this chapter we shall be concerned with some further dimensions of the basic ideas contained in the notion of liberal democracy. We shall attempt to clarify some of the key ideas and theories that have given it life, as well as comparing it with rival nations. We begin by looking at the central ideas in the historical tradition of thought about democracy, before turning to consider the fate of these ideas in the modern world.

2.1 Direct and Indirect Democracy

We saw in the last chapter that the meaning of 'democracy' was extended around the end of the eighteenth century to include 'indirect' as well as 'direct' democracy. And it is now time to consider the nature of these two ideas and the relationship between them.

Both ideas fall within our general definition of 'democracy' by virtue of the differing accounts of what are 'important matters of public policy' and differing interpretations of the notion of the people making decisions. In a direct democracy, decisions on most matters of public policy are made directly by the people; in an indirect democracy, although a few – the most important – are directly made by them, most decisions are made only indirectly by the people.

A direct democracy, then, is a political system in which the people directly make the policy decisions –'directly' in the sense that the decisions that are implemented are not merely 'derived' from, but *are*, the decisions the people have actually made. The usual idea about how this can happen involves many of the people being, and all having the chance to be, present and participating when the decisions are made; and the proportion of matters specifically decided by the people in this way being high. Given the relevant pre-supposition about the desirability of extensive popular decision making, then if the people *can* be assembled to make decisions there is no reason why all non-routine decisions should not be made by them. By contrast, in an indirect democracy although the determining policy decisions are still made by the people, to an important extent this is done indirectly. True, the fundamental decisions are made directly – at elections; but most others are actually made by elected representatives: it is these that are made only 'indirectly' by the people. But though it may be done indirectly there is still an important sense in which it is the people who make them, by virtue of the way in which the representatives are affected by, and are ultimately subordinate to, the direct electoral decisions. Beyond, or alongside, this basic idea, different democratic theories have differing ideas about the relationship between the representatives' decisions on the one hand and the opinions and interests of the people on the other. But in all cases – besides, or in association with the effects of, the electoral decisions – the representatives are in some sense or other deciding for, or on behalf of, the people.

Direct Democracy

Direct democracy is often viewed as the very archetype of democracy; and it is often held up as the ideal against which indirect democracy is to be judged. It is the most thoroughgoing form of democracy. And the original – and now highly esteemed – democracies of ancient Greece were of this type. Direct democracy therefore continues to have an important influence upon democratic thought. It is true that it is commonly considered to be totally impracticable in modern conditions of large industrialised societies and states of corresponding scale and complexity. Nevertheless it often continues to be seen as the ideal of democracy. And some do see modern forms of direct democracy as being made possible by modern communications technology – televised debates with viewer interaction via computer keyboards and so on (see, for example, Margolis (1979) and McLean (1986)). However, whether such arrangements would provide anything like the experience of discussion in face-to-face meetings of participants is another question. Be that as it may, the ideal of direct democracy still casts its spell and it continues to affect practice. First, there do exist today examples of direct democracy. True, these are not at the level of states, and they mostly involve relatively small-scale, non-state bodies – a students' union, where the general meeting has a key role, is one instance. But some examples are local government units; and although not at the level of the whole state, they are state institutions. The best known are the New England town meetings. (For a fascinating and detailed empirical study of two examples of direct democracy, one of them being a New England town meeting, see Mansbridge (1980).) Second, in recent times there has been a resurgence of interest in direct democracy and this has been central in current 'participatory theories'(see Chapter 3 below). Belief in, and calls for, participatory democracy often involve a denunciation of at least orthodox representative institutions, and a corresponding demand for an increased direct involvement by the rank and file in decision making. Third, as we shall see later, some form of direct democracy has a key place in Marxist thought about democracy; and Marxism continues to be – or is increasingly – an important influence in political thought, even in the West.

As already mentioned, the main inspiration and model for direct democracy has been the theory and practice of ancient Greek democracy. The all-important political unit in ancient Greece was more on the scale of a modern medium-sized town than of a modern state: the city-state or *polis*. Some of these city-states were direct democracies, albeit with a conception of 'the people' which modern democrats would not accept since women and slaves were excluded! And it has above all been Athens of the fifth and fourth centuries BC that has inspired subsequent democratic thought. The Athenian *polis* contained between 30,000 and 45,000 citizens and the quorum for the Assembly was 6,000. The Assembly made decisions on matters put to it by a council, which was itself chosen by lot and was a microcosm of the people. But these matters were the important ones; the

Assembly met frequently – over forty times a year – and it engaged in genuine and decisive debates. Political decision making, therefore, was in a very real sense directly in the hands of the Assembly. (On ancient Greek democracy see, for example, Jones (1964), Davies (1978) and Held (1987), Chapter 1).) It is of course usually held that it was the smallness and lack of modern social and technological complexities that made ancient Greek direct democracy possible. The question of the viability of something like direct democracy in the modern world will be one of the themes in our discussion of 'participatory theories' in Chapter 3.

Indirect Democracy

Let us now turn to indirect democracy. And we should remember that from the French Revolution onwards this came to be regarded as the only practicable form of democracy. It should also be remembered, however, that Jean-Jacques Rousseau, whose political philosophy is often considered one of the inspirations of the French Revolution, is usually seen as being in favour of direct, rather than indirect, democracy.[1] We shall have more to say about Rousseau later in this chapter.

As we have seen, indirect democracy means representative democracy: a political system in which the people elect representatives to act for them for certain purposes. As was said just now, the great disadvantage of direct democracy on the ancient Greek pattern is held to be its impracticability on a larger scale. The idea of representation was later incorporated into democratic thought as a device for overcoming this disadvantage. The concept and practice of representation emerged during the Middle Ages to develop and be utilised in the flowering of democratic theory, begining in the late eighteenth century, so that representation became an integral part of democratic theory. Indeed, in some instances representation was joyously seized upon as a miraculous solution to the problems of applying popular rule in large-scale societies. Tom Paine was of the view that, as the ancient 'democracies increased in population, and the territory extended, the simple democratical form became unwieldy and impracticable', though 'original simple democracy. . . affords the true data from which government on a large scale can begin. [But] it is incapable of extension, not from its principle, but from the

inconvenience of its form.' However, the system of representation is the
remedy for this defect of form, and 'by ingrafting representation upon
democracy we arrive at a system of government capable of embracing
and confederating all the various interests and every extent and
territory of population'(Paine 1969). James Mill proclaimed that 'in
the grand discovery of modern times, the system of representation, the
solution of all the difficulties, both speculative and practical, will
perhaps be found' (Mill 1955). As we shall see, not all theories of
representative democracy view representation as simply overcoming
the problems of size, although all would give it at least – if not only
– this function.

Representation: Concepts and Theories

The idea of representation, then, plays a central role in indirect
democracy. But what does this important idea amount to? The first
thing to notice is that there are several conceptions rather than a
single straightforward one. Arguably these are separate, though
related, ideas; but it may be that they are best seen as different
variations on one basic notion.[2]

The basic notion identified by Pitkin is that of *re*-presenting,
'making present' in some sense, that which is not literally there. But
this 'making present' can be thought of in different ways. Thus Birch
talks of three main usages of the term 'representative': (a) to denote
an agent who acts on behalf of his or her principal; (b) to indicate that
a person shares some of the characteristics of a class of persons; and
(c) to indicate that a person symbolises the identity or qualities of a
class of persons (Birch 1972).

A representative in the first sense is one whose duty it is to promote
certain interests or wishes of another person or persons – the 'principal'. (Birch sticks to the term 'interests' here, but this begs important
questions: as we shall see later, the relationship between interests and
wishes, or opinions, is important to the differences between the
various theories of representation). Sales representatives and lawyers
would be examples. As Birch points out, there can be a variety of types
of relationship between agent and principal. In the second sense the
term refers to the possession of characteristics typical of some larger
group or category within which the representative is included – and
of which he is 'representative'. Birch gives the example of a representative sample, as used for instance by public opinion pollsters, where
a 'sample of the relevant population [is] chosen by statistical methods

so that the main characteristics of the population will be mirrored in the sample' (Birch 1972). The third sense of 'representative' is less important in democratic theory. We came across it in the last chapter in those medieval notions of kingship in which the king 'represented' the corporate people. In this sense the representative 'stands for' or 'symbolises' that which is said to be represented, as a piece of sculpture might 'represent', say, courage.

There are differing ideas about *what* – as well as the *ways in which* – persons or groups are to be represented. And there are also varying ideas about the function of representatives in the political system as a whole. This number of variables entails the possibility of many different relationships. And, in part as a reflection of this, there are different theories of representation. We, however, are concerned only with those theories which occur in democratic theory. (It is often assumed that theories of representation are necessarily democratic. But this is not so: the groups being represented need not comprise the whole people. Even where it is the whole people who are represented this need not involve them in making decisions: for example, in the medieval notion according to which the king represented the people it was the king who made the political decisions. As already indicated, the concept and practice of representation in fact pre-date theories of representative democracy – see for example Pitkin (1967).)

In democratic theories of representation the whole people are represented; and the whole *people decide* who are to be their representatives and, roughly at least, what they are to do. It is, of course, essentially through the electoral process that this is achieved: through the process of electing representatives the people decide how and by whom they are to be represented. It should be noted, however, that the democratic selection of personnel need not be by elections – though without them an indirect democracy would need some alternative mechanisms, such as the use of referenda, for the actual making of (at least the basic) decisions by the people. Selection by lot was used in ancient Greek democracy, but it would usually be held that this method had grave disadvantages in modern indirect democracies. For a useful discussion see Dahl (1970); for an interesting recent – but only ambiguously democratic – argument in favour of selection by lot see Burnheim (1985).

Different theories of representation arise through (amongst other things) differing accounts of the relationship between electors and their representatives. But in all of these a key idea is that the fact of being elected ensures that those elected do actually behave as representatives. The important arguments here are that the members of an assembly who are elected by their constituents will, largely *because* of this election, actually (a) behave as agents of, and/or (b) have the same characteristics as, those constituents. (In fact (b) is much less likely to obtain than (a) – a point which is developed in Burnheim's important book (Burnheim 1985).) 'Symbolic representation' is of only minor importance here.

There are four main ideas about the manner in which election is supposed to ensure representation in these ways. First, there is one of the ideas behind argument (a), that only those persons will be chosen who say that they will advance the opinions or interests of the electors. Second there is the idea in argument (b) that election will help to ensure that those chosen as representatives will have characteristics typical of their electors. With each of these first two ideas the assumption is that the electors will vote only for such candidates as will be representative. The third conception, which relates to argument (a), is that electors will make sure that the representative will behave in the appropriate way after election. The idea here is that members of the assembly who in fact fail to do what they were elected to do will not be re-elected by their constituents. This has the double effect of helping to ensure that most members will remain representative, and of removing any that do not. These ideas concerning the continued representativeness of the elected members rely on the notion that the members will wish to be re-elected and that they will therefore see to it that they do nothing to prevent this happening. This conception is sometimes expressed in terms of the 'rule of anticipated reactions'. A fourth idea, again relating to argument (a), concerns the insecurity of tenure implied by election. Representatives will, it is argued, refrain from promoting legislation that could later affect them adversely as ordinary members of the public.

It is, then, the system of election that provides for the people to decide, at least in broad outline, the policy to be pursued by their elected representatives. And it is because, or to the extent that, this is so that a system of representative government is a democracy. Again it is 'agent representation' that most directly fits the argument. 'Sample representation' – in so far as it is separated from agent representation – fits it indirectly. The expectation of legislators being elected because they have characteristics similar to their electors carries with it the further expectation that similar characteristics will imply similarity of interests and policy views.

Representation as such, though, is also important in its own right; indeed, in a representative democracy there is a double form of responsiveness to the people. The people make the basic decisions through elections. But, over and above this, the representatives have the inherent function of promoting the people's interests and/or views. This function exists even apart from elections, although elections are extremely important in ensuring that the function is actually performed.

The different theories of representation in democratic theory centre on differing ideas regarding (a) the degree of autonomy of the representative in relation to his electors; (b) whether there is a difference between the representation of constituents' interests and representation of their opinions, and, if so, how they relate to each other; and (c) the extent to which it is the function of the representative to promote the national interest rather than – if there is a difference – the interest(s) or views of particular constituents. The issues here are interrelated and the ways in which they are treated in different theories of representation are interconnected. We shall now turn to these theories and look at them as key elements in traditional liberal democratic theory. We should note, though, that conceptions of representation were modified by the development of mass political parties and ideas about their functions in a democracy. As we shall see, these conceptions became 'grafted on' to traditional democratic theory. But let us look first at the original democratic theory that pre-dated these developments.

2.2 Traditional Democratic Theory[3]

A theory of democracy, or democratic theory, is a body of thought that provides and analyses a conception – a model – of democracy; and justifies and explains the actualisation of the model in the world. There is also another use of the term 'democratic theory', meaning something like a scientific theory, where the reference is to a body of theory concerning the workings of actual political systems that are presumed to be democracies. We shall not be concerned with this sense here.

There are, of course, different models of democracy that can fit within the general idea of liberal democracy; and, indeed, there are different democratic theories. Broadly speaking these theories may be divided into 'traditional' and 'modern', though some twentieth-century theorising consists, essentially, in restatements or refinements of traditional democratic theory. In this section we shall be concerned with traditional democratic theory, sometimes called 'classical democratic theory'.

We should really talk of traditional democratic theor*ies*, since there are different types of theory that fall under this heading. The differences are in fact important, though often overlooked. However, the different theories nonetheless do also have certain common features. Perhaps the chief reason for grouping them together under the same label is historical: they were all formulated in the same general period, over a century ago. Traditional democratic theory, then, consists of theories of democracy formulated in the period roughly between the middle of the eighteenth and the middle of the nineteenth centuries. Theories relating to ancient Greek democracy were often influential in their formulation, but the term 'traditional democratic theory' is usually taken as referring to the theories of *in*direct[4] democracy relating to this later epoch.

Traditional democratic theory, then, did not really emerge until the second half of the eighteenth century, as part of the Enlightenment. There had, though, been anticipations of it in the thought of the Levellers of the mid-seventeenth century (Gooch, 1954). And we must also recognise the importance of the political philosophy of John Locke.

Locke is not really a democratic theorist and yet his political theory has been extremely influential in democratic thought, especially in the United States; indeed, he is often regarded as the founding father of liberal democratic theory. This paradox arises because, on the one hand, Locke is an important thinker whose influential political philosophy has important democratic features; whilst, on the other hand, these features – although developed by later theorists into a full-scale theory of democracy – are but aspects of a theory that ultimately is not democratic. The democratic elements of Locke's political philosophy are his theories of popular consent and of majority rule. But these are set within an overall theory which does not properly give the people constitutional power. Although the whole people have power in the sense of having an ultimate right to revolt if they find that the governors have abused their trust, there is no constitutional mechanism for exercising this right. Nor, apparently, does Locke believe that *all* the people, the masses, should have the vote,[5] although this has now been called into question by Richard Ashcraft's scholarly work on Locke (Ashcraft 1986).

Whatever the 'democratic status' of Locke's own political philosophy, it fathered what can be regarded as the two main streams of Anglo-American traditional democratic theory (we shall discuss later the relationship between 'Anglo-American' and 'Continental' democratic theory). We can characterise these streams as follows.

Types of Traditional Theory

On the one hand there is what we might call 'conventional democratic theory'. This inherits Locke's view of the government as an entity separate from, and 'above', the people and sees this entity as having a positive and independent function. The people have a negative and passive – although in the end decisive – role. The term 'conventional' is used principally because of the extent to which the theory became part of the conventional view of the British political system. Historically the British system was the chief object of theorists' attention, although the American political system has a somewhat similar status here. In a dialectical relationship the theory's model of democracy was perceived to fit, but also inspired and legitimised, the conventional view of the nature of the British political system. The term 'liberal democratic theory' is sometimes used to refer to what I here call conventional democratic theory. There are some good reasons for this, but there is the risk of confusion since 'liberal democratic theory' also has the generic sense in which it means *all* theories about liberal democracy.

In conventional democratic theory an important notion, connected with the people's negative role, is the idea of government by consent – i.e. government with the consent of those, the people, who are being governed. Where consent is required for the performance of some action(s), those who give or withhold that consent can be seen as playing a decisive but negative role – 'decisive' because their decision is necessary before the action(s) can be performed; 'negative' because they merely respond to initiatives put to them by someone else. One can also stress the 'negative aspect' of consent by distinguishing on the one hand between a 'self-assumed obligation' as the 'free creation of a relationship', as in making a promise; and on the other hand consent *to* something already in existence, as in agreeing to abide by the rules of an institution (Pateman 1985). In the idea of 'government by consent', then, the people can be seen as performing a decisive but negative role. They are viewed as giving consent to – or withholding consent from – the government; and this can incorporate the idea of the people having negative power over the government.

It is not, however, always realised just how complex and vague is this notion of government by consent. Indeed, in some renderings the idea is not even necessarily connected with democracy. For example, consent by the people simply to the existence of a regime – rather than to the policies pursued by its government – does not amount to the people making the basic policy decisions: in fact it might be that the people consent to a non-democratic form of government. To further indicate some aspects of this vagueness and complexity, we can say that the meaning of 'government by consent' varies principally along two main dimensions. One dimension concerns that to which the people consent. At one end of the scale it is consent to the existence of government as such. This varies through consent to particular forms of government and particular governments to, at the other end of the scale, consent to the policies pursued by the government or even to particular legislative or administrative acts. The other dimension concerns that which constitutes consent. This varies from acquiescence under duress, through various kinds of manipulated, habitual and traditional acquiescence – and also the process of 'socialisation' – to freely and deliberately choosing to give assent, which may involve the giving of permission. For further discussion of government by consent see, for example, Partridge (1971) and also Pateman's important book (Pateman 1985) which explores what she regards as the manner in which the ambivalences of consent theory have been 'exploited' to mask the non-voluntarist character of the modern liberal democratic state.

The other stream of traditional democratic theory fathered by Locke contains theories we can label as 'radical democratic theory'. In effect Locke's right of revolt is here developed into a positive, initiating role for the people. Rather than the people merely responding to initiatives put to them by the governors (actual or potential), as in conventional democratic theory, it is the governors who respond to initiatives from the people. We shall look further at conventional and radical democratic theory in a moment. Before that, though, there are a couple of important points to note.

First, the division of traditional democratic theory into just two types in this way is something of an over-simplification – although, I would suggest, a permissible and helpful one. The point being, of course, that there is more than one way of grouping and distinguishing the various different theories that go to make up traditional democratic theory.

In particular we should note another significant category of distinctions that cuts right across that between 'conventional' and 'radical' democratic theory – distinctions reflecting the differing basic philosophies or underlying theories with which thinkers have linked the democratic idea (further discussed in Chapter 4). Broadly speaking we can, perhaps, discern three main types of theory when we look at it in this way. First, there are theories in which the idea of a democratic form of government derives from, or is intermeshed with, a basic theoretical or philosophical analysis in which fundamental moral principles are seen as having a central role. Such theories have often been centred on conceptions of natural law and natural rights: Tom Paine's *Rights of Man* is a leading example (Paine 1969). But bases for theories which see democracy as necessary for the realisation of fundamental moral principles have also been found in Christian philosophy and the philosophy of Kant (1724–1804). An important modern example of something like a Kantian basis for democratic theory is to be found in John Rawls'*A Theory of Justice* (Rawls 1972). In theories of a second type the idea of democratic government flows from an analysis of how interests are best protected. These are utilitarian theories of democracy, the classic exponents of which are Jeremy Bentham (1748–1832) and James Mill (1773–1836). In a third category are theories which see democracy as necessary for the proper development of the individual. To what extent this is properly a category of traditional liberal democratic theories is debatable. Such 'developmental theories' tend to have roots in Rousseau rather than in Locke; and some central ideas are considered when we discuss 'participatory theory' generally in Chapter 3. Anglo-American examples have mainly been twentieth-century products: 'neo-Idealist' democratic theory and 'citizenship theory' are referred to later in this chapter. But, having said this, it must also be pointed out that one of the central figures in traditional liberal democratic theory, John Stuart Mill (1806–73) – James Mill's son – does appear in this category. In fact John Stuart Mill is something of an eclectic theorist of democracy. He considered himself to be a utilitarian,[6] and important aspects of his theory focus on democracy as a means of protecting people's interests. But at least as important in his theory is a 'developmental' view of democracy:[7] democracy being seen, and valued, as promoting the proper development of the individual.

The second important point to note is that, as implied just now, there is a very important theorist of democracy whose thought we are not counting, for the moment, as part of traditional democratic theory – Rousseau. There are two, interconnected, reasons for leaving him aside at this point. First, Rousseau differs importantly from the other thinkers we are here concerned with in being a theorist of *direct* democracy: he is, indeed, usually understood as being against representative government (but see note 1). Second, as will be remembered, our concern is in fact with traditional *liberal* democratic theory. And Rousseau's political philosophy and the sort of democratic theory he inspired is arguably not 'liberal' democratic theory. We shall in fact be discussing this matter in the next section when we compare 'Anglo-American' and 'Continental' democratic theory. But we must acknowledge right away that despite not counting him at this point as a traditional liberal democratic theorist, Rousseau's political philosophy has been extremely important here. 'Continental' democratic theory, stemming from Rousseau, is itself very important; but the immediate point is that Rousseau's thought – striking and profound as it is – has directly influenced traditional 'Anglo-American' democratic theory by virtue of its similarities with, and the inspiration it has given to, aspects of radical democratic theory.

But let us return to traditional liberal democratic theory. We saw a moment ago that there are differences among the theories within this general category as well as the differences which separate the category from others. But there is of course also an important common element in the theories. This can be summed up as a form of 'individualism'. All liberal democratic theory is individualist to an extent; but what characterises traditional liberal democratic theory is the prominence of a form of individualism – in contradistinction to 'modern' democratic theory, which ascribes an important role to groups rather than (or as well as) to individuals. True, some traditional theories contain contrary tendencies. For instance John Stuart

Mill was very conscious of the general influence of society and of majority groups; and some American theories – such as those of Madison and Calhoun – which historically, and on the whole conceptually, are part of the mainstream of traditional democratic theory, focus on the role of groups. But it is still a predominant individualism that is typical of traditional democratic theory.

What is this form of individualism? We shall be discussing individualism in more detail in the next chapter, but for the moment we can say that in a general sense 'individualism' has two main aspects. First, 'moral individualism': this term indicates viewpoints which give great moral importance to the individual. They are typically expressed by statements such as 'the individual ought always to be treated as an end in himself and never only as means'. Moral individualism is central in some varieties of traditional democratic theory – in John Stuart Mill, for example. But it is not (or, at least, it is crucially qualified) in others: utilitarian theory notoriously yields interpretations which give greater moral importance to general happiness than to the just treatment of an individual.[8]

Second, there is what we might call 'ontological individualism' – 'ontological' meaning having to do with the nature of being or reality, in this case the nature of social reality. Individualism in this sense involves seeing society as composed only of individuals and having its character determined by the characteristics of its constituent individuals. Groups, institutions, processes, structures, cultures, communities and so on are viewed merely as collections of individuals and the patterns they set up in their relationships. The nature, validity and significance of ontological individualism will be discussed in the next chapter; but here we should note that ontological individualism is especially important in traditional democratic theory. We are not just talking of the theory's individualist views of social reality generally. Rather, we are saying that there is a typical view of the political system itself in which the behaviour of individuals is central. The functioning of institutions and the political process generally is seen primarily in terms of the decisions and interactions of individuals. In 'modern' democratic theory, by contrast, even though there is an underlying ontological individualism, the functioning of the political system is seen primarily in terms of group interaction. (We shall see later, though, that traditional theory was itself subsequently modified by the 'grafting on' to it of theories about key groups in the democratic process – political parties.)

Conventional and Radical Democratic Theory

Let us now go back to 'conventional' and 'radical' democratic theory. We have already seen that the basic difference between them concerns the difference in roles ascribed to the people, and we shall now say a little more about this.

In conventional democratic theory the people have the negative role of choosing, at elections, among options presented to them. The options involve personnel and policies – different candidates and their various plans – and the choice of personnel is important as well as the choice of policies. Indeed, the policy choices by the electorate are seen as being only general and broad rather than detailed and specific. This is associated with the expectation that the representatives will be wiser and more knowledgeable than the people who elect them. There is considerable autonomy for such representatives in the making of political decisions, although they act within the general control of their constituents.

In radical democratic theory, on the other hand, the positive, initiating role of the people involves the idea of elected representatives being closely controlled by their electors, so that they act as little more than messengers conveying the policy decisions of their constituents. In a word they are *delegates* – in the well-known sense of this word in which a 'delegate' is contrasted with a 'representative', the latter being one who exercises personal judgement, rather than simply conveying the views of electors. (It should be remembered, though, that both these conceptions fall within the generic or general meaning of 'representative'. Somewhat confusingly, then, both representatives – in the specific sense of those who use their own judgement – and delegates are representatives in the generic or general sense of the term.) The electors' decisions not only initiate the policies the delegates are to follow, but these policy decisions are fairly detailed and specific. Indeed there is a sense in which the ideal system for radical democratic theorists remains a direct democracy, with a system of representation being favoured merely as an unfortunate necessity for dealing with the problem of scale. By contrast, in conventional democratic theory representation is rather seen as having virtues of its own: as a means to 'refine and enlarge the public views, by passing them through the medium of a chosen body of citizens whose wisdom may best discern the true interests of their country' (Madison 1961). With some radical democratic theorists – for example Thomas Jefferson (1743–1826) and Richard Price (1723–91)[9] – active popular 'participation', other than just voting at elections, is seen as an important part of the positive role of the people. (As we have seen, the conventional theorist John Stuart Mill also sees participation as very important. It may be that there is an inconsistency in his thought here as Pateman argues (Pateman 1970), but since Mill focuses on participation in *local* government this, arguably, does not clash with his 'conventional view' of the role of representatives at the national level.) Here there is notable parallel with democratic theory stemming from Rousseau. Indeed, this important theme of popular participation has at least as much to do with Rousseau as with traditional liberal democratic theory and is not a feature of all varieties of radical democratic theory. It has in fact been much discussed in recent times in the context of critiques of liberal democracy, and we shall postpone further consideration until the next chaper.

The models of democracy in both conventional and radical democratic theory consist, then, of political systems in which the people make decisions by electing representatives to govern them. In the radical model these elections also constitute specific decisions, or sets of decisions, on the policies to be followed by the representatives. In the conventional model, on the other hand, elections, although they do also decide policy to an important extent, are decisions of a far looser and broader kind; and as such, representatives are left room for considerable autonomy in decision making.

In order to highlight some other important aspects of traditional democratic theory we shall now expand our remarks on the role of representatives to include other important aspects of, and differences among, the various conventional and radical models of the democratic process.

Traditional Models of the Democratic Process

The democratic process here essentially consists in the making of decisions by numerous individuals and the combining of these into decisions by the people. This involves more than, but includes, the process by which those decisions are transmitted into government action. (The issues are different from those that were indicated in the discussion of majority decision making in the Appendix to the previous chapter, although they also overlap with them.) The ideas involved relate to what it is that decisions by individual electors express; and also the relationship between these decisions and the functions and activities of the electors' representatives.

Opinions and Interests

First, then, let us look at the individual electors' decisions. Ideas within different democratic theories reflect differing responses to a key question: whether it is interests or opinions that are expressed by these decisions. (A decision which expresses an interest links a conception of what the interest is with a decision to advocate its promotion. Similarly, one which expresses an opinion links an indication of what the opinion is with a decision to advocate promotion of action in accordance with it.) It is true that electors' decisions do not necessarily always fall neatly into this interest–opinion dichotomy. And the relationships between 'interests' and 'opinions' can become quite complex and the distinction very blurred in the thought of some theorists. Nonetheless, in a rough-and-ready way key differences are highlighted by drawing such a distinction.

We can say that the individual's interest(s) – or that which is in the individual's interest(s) – is that which benefits him or her.[10] A significant and complicating point is that an interest can be said to exist independently of the individual supposed to have it. An opinion, on the other hand, is simply what its holder conceives it to be (the question of its *validity* is another matter). This difference can have far-reaching implications.

Within traditional democratic theory it is above all the utilitarian theory of democracy that focuses on individuals expressing interests.[11] Utilitarianism became an influential moral and political theory in nineteenth-century Britain.[12] It was most widely known, and was incorporated most clearly into traditional democratic theory, in the work of Jeremy Bentham and James Mill. (John Stuart Mill was a more profound thinker, but despite his claimed or modified utilitarianism his was a crucially different theory of democracy, as we shall see further below.) We may characterise utilitarianism as asserting that happiness is pleasure, and the absence of pain; that pleasure is good; and that the equal pleasures of any two or more people are equally good. From this was derived the famous criterion of moral action: that which is right is that which produces the greatest happiness of the greatest number.

Utilitarianism also asserts that individuals do in fact seek pleasure and avoid pain; that they obtain pleasure by fulfilling their desires (doing that which is pleasant); and that doing that which is pleasant is what benefits them. In other words the promotion of individuals' interests consists in fulfilling their desires. Now, since only the individual concerned knows what desires he or she has, and knows best how to fulfil them, it follows that each individual is the best judge of personal interest. And this implies that individuals should themselves decide how their interests are to be promoted. And it is from this that utilitarian democratic theory springs: the idea of people themselves deciding how their interests are to be pursued leads naturally (despite some difficulties and inconsistencies that are touched on below) to the idea that the people should govern themselves. It is in fact a species of radical democratic theory that is generated in this way, since it follows from the notion that people are the best judges of their own interest that they should have full and detailed control over how their representatives pursue those interests. One of the most succinct statements of utilitarian democratic theory is to be found in James Mill's *Essay on Government* (Mill 1955; see also Lively and Rees 1978). Mill had some rather odd ideas on the extent of the franchise and C. B. Macpherson, for example, sees them as fatal to the view that James Mill is properly a democratic theorist (Macpherson 1977a). However, they need not be seen as integral to his theory – the central logic of which is radically democratic.

In conventional democratic theory, individuals' decisions are not typically seen as expressing interests. This is not because the concept of interest plays no part in conventional theory. Rather it is because central to such theory is the view that ordinary people do not properly, or clearly, *know* their own best interests. One reason for this is that interests are not viewed simply in terms of the fulfilling of desire (even Bentham is pushed in this direction at times). Wise representatives can best know their electors' interests; but only if they are aware of those electors' opinions. Hence it is opinions that are seen as being expressed in voting decisions; and it is the representatives who, taking account of these expressions, decide what the interests of the electors are. Conventional democratic theory here echoes the famous words of Edmund Burke (1729–97) – although he was not himself a democratic theorist – when he said that a representative owed his constituents a 'devotion to their interests *rather than* to their opinions' and should if necessary go as far as maintaining their 'interest even against [their] opinions' (Burke 1949). Such conceptions are incorporated into democratic theory by John Stuart Mill, the most influential British conventional democratic theorist. His ideas are in many ways different from those of Burke, but with respect to the nature and role of voters' decisions as expressions of opinion, there are key similarities.

In conventional democratic theory, then, individuals' decisions are typically seen as expressing opinions; whilst in one of the main forms of radical democratic theory – utilitarian – such decisions are seen as expressing interests. But there is not always this kind of line up.

On the one hand there are important varieties of radical theory in which the electors are, implicitly, seen as expressing opinions rather than interests. Jefferson and Tom Paine, for instance, focus primarily on the will of the people; the views of individuals are then seen as but constituent elements of this popular will. And, since the popular will has as its object the benefit of the (whole) people, this too must be the object of the constituent individual wills. Individuals, then, are expressing opinions about the good of the community, the whole people, rather than concentrating on their own particular interests. (It is true that the second part of Tom Paine's famous book, *Rights of Man* (Paine 1969), is essentially utilitarian in character, but this is not true of the more widely read Part One.)

On the other hand the expression of interests does play some part in conventional democratic theory. For example, the notion of class interests has a place in John Stuart Mill's thought, where an important element is the notion of the more enlightened representatives holding the balance of power between the opposed class interests that find expression in the legislature. But, more than this, there is one important figure, James Madison (1751–1836), who should be counted as a conventional democratic theorist and in whose thought the expression of interests plays a central role. Madison has the conventional democratic theorist's typical view of the role of a representative, and his thought as expressed in his contribution to the *Federalist Papers* (Madison 1961) has a standing in the American tradition of democratic thought not unlike that of John Stuart Mill's *Representative Government* in the British tradition. Madison, however, is untypical of traditional democratic theory in that he concentrates on the role of groups rather than on individuals. (In some ways his thinking has more in common with modern, group-orientated, pluralist democratic theory than with individualist, traditional democratic theory. Unlike pluralist democratic theorists, however, Madison is worried about the power of groups: he accepts their presence as inevitable but seeks to 'tame' them – to deal with the 'evils of faction'.) For Madison it is group interests that are at the heart of the democratic process. Like the utilitarians he conceives of individuals as themselves knowing their own interests. However, in contrast to utilitarianism, these are

not the interests of each particular individual but the interests of the
group or 'faction', to which the individual belongs. An individual who
is a farmer knows his own interests, but these are his interests as a
farmer. Also in contrast to utilitarian democratic theory, the idea that
individuals know their own interests does not lead to a delegate view
of representation. This is because utilitarian theory fails to come
properly to grips with the problem of the relationship between individual interests and the general interest, and it sees representation
simply as a means of translating individuals' interests into legislative
action. In Madisonian theory, however, to protect the general interest, groups' interests and their expression are to be tamed by the
actions of representatives in the legislature. This brings us to the issue
of the relationship between the electors' decisions and the behaviour
and functions of their representatives.

The Functions of Representatives

There are, in fact, two important and different, but overlapping,
issues here: the first concerning the representative's proper role with
respect to his or her own particular constituents, and the second
concerning the relationship between this and the representative's role
with respect to the nation as a whole.

The first issue gives us the line of divide between conventional and
radical democratic theory that we have already noted. Radical theory
views representatives as delegates only, while conventional theory
emphasises the relative autonomy of representatives. Conventional
democratic theory, indeed, sees representation as something more
than simply a device to deal with the problems of scale. The 'something more' is provided by the special wisdom and expertise of the
representatives as compared with the ordinary person. In fact, in
conventional democratic theory representative institutions are viewed
as a way of combining the merits of democracy with the merits of rule
by an educated and informed elite. John Stuart Mill is in favour of
'Parliament . . . containing the very elite of the country' (Mill 1912).
And Madison sees the public's views as being not so much directly
expressed as refined and enlarged 'by passing them through the
medium of a chosen body of citizens, whose wisdom may best discern
the true interest of their country', and 'it may well happen that the
public voice pronounced by the representatives of the people, will be

more consonant to the public good than if pronounced by the people themselves . . . ' (Madison 1961).

In short, in conventional theory the people choose representatives to govern for them. But, if this is so, can it really be said that it is *democratic* theory? The answer is a qualified, but nonetheless definite, yes. Both Madison and Mill have their undemocratic aspects, but when it comes to the crunch the people are the masters. 'The meaning of representative government is that . . . the people . . . exercise through deputies periodically elected by themselves, the ultimate controlling power . . . This ultimate power they must possess in all its completeness' (Mill 1912). For Mill 'the people ought to be *masters*, but they are masters who must employ servants more skilful than themselves' (Mill 1859, italics added). The people may choose representatives to govern for them, but in doing so the people make the ultimate, the basic, decisions on important matters of public policy.

Conventional democratic theory's view of representation is best summed up by Hanna Pitkin:

> The wonderful theoretical advantage of representation as Liberalism sees it, then, is this: representation makes it possible for each to participate in government as the final judge of whether his particular shoe pinches; yet it allows the rulers to use their wisdom and information to further people's true interests, where direct action would be misguided by short-range, hasty decisions. And, at the same time, representation makes it to the interest of the ruler to act in the interest of the subjects – not to give in to their passing whims, but to act in their true interest. For if he gives in to their passing whims, they will not really be pleased; the shoe that looked so attractive in the store will turn out to pinch. Only if he uses his wisdom to promote their true, long-range interests will they be truly pleased, and support him at the polls (Pitkin 1967).

In contrast to conventional democratic theory, the delegates of radical democratic theory are elected to the representative assembly simply to convey the wishes of their constituents: to act as messengers, or to act as their constituents would have done had they been there. This is clear in Paine if less clear in Jefferson. (Jefferson recognises a need for above-average intelligence in representatives. But he nonetheless thinks they should be very frequently accountable to the people; and he is, moreover, in favour of direct popular participation wherever possible.) The logic of utilitarian theory – despite some qualifications by Bentham – leads clearly to a delegate view of representation: if people are the best judges of their own interests it follows that those interests can be properly pursued only by representatives who are guided by the express directions of the people. This argument is complemented by another, succinctly expressed by James Mill:

> There can be no doubt, that if power is granted to a body of men, called Representatives, they, like any other men, will use their power, not for the advantage of the community, but for their own advantage, if they can. The only question is, therefore, how can they be prevented; in other words, how are the interests of the Representatives to be identified with those of the community?
>
> Each Representative may be considered in two capacities; in his capacity of Representative, in which he has the exercise of power over others, and in his capacity of Member of the Community, in which others have the exercise of power over him.
>
> If things were so arranged, that, in his capacity of Representative, it would be impossible for him to do himself so much good by misgovernment, as he would do himself harm in his capacity of member of the community, the object would be accomplished (Mill 1955).

And the way to achieve this is to have frequent elections. It is then always apparent to the representatives (a) that they may at any time revert to being members of the community, and (b) that in order to remain in office they must promote their electors', and not their own, interests.

We might note here that utilitarian democratic theory, which focuses on individuals and their interests, is paralleled by a group theory – rather as the more individualist strand in conventional theory is paralleled by Madisonian theory. This is the theory, important at least in America, put forward by John C. Calhoun in his 'Disquisition on Government' (Calhoun 1851). Like Madison, Calhoun accepts the idea of the representation of sectional interests. But, unlike Madison, he thinks that representatives should *merely* reflect these interests and act *primarily* as spokesmen for their constituents. Control by elections would make 'those elected the true and faithful representatives of those who elected them instead of irresponsible rulers as they would be without it; and thus by converting it into an agency and the rulers into agents, to divest government of all claims to sovereignty and to retain it unimpaired to the community' (Calhoun 1851).

Let us now turn to the second of the issues involved in ideas about the relationship between representatives and their constituents. This concerned the local constituency and the national interest: is the representative merely to promote the opinions and/or interests of his particular constituents, or primarily to identify and promote the *national* interest, the interest of the *whole* community? Is there, indeed, a conflict here at all? The answers to these questions are enmeshed with the accounts of electors' decisions and representatives' functions that we have just been discussing.

In conventional democratic theory there are a number of factors at work. To begin with there is the central idea that the representative is wiser than his constituents and should exercise his own judgement. This becomes closely associated with the idea that the representative is best able to discern the national interest and that he has an overriding duty to pursue it: the representative's judgement here is likely to be superior to his constituents' opinions.

Where electors are regarded merely as expressing opinions this settles the issue. Where, however, as is sometimes the case in conventional theory, it is electors' interests that are focused upon, the matter is a little more complicated, but two basic ideas intermingle.

First, there is the idea that the national interest ought to prevail over the interests of particular constituencies. Again, it is the enlightened representative who has the capacity and the duty to discern and promote the national interest. And in doing so he or she is acting as something other than simply an agent for constituents' interests. And, again, it is Burke who is often echoed in conventional democratic theory. In his famous words, speaking to the electors of Bristol:

> Parliament is not a congress of ambassadors from different and hostile interests, which interests each must maintain, as an agent and advocate, against other agents and advocates; but Parliament is a deliberative assembly of one nation, with one interest, that of the whole – where not local prejudices ought to guide, but the general good, resulting from the general reason of the whole. You choose a member, indeed; but when you have chosen him he is not a member of Bristol, but he is a member of Parliament' (Burke 1949).

John Stuart Mill focuses primarily on opinions. But he does also recognise that interests will find expression; and in so far as this is the case the national interests should prevail over local or sectional interests. This should in part be achieved by the wise action of representatives: or, at least, by the wise action of the most enlightened representatives, who should hold the balance of power in the legislature. But Mill also seeks to discourage the expression of local interests by advocating a system of proportional representation that plays down local constituencies and allows voters to choose from among candidates throughout the country. Madison, too, values the pursuit of the general interest above sectional interests. In his case, however, there is not the confidence that representatives will always be capable of rising above sectional interests.[13] He is therefore in favour of sectional interests gaining expression in the legislature so that they can be balanced against one another and thereby neutralised. In this way representation is 'a way of bringing dangerous social conflict into a single central forum, where it can be controlled by balancing and stalemating' (Pitkin 1967).

The second idea denies that there is, essentially, any conflict between the national and particular constituency interests – even where there appears to be. What might *appear* as particular interests, in conflict with the general interest, are in fact not so; they are not the genuine, long-term interests of those involved. It is an important aspect of the representative's superior wisdom that he can see this even when his constituents cannot. (The electors do have the last word – conventional theory *is* democratic – but by that time they will probably have seen, and approved, the wisdom of their representatives' decisions.)

Particular Interests and the General Interest

In radical democratic theory there is, typically, no particular issue regarding a representative's respective duties to his constituents and to the national interest. This is because, as we have already seen, the *sole* duty of a representative (delegate) is to convey his electors' opinions and/or their own conception of their interests. Now, this means that the problem of the particular *versus* the general does not get discussed at this point, and remains as an issue unrelated to the specific question of the role of representatives. In the case of those radical democrats who think in terms mainly of opinions and their representation, the problem tends simply to be ignored. It is assumed that what individuals decide in favour of will constitute the national interest. This is part of a general failure to perceive that the whole people are not the same as a single individual 'writ large', and that there are fundamental problems regarding the relationship between particular individuals and the sum total of individuals. (As we saw in the last chapter, there is a tendency in these theories to assume that the only important issues regarding the relationship of the individual to the state are those that concern the individual's relationship with the government – which ignores the relationship with the people as a whole.)

In the utilitarian variety of radical democratic theory we can see how the problem is, in part, obscured by the delegate view of representation. The delegate view does not push to the fore the question of differing – possibly conflicting – functions of representation. Unlike the representative of conventional theory the utilitarian delegate's only duty is to pursue constituents' own conceptions of their interests, since this is what those constituents' interests *are*. The delegate has no duty to focus on any other objective; and therefore other, and possibly conflicting, objectives – such as a 'national interest' – do not really come into the picture.

But there are deeper reasons than this. There are in fact crucial difficulties in utilitarian theory regarding the relationship between particular interests and the general interest. The particular interests focused upon by the original utilitarian theorists were those of individuals, and the constituency/general interest problem in effect becomes submerged in the individual/general interest problem.[14] At one level, utilitarian theory really implies that there is no such thing as a general or national interest that could be in conflict with anything. The only interests that exist are those of individuals, and the 'general interest' can mean nothing other than the interests of all the individuals somehow 'added together'. But this view is not consistently held to; indeed it cannot be, since it becomes incoherent.

In fact there is also in utilitarianism another, typically liberal individualist, account of the general interest. Here there is the postulate of some kind of harmony among, rather than a simple 'addition' of, the individual interests. In this way, in fact, the general interest consists in the *harmony* among particular interests, and not in the *interests* themselves – not even the alleged 'sum total' of interests. The assumption that there will be harmony among particular interests, plus the assumption – fundamental in utilitarianism – that each individual is the best judge of personal interests, supports the idea that harmony results from leaving each individual unfettered in the pursuit of his or her interest. This is a central conception in classical liberalism and reached its most famous expression in the classical economists' notion of *laissez-faire*, in particular in Adam Smith's conception of the 'invisible hand' which ensures that the pursuit of private gain results in the promotion of the interests of society as a whole. Here the focus moves from the fact of harmony to its beneficial results. According to such views as these, there seemed little need for government of any kind – even democratic government. However, utilitarianism did, also, recognise that government was necessary. As Hobbes had earlier argued, life without government would be insecure. Individuals would be in mutually destructive competition for limited resources. In other words, individual interests are not naturally harmonious and need to be 'artifically' made so.[15] This is the task of government. 'Government . . . is to make that distribution of the scanty materials of happiness, which would insure the greatest sum of it in the members of the community, taken altogether, preventing every individual or combination of individuals, from interfering with the distribution, or making any man to have less than his share' (Mill 1955). But there is a problem: the government will be composed of persons who, like all individuals, will have to pursue their own private interest. We saw earlier how this problem is solved: the representative system was conceived to get over this difficulty and ensure that the interests of the representatives are made to coincide with those of the community as a whole. The idea is that if the people control their rulers, then the interests of the people rather than those of the rulers will be promoted.

There is, of course, a crucial difficulty in this argument. Government is necessary to control the clash of particular interests among the people at large. How, then, can the people at large have *an* interest, and have control of the rulers to ensure its promotion? (The harmony of interests idea cannot be invoked here since it is this idea's deficiencies that make government necessary in the first place.) James Mill seems unaware of this difficulty. 'Sometimes the Utilitarians simply ignore this difficulty, speaking of the people only as a unified whole with one interest [thereby contravening the individualist basis of utilitarianism]. That is James Mill's solution, and one sometimes used by Bentham' (Pitkin 1967). Bentham, though, does have a more sophisticated side to his theory. This involves a recognition of individuals having shared public interests as well as ethically inferior selfish and private ones. It also involves a contradiction of the original axiom that each individual is the best judge of personal interest, and a departure from the delegate view of representation.[16] It is, however, the simple – and inconsistent – theory exemplified by James Mill that has been regarded as the typical utilitarian legacy.

Finally, on this question of the general and particular interests in radical democratic theory, we should note that Calhoun's 'group theory' tends to get into the same sort of muddles as the utilitarian democratic theory that it 'parallels' – with the particular interests in this case being those of groups rather than of individuals. However, there is also in Calhoun a 'weak' theory of the general interest, that later was to become important in modern democratic theory in the notion of 'consociational democracy'. It is a negative conception of the general interest as consisting in not harming any particular interests. That which is in the general interest is that which offends no group's interests. According to Calhoun, the political institutions should be such that it is 'impossible for any one interest or combination of interests or class, or order, or portion of the community, to obtain exclusive control', thus preventing 'any one of them from oppressing the other'. This forces the different interests 'to unite in such measures only as would promote the prosperity of all, [since this is] the only means to prevent the suspension [by mutual veto] of the action of the government; – and thereby, to avoid anarchy, the greatest of all evils' (Calhoun 1851).

Traditional Democratic Theory: Modifications and Assumptions

Before we leave Anglo-American traditional democratic theory there are a couple more things we should notice.

The first of these concerns the relationship of ideas about political parties to traditional democratic theory. The essential point is that the relationship is ambivalent: political parties and their role are seen both as being discordant with, and as important complements to, traditional theory.

The discordance is partly a matter of the relative unimportance of political parties at the time when traditional democratic theory was being formulated. There is very little in traditional theory about parties; and what there is, is largely hostile. Essentially, the hostility has two, interrelated, sources. First, there is the tension with individualism: political parties and their operations do not accord with the individualist view of the polity typical of traditional democratic theory. With parties playing an important role, the electoral decision becomes a highly structured and limited mass choice among a relatively small number of parties rather than the aggregation of unfettered decisions by separately acting individuals. Moreover, the elected legislature becomes a forum for group entities – political parties – rather than for individual representatives. And the relationship between parties and the electorate subverts that between individual representatives and their constituents. The second basis for hostility to political parties comes back to the question of the general interest again. Despite traditional theories' own difficulties with analysing the general interest and the popular will, when it comes to political parties it tends to be assumed that these conceptions are clear and that they are subverted by political parties. Parties are then seen as groups with particular interests that interfere with the people willing what is in their – i.e. the general – interest. This view of parties as factions with partial or particular interests is to some extent an echo of Rousseau's hostility to partial groups, which he sees as interfering with the people seeing and willing the common good of the overall community, the general will. But within Anglo-American theory there is a classic discussion, to which we have already referred, of the dangers of faction and how to cope with them: Madison's famous 'Paper 10', of *The Federalist Papers* (Madison 1961).

Although echoes can still be found in arguments in favour of multi-party systems, and against 'restrictive' two-party systems with their limitations on electoral choice and legislative behaviour, this predominantly hostile view of parties did not persist. Hostility to the pursuit of particular interests directed itself instead to pressure groups, and parties in fact came to be very widely seen as essential components of democracy. Burke's conception of a political party became widely accepted: 'a body of men united, for promoting by their joint endeavours the national interest, upon some particular principle in which they are all agreed' (Burke 1861). Concern about restrictions on individual choice and behaviour was overlaid by a perception of the ways in which political parties made electoral decision making and control more effective. Parties came to be seen as mechanisms invaluable for organising millions of separate individual votes into unified policy decisions: and for keeping those in government in touch with, and accountable to, the electorate. Indeed, appreciations of the democratic functions of political parties virtually became incorporated into traditional democratic theory – grafted on, as it were. In combination with conventional democratic theory we get a view of parties as providing, on the one hand, the leadership and organisation necessary for firm and wise government, and on the other hand, structures through which governmental organisations can be held ultimately responsible to the electorate. In the case of radical democratic theory, the doctrine of the mandate emerges: parties and their programmes are viewed as instruments of the popular will, so that a (party) government must, and must only, pursue such policies as it was elected to carry out.[17]

The second point to notice here about traditional democratic theory concerns the assumption of rationality that is said to underlie it. It is commonly held that traditional democratic theory assumes that people are rational and, in particular, that electors vote rationally. (It is important to notice that from some viewpoints – but not those of traditional democratic theory, apart from what might be implicit in utilitarian theory – it may not be rational for an individual to 'vote rationally'. In terms of cost–benefit analysis it can be argued that the 'costs' involved in, for example, an individual acquiring the information necessary to vote rationally, far outweigh the benefits obtainable from rational voting. Indeed, looked at in this way it can be shown that the 'costs' to any one individual of simply voting – in terms of the effort needed to get to the polling station, etc. – outweigh the benefits that can be obtained from that vote, virtually unnoticeable as it is among the thousands or millions of others. In fact, quite a literature has grown up around this subject, really starting with Downs (1957).[18] The assumptions on which such arguments are based are strongly disputed by 'participatory theorists' of democracy, who argue that any political participation, including voting, far from being a 'cost' has inherent virtue.)

Rationality is a complex notion but the focus here is primarily on the idea that the rational individual is the one who uses reason in seeking to obtain objectives and has sufficient relevant knowledge to do so. What, and what degree of, knowledge is 'relevant' and 'sufficient' can obviously be a controversial matter. But in the case of traditional democratic theory and voting the criteria are essentially given by the theories. To be rational is to use reason based on knowledge in a way that enables one's voting to express the sorts of decision which a theory postulates as being taken by the people. Thus, according to radical theories of democracy, in order to be rational voters need sufficient knowledge to express detailed policy views.

We shall see when we look at the 'academic challenge' that traditional democratic theory has often been criticised for its 'unrealistic' assumptions about the rationality of the people. We shall comment on this later, but it should be pointed out here that such 'criticism' properly applies only to radical democratic theory. One of the features of conventional theories of democracy is their idea of the limited nature of popular decision making: the electors are neither expected nor presumed to have the substantial degree of rationality necessary for the kind of detailed decision making postulated in radical theories.

'Anglo-American' and 'Continental' Democratic Theory

Let us now return, for a moment, to the question of the general and particular interests. As already indicated, our analysis so far has really been concerned with Anglo-American traditional democratic theory, including the discussion of the issue of the general and particular interests. But it is very important to realise that this issue does not arise – or, at least, that it is treated entirely differently – in another tradition of democratic theory which we can call 'Continental'. It is time now to have a brief look at this and to compare it with Anglo-American traditional democratic theory.

In fact the term 'traditional democratic theory' is to some extent ambiguous here; or, at least, it is in an Anglo-Saxon context. Sometimes, as has been the practice in this chapter so far, 'traditional democratic theory' is used only to refer to Anglo-American democratic theory. This can be because of hostility to Continental democratic theory and the wish to distance it; and it certainly points to some crucial differences between Anglo-American and Continental theory. At other times 'traditional democratic theory' is used in a way that includes both types of theory.

Continental Democratic Theory

What is meant by 'Continental' democratic theory? What sort of democratic theory is sometimes called 'Continental' – or, perhaps, 'French'? We shall attempt to characterise it by briefly sketching in its main features, comparing it with Anglo-American theory and asking whether, or in what sense, it is a species of liberal democratic theory.

Frequently in talk about democracy, distinctions are not drawn between different types of Western democratic theory. However, in more thoughtful discussion it is not uncommon for an important distinction to be pointed up by the use of a term such as 'Continental democratic theory'. It refers to that kind of democratic theory characteristic of Continental Europe and especially of France. There is a special connection with France because of the origins of this type of thought in the political theory of the French philosopher Rousseau, and in the happenings and understandings of the French Revolution.

Indeed, as Sabine shows so lucidly, the contrast between the Anglo-American and Continental democratic traditions stems essentially from the contrasts between Locke and the English Revolution on the one hand, and Rousseau and the French Revolution on the other (Sabine 1952).

Continental theory's model of democracy has a distinctive account of the nature of the people and the way in which they wield power. One of the key features of this account is that the people are – indeed it is perhaps more accurate to say the people 'is' – a corporate entity with a single will. This is partly a matter of a tendency to employ a 'juristic notion' according to which 'the people' refers to a legal category rather than directly to an actual group or set of persons – rather as there is a crucial difference between, say, a parish legally defined and an actual assembly of its inhabitants in a parish meeting. But this is only part of the story since Continental theory contains important propositions about how the people act. Anglo-American theory – with its focus on an 'empirical' rather than a juristic notion – sees the people as a collection of individuals, with the 'will of the people' being some kind of aggregate of separate individual wills; indeed, it gets into great difficulties here. Continental theory, on the other hand, conceives the people as being, in a significant sense, a single entity with its own, single will. In a similar way one talks about organisations of people such as, say, ICI as single corporate entities being possessed of wills – they plan, they act and so on. (It is important to note that the idea of the people as a corporate entity is, somewhat paradoxically, combined with a radical individualism. The constituent parts of the entity are of only one kind – individuals. There is here an important contrast with that appreciation of the importance of groups and sections of society which so often modifies Anglo-American individualism. Indeed, in Continental theory there is a positive hostility to any 'partial groups' which would divert attention from the overall community and the common good.) The other key feature of Continental theory's account of the people and their power is a very strong notion of popular sovereignty which stresses the idea that there is no proper limit to the people's authority. The will of the people is supreme: there is nothing they are not entitled to do. By contrast Anglo-American democratic theory is much preoccupied with the limits to state action, even – or, in some cases, especially – when such action is the embodiment of the will of the people.

These differences between Anglo-American and Continental theory largely reflect those between Locke and Rousseau. We have already said something about Locke and we should here focus on a key feature of Rousseau's political theory:[19] his notion of the general will. As already remarked, in Anglo-American democratic theory the 'will of the people' is viewed as some kind of aggregate of the *separate* wills of the individuals, the collection of whom makes up the people. According to Rousseau, however, there is an important sense in which all individuals can have the *same* will by willing the same thing; in fact this possession of a single will is a key aspect of the way in which individuals constitute a single corporate entity. This is the 'general will', which consists in every individual willing the common good (or the 'general good' or 'general interest').

There are three important points to note here about the idea of the general will. First, it assumes that there is no disagreement in principle about what *is* for the general good. Conflict can arise between apparent, short-term particular interests and the general interest. This may blind people to the common good and cause dispute about what to do, but this does not mean disagreement about what genuinely is for the common good. Secondly, it does recognise that individuals are indeed sometimes distracted in this way from focusing on the common good, by apparently willing what is in their own particular interests – as could happen if every individual were offered relief from jury service. But everyone opting for this could constitute what Rousseau would call the 'will of all'; the *general will* of citizens might well be for the maintenance of the jury system. In fact, when distracted in this way individuals are only *apparently* willing what they see as their particular interests.[20] They are responding to a question about their particular interests rather than to one concerning what they see as being in the general interest. They are being asked the wrong question, as Rousseau would say; they still *really* will the common good (note the connection with the notion of 'positive freedom'). The third point follows on from this: all individuals can be said to be willing the same thing – the common good – even when, apparently, they are not. Indeed, that it *is* the will of every person is a defining characteristic of the general will: the subject of the will is general as well as its object (the general good).

This idea of the existence of a single will, even where there is an apparent diversity of wills, cuts through the difficulties Anglo-American theory experiences in trying to give an account of *a* will of the people. It also cuts through the difficulties concerning the relationship between – and the proper roles for participants in pursuing – the general and particular interests. It is clear that the general interest is distinct from (narrowly conceived) particular interests, that it is morally superior to them and that democracy requires that it motivate everyone's political behaviour.

Besides the difference between Locke and Rousseau, the contrast between Anglo-American and Continental theory has much to do with the historical contrasts between the English and French Revolutions, and between English and French historical experience generally. There are many facets to this (Sabine 1952), but their main effect is to emphasise, on the one hand, the pragmatic nature of Anglo-American theory together with its focus on the limitation of state power and on the importance of non-state groups and structures; and on the other hand, the 'rationalistic' character of Continental theory and its preoccupation with the unlimited power of that overall abstract entity, the sovereign people. Sartori has similar things to say about the differences between 'empirical' (Anglo-American) and 'rational' (French or Continental) democracies (Sartori 1965 and 1987).

Is Continental Theory a Form of Liberal Democratic Theory?

Let us now turn to the question that has so far been left hanging in the air. Is Continental theory a form of liberal democratic theory? Should Continental theory's model of democracy be counted as a *liberal* democracy? The answer is a little complicated, and is best arrived at by looking at the cases 'for' and 'against'.

First, what is the case against counting Continental theory as a form of liberal traditional democratic theory? To begin with, it can be said that Continental theory gives more importance to equality than to liberty (Sabine 1952). But this is an assertion hard to pin down and assess. More important here is the view of the Continental model as being an 'absolute' rather than a 'liberal' or a 'limited' democracy. There are two aspects to this: the Rousseauist theory itself and the practice with which the theory became associated. In the theory we have seen that the will of the people is sovereign and that it should be subject to no limits. Indeed, as the general will is the true, moral will of each individual it would make no sense to try and limit it. There should not, then, be any limits to the democratic state's activity : its power should be absolute. This is obviously in stark contrast to the idea, central to the notion of *liberal* democracy, that power of the state – even a democratic state – should be limited. Even more clearly illiberal is the practice which was to an important extent inspired, and/or explained and justified, by Rousseauist theory. To put the matter bluntly, Rousseauist theory was to be called in aid of such grossly illiberal regimes as the Napoleonic dictatorships and the twentieth-century totalitarian systems. Indeed, as we have already noted, it is not uncommon for Rousseau to be regarded as the origin for the theory and practice of *totalitarian* democracy (Talmon 1952).

What, then, of the opposing case – the case for counting Continental theory as a form of traditional liberal democratic theory? First, despite what the Anglo-American liberal would say, Continental theory *is*, in its own terms, concerned with democracy as the way to promote freedom. But it is a different conception of freedom. We saw in the last chapter that Rousseau has a 'positive' conception of freedom. Now, in a properly constituted democratic state, laws are expressions of the general will – which means that such laws ensure that people do what they really want to do. In other words laws, the manifestations of state power, assist people to act freely so that the *un*limited democratic state, far from threatening or extinguishing freedom, is a necessary condition for it. However, the Anglo-American liberal does not, typically, accept this account of freedom and persists in seeing unlimited democracy as a threat to it as properly understood. In any case, even if the Rousseauist *theory* is given some credence, the practice of certain of the 'democracies' inspired by the theory has very clearly threatened and diminished individual freedom on any understanding of the concept. But now we come to another argument. This starts from the point that, although they might *claim* otherwise, those regimes which are illiberal and totalitarian may in fact owe their nature to something other than Rousseauist theory. Indeed, their nature may be crucially different from that theory's model of democracy. It may be that it is *mis*interpretations of Rousseau that have contributed to the non-Western, non-liberal theories of democracy, as in the 'people's democracies' of Eastern Europe. But there are other, *Western*, democracies which also see Rousseau as their inspiration and which are not illiberal and totalitarian – most notably in France. The practices of French democracy, indeed, have much in common with those of Anglo-American democracy: free competitive elections and so on. This is partly because both democratic traditions have in fact been called on in France. But so, conversely, have Britain and America called upon the Continental tradition to some extent: 'the evolution of democratic government throughout the nineteenth century continually drew upon both [traditions]' (Sabine 1952). Both traditions have important similarities as well as differences; and both have common origins in Western political theory and experience (Talmon 1952, Introduction).'The two traditions have remained persistently linked, both in the sense that they were felt to express only different aspects of a single ideal and also in the sense that practical democratic politics made drafts as occasion dictated almost indifferently upon both traditions' (Sabine 1952).

Continental traditional democratic theory, then, can certainly be seen as a variety of Western democratic theory; although whether it is properly described as 'liberal' is less certain. Be that as it may, it remains important in understanding liberal democracy because of the influence it has had not only on the practice but also on the theory of the archetypal liberal democracies,[21] where it has especially been reflected in radical democratic theory.

Neo-Idealist Democratic Theory

Finally, before we leave Continental theory, we should notice that its intermixing with Anglo-American theory in effect became a central feature of a kind of 'hybrid' form of democratic theory which was important in the earlier part of this century. Some of its ideas have come to the fore again in contemporary radical critiques of mainstream liberal democracy; and it does, indeed, provide something of a bridge between traditional and some contemporary theorising about democracy.

This type of theory is much influenced by Rousseau and collectivism but also contains distinctively Anglo-American ingredients; indeed, its authors were English and American. We can perhaps refer to it as 'neo-Idealist' democratic theory since some of its most important exponents were influenced by the philosophical Idealism[22] of the German philosopher Hegel (1770–1831) through the medium of the English philosophical Idealists T.H. Green (1836–82), F.H. Bradley (1846–1924) and B. Bosanquet (1848–1923). But it has connections with a wider stream of democratic theory contained in the work of writers – American as well as British, and including such thinkers as

John Dewey (1859–1952) – who have been referred to as 'citizenship theorists' (Thompson 1970).

The best-known neo-Idealist democratic theorists are A.D. Lindsay and Ernest Barker (see especially Lindsay (1935) and (1943), and Barker (1942)). The key feature of their theories of democracy is a variant of Rousseau's idea of the general will – called by Lindsay 'the spirit of the common life' – which emerges from the democratic processes of *discussion*. Here we have elements of Continental theory – the general will – developed by Englishmen with typical Anglo-American democratic ideas: the process of discussion, after all, requires those (negative) liberties of the individual that are central in Anglo-American liberal democratic theory. Indeed, in this sort of synthesis we have the most convincing kind of liberal democratic theory: with the emphasis on the generation of views about the common interest, through a process of discussion, the difficulties of liberal democratic theory which focuses only on individuals and their preferences are greatly diminished.[23]

2.3 Liberal Democracy versus One-Party Democracy

With neo-Idealist and citizenship theory we have come to the twentieth century and we shall be turning to 'modern' liberal democratic theory shortly. But before that we need to look at a twentieth-century challenge to liberal democracy. This, as many see it, stems ultimately from Rousseau, and we have just seen how this is a key factor in the ambivalent status of Continental theory in liberal democratic theory. We shall, then, flesh out the reference above to non-Western, non-liberal forms of democracy and look briefly at 'one-party democracy'. One-party democracy can, in fact, be seen as a powerful and challenging alternative with its competing models of democracy being embodied in the political systems of (sometimes powerful) states, hostile to liberal democracy. These are the 'people's democracies' and the 'Third World one-party democracies', which form such a large proportion of the world's states. (There are direct connections between this challenge to liberal democracy and the kind of theoretical critiques of liberal democracy discussed in the next chapter. But the nature of these connections is somewhat ambivalent.[24] In any case, in considering one-party democracies here we are focusing on the 'practical' as much as the theoretical: it is the actual existence of alternative political systems that constitutes the challenge and makes it potent.)

In his influential little book *The Real World of Democracy*, C.B. Macpherson states that 'democracy is not properly to be equated with our unique Western liberal democracy, but that the clearly non-liberal systems which prevail in the Soviet countries, and the somewhat different non-liberal systems of most of the underdeveloped countries of Asia and Africa have a genuine historical claim to the title of democracy' (Macpherson 1966). Its validity we can leave on one side for the moment, but it is certainly true that there exists an important claim here; and the ideas involved require to be understood.

The two forms of this 'non-liberal democracy' Macpherson calls the 'communist variant' and the 'underdeveloped variant' (Macpherson 1966), and we shall look at them in a moment. But first, what do they have in common: what are the distinctive features of 'non-liberal democracy'?

The most visible feature is the single party: non-liberal democracies are one-party systems. This finds its basis in, and is an expression of, a social unity that produces and is maintained by what amounts to a Rousseauean general will. Perhaps this is more apparent in the case of the 'underdeveloped' than the 'communist' variant, but essentially the basic idea is that there is a general will which expresses itself through, and only through, a single party. As it is the general will – the single genuine will of the people – that the party expresses, it follows that there is no legitimate democratic function for any other party and that there is no limit to what the governing party can properly and democratically do. For critics, this is the notion of totalitarian democracy again.

'The people', then, is conceived as a social unit. There are some differences between the variants here but, in contradistinction to liberal – individualist conceptions, they share the idea of the people as some kind of communal, corporate entity. The differences are in the nature of the entity focused upon, but in each case there is something of the original, 'Aristotelian' meaning of 'the people': the common people, the hitherto oppressed.

Before looking at each of the variants, there are two important general points to be dealt with. Both arise in Macpherson's analysis. First, part of Macpherson's argument is that even if, or where, non-liberal democracy does not qualify as democracy in the narrow sense of a system of government, it does qualify in the 'broader social sense' of a kind of society (Macpherson 1966). Now this may or may not be so, but as we have already suggested, although Macpherson would not agree, this 'broader sense' is but a secondary meaning of 'democracy'. And in any case the really important and interesting question is whether non-liberal 'democracy' qualifies as democracy in the narrower, primary sense.

This brings us to the second point. With regard to the narrow meaning, Macpherson states that for non-liberal democracies 'democracy has had something like its original meaning, government by or for the common people' (Macpherson 1966). But democracy does not mean, and never has meant, government *for* the people (the 'common people' or otherwise); rather it means government *by* the people (see, for example, Sartori (1987) Chapter 15, Section 5). And to suggest that 'government for' is the 'original meaning' as in Aristotle, is wrong: 'Macpherson is, quite simply, untrue to Aristotle. As has been correctly observed, "Macpherson's view that democracy means originally 'rule by or in the interests of the hitherto oppressed class' is doubtful. It would be a truer account . . . to say that it has meant rule by and *therefore* in the interests of the poor" [Lively 1975]. Aristotle . . . said that democracy was a rule in the interest of the poor (and/or the many) *because* democracy — the direct Greek democracy — was government *by* the poor . . . Hence, Aristotle said what has been said ever since: The interest of the poor, or the many, is affirmed when the poor or the many can themselves affirm it' (Sartori 1987). And in fact the key question about non-liberal democracy — the question on which the significant controversy and the deep theoretical issues centre — is whether in any sense it *is* government *by* (even if it is government for) the people. And this is certainly the question we shall ask here about one-party democracy.

People's Democracy

Let us now look briefly at the two varieties of one-party democracy, starting with the 'communist variant'. What we are essentially considering here is 'people's democracy': the 'democracies' behind the Iron Curtain, the Eastern European 'democracies'. Strictly speaking the term 'people's democracy' does not refer to the Soviet Union itself, but only to former and present satellites including China. One of the 'differences' here is that the latter allegedly have multi-party govern-ments, a number of parties united in a coalition. However, 'the decisive characteristics of the . . . governmental form [of the people's democracies] was the leading role of the working class, represented by its "vanguard", the communist party'. And there is an 'essential identity between the . . . patterns of government' of the Soviet Union and its satellites (Kase 1968). We shall therefore treat 'people's demo-cracy'as including the Soviet Union.

In people's democracy the single will of the people is elicited and implemented by a single vanguard party, the Communist party. We shall sketch in the nature of the system by indicating the key features of these ideas – the people, the vanguard party and the eliciting of the people's will.

People's democracies are based on Marxist-Leninist theory. The question of the place of democracy within Marxism-Leninism is complex and controversial. Arguably, Marx himself equated demo-cracy with the final, classless communist society. But the dominant idea in Lenin is that democracy occurs before that, when the proleta-riat come to power after the revolutionary overthrow of the capitalist power structure, i.e. during the phase of the 'dictatorship of the proletariat' (we shall be saying more about Marxism-Leninism in the next chapter). And people's democracy is seen as being the form now taken by the dictatorship of the proletariat (Kase 1968).

The idea of the people, then, is in this theory essentially a class concept. There are some complications and modifications – which we shall look at in a moment – but the basic notion is of the people as the working class, the proletariat. Two, overlapping reasons are usually given for counting one class only as equivalent to 'the people'. First it is pointed out that the proletariat are (at least in the sort of societies Marx originally had in mind) the most numerous class, the majority. And since, it is argued, rule by the people in a democracy actually means rule by a majority, the proletariat are 'operationally' equi-valent to the people. 'The dictatorship of the proletariat . . . will, for the first time, produce a democracy for the people, for the majority' (Lenin 1960). In fact, as we saw earlier, the whole idea that demo-cracy amounts to rule by a majority is fraught with difficulties, but these do not come within the purview of Leninist theory. Indeed, the existence of what the liberal democrat sees as the strange and obnoxious idea of democracy being constituted by the *dictatorship* of the majority – the dictatorship of the proletariat – is related to a failure to focus on the proper qualifications to the idea of democracy as majority rule. Second, the proletariat are seen straightforwardly *as* the people, in the traditional 'Aristotelian' sense of the people as the poor or 'the hitherto oppressed classes'. Here rule by the proletariat simply is rule by the people, without the qualifications and difficulties of saying it is merely rule by a majority of the people.

There is an overlap between these two ideas since the traditional Aristotelian sense of the people connects up with the (now) dominant meaning of the people via the assumption, made also by Aristotle, that the poor are nearly always the most numerous. There is also another dimension to this connecting up of the people-as-proletariat with the primary idea of the people as the whole population. In Marxist theory the overthrow of capitalist society by the proletariat – the proletarian revolution – is the decisive step towards the communist, classless society which will be for the benefit of *everyone*. Action by the proletariat, then, frees, and is on behalf of, not just the proletariat but the whole of humanity; or, at any rate, all the humans in the state in which the revolution occurs (Marxist theory originally held that the proletarian revolution would transcend state divisions). Rule by the proletariat, then, is on behalf of the whole people.

One complication is that Leninist theory recognised that the proletariat were not necessarily actually in a majority. In this case either the proletariat were the vanguard of the rest of the people ('the non-proletarian working masses', mainly the peasantry); or else the proletariat jointly constituted the people: 'On the continent of Europe, in 1871, the proletariat did not in a single country constitute the majority of the people. A "people's revolution" . . . could be such only if embracing both the proletariat and the peasantry. Both classes constituted the "people" ' (Lenin 1960). However, it was later said that the people's democracies have 'all, including the Chinese people's democratic dictatorship . . . reached the stage of full proletarian dictatorship' (Kase 1968). In the Soviet Union itself, the official view became that the dictatorship of the proletariat had been superseded by a state of the whole people, but this seemed to make little difference to the basic ideas of people's democracy (see Reglar and Young(1983) for a useful discussion).

For Marx, it seems the rule of the proletariat (he himself uses the phrase 'dictatorship of the proletariat' very infrequently) means rule by the whole proletariat. This might be through radically democratic processes, inspired by the notion of direct democracy, as in the Paris Commune of 1871. In Lenin, however, the dominant idea is that of the dictatorship of the proletariat being exercised in the form of rule by the vanguard of the proletariat – the Communist party. This is necessary partly for organisational reasons, but also because Lenin, unlike Marx, does not really think the proletariat, unaided, are capable of developing a revolutionary consciousness and discerning their true interests. Instead they will have induced in them, as victims of capitalist society, a 'false consciousness', a 'trade union consciousness'. This will lead them merely to attempt to ameliorate their position under capitalism, by trade union activity and so on, rather than trying to overthrow it.

It is the vanguard, then, that actually exercises power – on behalf of the proletariat. This is government *for* the proletariat, government for the people. But is it government *by* the people? This is a crucial but tricky question. There is, it is true, often a tendency simply to talk of government for the people. Macpherson, as we have seen, talks of government 'by or for' the people. However he also admits that in the 'narrow sense' of democracy a vanguard state is not a democracy, since it is not government by the people (Macpherson 1966, Chapter 1). And we have already argued that for democracy to exist there must, indeed, be government by the people.

In fact, there are also arguments to the effect that rule by the vanguard party *is* government by the people. One of these plainly will not do, though. This is the argument which points to rule by the vanguard being essential for bringing about a situation – the eventual communist society – in which people are truly emancipated and in which they really do rule themselves in the fullest possible sense. This could be a very important argument, but the most it could establish is that vanguard rule is a necessary condition for establishment of, not that it actually *is*, rule by the people.

The more fundamental argument makes use of what is very like a variant of Rousseau's idea of the general will; and it is here that we come back to connections between Continental theory, 'totalitarian democracy' and the theory of people's democracy.[25] The basic general idea involves distinguishing between people's apparent and true wills, and focusing on the true will for what is in the real interests of the people. Now, in Marxist-Leninist theory, the people is constituted by a class; and what is in the real interests of a class, and therefore of the people, can be objectively identified by those with the necessary knowledge, including knowledge of Marxist theory. The real will of the people can, then, be identified by those with the requisite knowledge. Lenin, as we just said, thought that only the vanguard party, rather than the mass of the proletariat, had the necessary knowledge. And in taking action to realise the true interests of the people we could say the vanguard party is doing nothing other than implementing the true will – the 'general will' – of the people. In fact in Lenin's own thought there is a certain ambivalence between a 'hard' and a 'soft' version of this theory: in the hard version the vanguard party simply tells the proletariat what their will is;[26] but in the soft version there is the idea that through mass participation under the leadership of the party – and such leadership *is* vital – the proletariat come themselves to know their interests correctly. Perhaps a synthesis of the two versions best expresses the essence of Lenin's thinking: the vanguard party knows the 'correct' policy to implement, but the masses must come to realise that this is the correct policy, through direct political participation in which they are led and educated by the party. There is here still a connection with Rousseau's own insistence that for the general will to exist the people must at some point actually, overtly, will what is in their real interests.

Be that as it may, however, the experience of people's democracies has been one in which rule is actually by the party and only the hard version of the theory can be said to apply. Here, unlike in Rousseau, one is required to accept that there is a meaningful sense in which people can be said to will – decide in favour of – that which is in their true interests, even when they do not themselves actually, subjectively, do so. This raises important issues, some of which will be discussed later, but two points need to be made now. First, the liberal democrat cannot accept that there is any sense in the notion that people will or decide things which they do not actually, 'empirically', will or decide. (The hard version of the Leninist theory ultimately turns on the conception of the proletariat as an objectively defined social entity; whereas the liberal democrat sees essentially autonomous individuals who can be only what they themselves conceive themselves to be. Again this raises deep issues which will be taken up later.) Second, the liberal democrat will very sensibly insist that whatever is to be made of the *theory* of people's democracy, the *practice* amounts to unbridled power being in the hands of the vanguard party, or its leading organs or individuals. Not only is this undemocratic, it is illiberal and dangerous. One need not accept without

qualification Lord Acton's dictum to the effect that all power tends to
corrupt and absolute power corrupts absolutely. But one can still
recognise that self-interest, and/or particular individual ideas on the
use to be made of power, will tend to exert a dangerous influence on
those whose power is not effectively limited, and that the liberty of
citizens is likely to suffer accordingly.

Before we leave people's democracy, though, we should notice the
very important recent developments in the Soviet Union, summed up
under the idea of *glasnost*, which might in time very significantly
change the nature of the Soviet political system and, perhaps, the
people's democracies generally. Particularly significant has been Gor-
bachev's talk of the importance of democracy and his introduction of
contested elections and secret ballots in respect of some regional party
bodies. If such arrangements were to be developed throughout the
party, and especially in respect of the top party posts, then a different
kind of judgement on the question of the existence of democracy in the
Soviet Union might be needed. For Macpherson, existing vanguard
states are not democratic in 'the narrow sense', i.e. the primary sense,
but 'a one-party state can in principle be democratic even in the
narrow sense' provided that certain conditions are fulfilled (Macpherson 1966). One of these is that there should be full intra-party
democracy – that the party itself should be democratically controlled
by its members. A liberal democrat would not accept this as sufficient
since choice is restricted within a party ideology, and is made only by
party members; although another of Macpherson's conditions is that
membership of the party should be open to all. This is not sufficiently
open to allow a genuine decision by the people. And in any case, one
can be sure that in practice the party leadership in the Soviet Union
will, for the time being at least, continue to keep a pretty tight rein
on the candidates able to stand for election to party posts. Nonetheless, such significant changes may develop a dynamic of their own.
And, at the very least, in the ideas involved in *glasnost* and Gor-
bachev's use of the conception of democracy, including calls for
increased participation, it is the soft version of Lenin's theory that is
being invoked.

Third World One-Party Democracy

We will turn now to the 'underdeveloped variant' of non-liberal
democracy – one-party democracy in the Third World. Little needs

to be added specifically on this as much of what has already been said about non-liberal democracy covers both variants.

In what way, though, does the 'underdeveloped' differ from the 'communist' variant? (We should notice, incidentally, that Marxist-Leninists are prone to argue that the communist variant itself should be applied to the Third World. Indeed a variety of the conception of people's democracy – 'national democracy' – was specifically devised to fit the developing countries (Kase 1968).) The chief difference is that the idea of class plays no part. There is still some notion of democracy being rule by and for the oppressed people, but the erstwhile oppressors are not a class but the former colonial rulers. 'The people' is the whole, undivided, nation and so we have the notion of a unified community uncomplicated by a theory of class conflict.

The idea of a community, and of community being expressed and sustained by a single unified will and manifested in the rule of a single party, is indeed absolutely central. There are clearly 'strong echoes of Rousseau' here (Macpherson 1966), and a student of African political theory tells us that 'it is to the theory of Rousseau that one is immediately drawn because of the striking parallels between his ideas and those of African theorists [and whilst] there is no evidence that Rousseau's ideas have been directly borrowed . . . that his political theory had an influence on the western-educated proponents of African democracy is indisputable' (Nursey-Bray 1983). But the inspiration for focusing on the importance of community and a single unified will is also home-grown. In Africa there is a harking back to pre-colonial days and 'African traditional society [which] is envisaged as an ideal communal society' (Nursey-Bray 1983). More generally, there is the importance of the independence struggle itself and the subsequent fight to develop economically and to create a cohesive nation. These both involved ideological leadership, disciplined organisation and the rejection of divisive views.

Such factors clearly point to a vanguard role for the single political party. And indeed there are strong similarities here between people's democracy and Third World one-party democracy. The ideas, though, are more like the soft version of Lenin's theory; and, largely due to the absence of ideas of class and class-consciousness, the 'vanguard' is not so sharply differentiated from the masses. 'The new [Third World] states were indeed brought into existence by mass movements headed by a strong vanguard, but the vanguard was not generally as separated from the mass as it was in the Communist revolutions' (Macpherson 1966). In fact there is quite a variety of single-party systems in (what are claimed as) Third World democracies – not including the *liberal* democracies (see Chapter 4). There are systems under the tight control of one highly disciplined party, perhaps actually inspired by Marxist-Leninist theory. There are countries where only one party exists but the party itself allows some genuine rank-and-file participation in its control. And there are systems in which two or more political parties exist but where one party is dominant and, by various means, is able to ensure it always wins elections.

Assessment of One-Party Democracy

Finally, what are we to make of one-party democracy and its claim to be an alternative – and, indeed, a superior – form of democracy? As indicated already, a full discussion of the issues raises fundamental questions that are taken up in the next chapter; but one or two remarks should be made.

The guiding thread of the one-party alternative is provided by the ideas of unanimity and a single will of the people. By contrast, liberal democratic theory, as we have seen, typically gets itself into many difficulties in trying to make sense of the notion of a decision by the people as consisting in many disparate individual decisions. But liberal democratic theory's focus on choice, which is to an important extent the source of these difficulties, is also its great strength. To simplify drastically, the key point is that in one-party democracy what is claimed to be the general will of the people need not be, and probably is not, any such thing. This is because unless the individuals who constitute the people can themselves choose policies it can never be known what their wills are. Rousseau provides important insights concerning the conflict between selfish decisions and decisions about the public interest and the common good. But even when all due allowance has been made for this, it must still be recognised that there are genuine differences of view about what *is* in the public interest; and these must be given expression. Moreover, even if the theory of one-party democracy and the single will of the people has something to be said for it, there is still the profoundly important point that in practice those with unchecked power are liable to depart from a concern with the general will. In short, the only meaningful and safe approach to achieving rule by the people – even if it is merely an *approach* and needs supplementation – is to give the people the opportunity to register different opinions and make explicit 'empirical' choices between alternative policies and candidates at regular contested elections.

2.4 The Academic Challenge to Traditional Democratic Theory

The ideas of one-party democracy constitute one kind of challenge, an 'ideological challenge', and alternative to traditional liberal democratic theory. But there is another and very different kind of attack: an 'academic challenge'. This gives rise to correspondingly different alternative theories of democracy, and it is time now to look at these. Such theories do, though, fall within the general notion of liberal democracy. In short, whilst in the previous section we considered rivals to traditional *liberal* democratic theory, the subject of this section is the opposition to *traditional* liberal democratic theory. (Henceforth, where the meaning is clearly implied by the context, the word 'liberal' will be dropped and the less cumbersome label 'traditional democratic theory' will be used.)

Traditional democratic theory was historically important, providing the theory that accompanied and inspired the development of democracy in the nineteenth century. But it also remains important today, continuing to provide for most people their account of what democracy is, and why it is desirable. For most citizens of Western democracies, traditional theory is the lens through which they see their systems *as* democracies; and so for them the traditional model of democracy remains fairly accurate as a picture of what those systems are like.[27] However, important though it continues to be, traditional democratic theory has been subject to a strong 'academic challenge' in modern times: traditional ideas have been measured against contemporary reality and then found wanting; empirical studies of the workings of Western democratic systems have seemed to show traditional democratic theory to be hopelessly unrealistic.

What precisely is meant by 'unrealistic' here, and why it should be taken as a fault, are matters we can leave aside for the moment. It is sufficient at this point to say that in the mid-twentieth century it became very widely held in politically knowledgeable circles that traditional democratic theory was deficient because its model of democracy was seriously out of accord with reality. The nature and functioning of actual democracies were revealed as being crucially different from what was portrayed in the model.

To be more accurate, it was the discrepancy between reality and *radical* democratic theory's model that was focused upon. The critics, though, did not always realise this: those who criticised it for being unrealistic seldom specified clearly what they meant by 'traditional democratic theory'; indeed, they often seemed not to appreciate how different the various theories are that cluster under the 'traditional' label. In fact, as we have seen, there are even significant differences in the theories under the 'radical' label. These latter theories do, though, have even more significant features in common, centring on the positive role of the people. And it is clear that it is democratic theories with these features that were being primarily challenged. Moreover, since it is from radical theory that the public tend to obtain their picture of democracy, it is theories with these features that constitute the operational form of traditional democratic theory. *Conventional* traditional theory is in fact in certain key respects less like this operational theory than the modern theories which were supposed to replace traditional theory (see the section on Modern Democratic Theory below).

But why did this widely accepted form of traditional democratic theory, radical theory, come to be seen as unrealistic? In summary, it was due to a changing perception in informed circles of the reality of the political systems, known as 'Western democracies', to which the theory was applied, so that the theory could no longer be regarded as being in accord with the reality. This changing perception resulted essentially from insights brought by developments in the academic study of politics, although it is hard to separate these from developments in the reality being studied. At all events, it was such things as the growth in the scale, scope and complexity of governmental activity, and an increased awareness of the nature of pressure groups, elites and the facts of voting behaviour, that led to the dismissal of radical democratic theory as unrealistic.

The argument from scale and complexity focuses on matters such as the sheer size of modern states, the development of science and technology, the complexity of modern economies and the involvement of governments in attempts to regulate them, and the modern responsibility of the state for social welfare. The quantity and difficulty of governmental decision making to which all this gives rise is said to make impossible the kind of detailed positive decision-making role for the people at large that is envisaged in radical democratic theory. This is a matter both of the organisational complexity of decision making by large numbers of people and of those people's inevitable lack of expertise and comprehension.

This type of argument overlaps with those based on studies of elites and of voting behaviour where, in effect, empirical evidence is said to confirm that there is no positive rule by the people. Some of the findings of twentieth-century sociology and political science have provided us with an account of the political systems of Western 'democracies'[28] in which they are shown in fact to be run by elites, with the mass of the electorate being ignorant and apathetic. This is clearly in stark contrast to radical democratic theory's model of a system which is run by an involved and politically rational citizenry.

To begin with, then, there was the study of elites, and a growing awareness of their existence and importance. Elites have come to be widely seen as playing a crucial role in all political systems. This includes the Western 'democracies', although whether, or to what extent, this amounts to elite control of the kind found in other political systems is something we shall take up shortly. Clearly, though, it amounts to something drastically at odds with the system of popular control portrayed in radical democratic theory.

But what are these elites that are said to be so important?[29] The meaning of the term 'elite' is hard to pin down, but roughly speaking we can say it means a minority group that is distinguished from the mass of the people by factors which give its members important advantages. Our concern here is with 'political' or 'power' elites where the particular 'advantage' in question is the possession of, and/or an especial ability to obtain, political power. That is to say, a political or power elite is one that holds, and/or is especially likely to hold, political power – perhaps because it *is* an elite. There is a long tradition of thought which regards political elites as being of crucial importance.[30] In a sense Plato was an elitist. But 'organisational elitism' – where elite power is seen as being required by the organisational needs of complex society – is relatively modern. It achieved its best-known expression in the works of the 'classic elitists' Pareto (1848–1923), Mosca (1858–1941), and Mosca's disciple Michels (1876–1936) with his famous iron law of oligarchy; but the work of the sociologist Max Weber (1864–1920) is also of profound importance.[31] Today, many political scientists see the existence of power elites as inevitable. But, since rule by an elite is the very opposite of positive rule by the people, this means that the non-existence of radical democracy is also seen as inevitable.

The elitist critique of radical democratic theory was linked with and further reinforced by judgements about the nature of the mass electorate. These arose from studies of voting behaviour, which seemed to deny the capacity of the mass of the people for positive rule. Modern empirical studies of voting behaviour have been of various kinds, but the most relevant here are those using questionnaires and the sample survey method to obtain direct – and sometimes very detailed – information about why people vote as they do. The pioneering studies of the 1940s and 1950s (mainly, but not only, in Britain and the USA) apparently demonstrated that electors are largely ignorant of, and uninterested in, the issues and policies before them at elections; and, more generally, that they participate but little in politics.[32]

The evidence was, broadly speaking, of two main kinds. On the one hand voting behaviour was correlated with social and demographic characteristics. The conclusion frequently drawn was that voting was more or less 'socially determined': a person's voting behaviour was seen as a reaction to social and demographic position rather than as a response to issues and policies. As one of the earliest studies put it: 'a man thinks, politically, as he is, socially. Social characteristics determine political preference' (Lazarsfeld *el al.* 1968). Other studies drew back from quite such forthright conclusions but still implied a large measure of 'social determinism'. Social class (Britain and the USA), ethnic group, religion and being urban or rural (USA) were seen as the main determinants. On the other hand there was direct evidence of what this social determinism implied – that voting was not the product of political knowledge and interest. Voters, in fact, seemed to lack knowledge and interest: answers to survey questions revealed a massive ignorance of the issues and policy proposals facing them at elections. Many American voters knew 'the existence of few, if any, of the major issues of policy' (Campbell *et al.* 1960) whilst of the British electorate it was said they are 'uninformed . . . The number who are well informed is probably no more than one-tenth of the whole electorate on the great majority of issues.' And 'the electorate is not only uninformed it is uninterested' (Abrams and Rose,

1960). The ignorance and apathy of the electorate was summed up in a leading study in these words: 'there seems to be widespread ignorance and indifference over many matters of policy. And even when opinions are held, many persons are not motivated to discover or are unable to sort out the relevant positions adopted by the parties' (Campbell *et al.* 1960).

According to the conception of rational political behaviour indicated earlier, this evidence shows the electorate – the mass of the people – to be irrational. As such the people cannot be seen as capable of running the country, of holding positive power. This clearly supports the idea that elites must rule. Thus, to return to the basic issue, studies of elites and of voting behaviour clearly seem to demonstrate that in reality the Western 'democracies' are not at all like the democracies portrayed in radical democratic theory. In a word, radical democratic theory is shown as unrealistic.

The focus in modern political studies on the role and importance of pressure groups also contributed to the view that radical democratic theory was unrealistic. 'Pressure groups' are bodies that seek to influence public policy by attempting to influence government: trades unions, business groups, farmers groups, campaign groups and the like (unlike political parties they do not seek to *become*, or become part of, the government).[33] Pressure groups have always been important, but they became more so with the increasing complexity of the economy, and growing government involvement with it. At all events, by the mid-twentieth century the study of their role in the political system had become a major concern of political scientists.

The implications of pressure groups for radical democratic theory are not, perhaps, so clear cut as in the case of elites and voting behaviour. This is partly a matter of some ambivalence in radical democratic theory: certain of the problems and differences in radical theories of democracy that we looked at earlier, are central here. (In a sense this ambivalence is reflected in the fact that, as we shall see, pressure group operations are actually the inspiration of some modern theories of democracy.) Nonetheless, a clear critique emerges of a model containing only certain features of radical theories of democracy, but which is quite often taken as an exemplification of traditional democratic theory. Such a model is one in which the people have a single, definite and unproblematic will. This all-important will of the people is embodied in the electorate's unified decision on what they see – and want implemented– as being in the general interest (the clear influence of Rousseau can be seen in this widely accepted model).

The critique maintains that a political system in which pressure groups are important is crucially different from this model of democracy. There are two key points. First, pressure groups, in seeking to promote the particular interests of their members are thereby acting against the general interest. (This point really relates only to those pressure groups which are 'interest groups', as distinct from those which promote a 'cause'; but it is interest groups which tend to be the more influential.) Since the government has been elected to implement the people's decision about what is in the general interest, to the extent that a pressure group successfully influences the government it is frustrating the will of the people. Second, pressure groups divert their members' attention away from the general interest and on to their particular group interests. To that extent, then, members ignore the general interest and fail to express their view about it. In short, on this analysis, pressure groups frustrate the generation and/or the implementation of the will of the people. And since, or to the extent that, studies show pressure groups actually to be key factors in the political process, government by the popular will is shown not to exist. Again, the – or a – radical model of democracy is shown to be unrealistic.

Assessment of the Academic Challenge

The 'academic challenge' to radical democratic theory has been powerful and fundamental. And this amounts to an undermining of traditional liberal democratic theory, since, as we saw, radical theory is its 'operative form'. But there are, in any case, certain features of conventional theory that are also challenged by modern studies of politics, most particularly the stress on the importance in the political process of groups – elites as well as pressure groups – rather than individuals.

What are we to make of this challenge to traditional democratic theory? In answering this question we must consider both responses that reject, and those that accept, the validity of the challenge. We shall leave the second type till the next section and turn now to the first.

In fact there are two types of response that reject the challenge to traditional theory, although they do overlap to some extent. On the one hand there is the argument that, properly understood, the findings of modern political science do not actually constitute a challenge to traditional democratic theory. On the other hand there are denials of the validity of some of the findings themselves.

The denial that there is in fact a challenge hinges on a central contention. This is that democratic theory generally, and traditional democratic theory in particular, is primarily *pre*scriptive rather than *de*scriptive: its purpose is to prescribe what ought to be rather than to describe what is. As Duncan and Lukes (1963) argued in an influential article, those who criticise traditional democratic theory as being unrealistic miss the point that such theory does not purport accurately to picture, describe or explain political reality. On the contrary, it is meant to be critical and to picture what does *not*, but what ought to, exist; in short, to hold up an ideal. If the reality is not like the theory it is the reality rather than the theory that is at fault.

There is a good deal in this kind of argument. But there is an important rejoinder to be considered: it might be granted that a democratic theory is prescriptive, but still, if it is *greatly* at odds with reality, it may, nonetheless fail – even as prescriptive theory. Even Duncan and Lukes acknowledge that 'if such a theory seems intolerably remote from reality, it may be charged with utopianism' (Duncan and Lukes 1963). And 'while idealised conceptions of our system may inspire both higher aspirations and performance in the real world, it is also true that too great a gap between democratic ideals and reality may inspire fanciful expectations whose frustration breeds cynicism' (Presthus 1964). Another, important and overlapping, type of argument centres more on the nature than the extent of the gap between ideal and reality. The principal contention here is that not only is there a gap but it is bound to remain, i.e. the key factor is its permanence rather than its extent. It is not the difficulty of greatly changing reality that is focused upon, so much as the impossibility of changing it at all in the relevant respects: the nature of voting behaviour, for instance, is seen as a manifestation of the permanent nature of man.

These arguments raise issues that are also central to the discussion of the radical critique of liberal democracy in the next chapter, so we shall not try and assess them here. But before we move on we should notice that there is an issue of another kind that can be involved in considering whether the findings of political science constitute a challenge to traditional democratic theory. So far, we have focused on denying the *existence* of radical democracy. But its *desirability* can also be questioned. This arises mainly from considering the implications of the voting behaviour studies: in essence the question is whether a system is desirable where power is in the hands of irrational people.[34] Again, we shall leave this on one side for the moment since it becomes part of the issues discussed in Chapter 4: in effect demonstrations of the irrationality of voters can be taken as supporting traditional arguments against democracy which stress the need for rule by the wise few rather than by the irrational mass of the people. We should simply note here that any 'challenge' to traditional democratic theory that is involved consists in the argument that such theory is discredited for advocating that which is undesirable. (It might be held that it is not just traditional but *all* democratic theory that is challenged in this way. However, it is again radical democratic theory that is most vulnerable since it gives the largest role to the 'irrational' people; indeed, conventional and modern elitist democratic theory modify the role of the people specifically to cope with doubts about their rationality.)

The second way of attempting to refute the challenge to traditional democratic theory is to dispute the validity of the findings of modern political science on which it is allegedly based. Once more the issues raised are ones which become part of those discussed in the next chapter. Nonetheless, some questions relating to the voting behaviour studies are fairly 'self-contained' and should be mentioned here.

The point is that the validity of the findings about the electorate's ignorance and apathy can be questioned. This is partly a matter of looking critically at the pioneering studies, their findings and the interpretations put upon them. The essential argument here is that a re-examination of those studies shows that the picture they give of the electorate is not in fact quite so dismal as at first appeared. The voters are shown to have *some* interest and *some* political knowledge and not to be completely socially determined.[35] But this kind of argument overlaps into another, and rather more important one, to the effect that more recent studies of voting behaviour have given us a significantly different picture of the electorate. In one of the seminal works it was asserted that 'the perverse and unorthodox argument of this little book is that voters are not fools' (Key 1966). Indeed, Key discerned 'an electorate moved by concern about central and relevant questions of public policy, of governmental performance and executive personality' (Maas 1966). Which view of the electorate is right – that of Key or the earlier voting studies – has continued to be a subject of controversy, but the weight of argument tends to favour Key. The critical factor in 'pro-Key' analyses has been study of the electorate in periods other than the 1940s and 1950s when the original studies took place. Key himself included data from the 1930s and subsequent studies have focused, obviously enough, on the 1960s, 1970s and 1980s. Many points have arisen, both substantive and methodological; but the main one has been that the electorate's behaviour does vary over time. It is pointed out that the 1950s was a politically quiescent time, so it was quite natural for there to have been a low level of concern with politics. It is contended that the pioneering studies mistakenly extrapolated from findings concerning this atypical period to universal generalisations about 'the nature of the electorate'. The periods before and after the 1950s – especially the 1930s and 1960s – were less bland; political events made more impact on voters and they became more concerned and knowledgeable about politics. Which *is* the 'typical' period and what is the 'typical' or 'natural' form of behaviour (or whether, indeed, there is any such thing as typical or natural behaviour here) are questions that raise fundamental issues, some of which are touched on later. All we shall do here is refer to some of the more recent voting studies and then come back to the significance of all this for traditional democratic theory.

Recent studies have emphasised, on the one hand, a decline in the importance of social position and stable party identification as determinants of, or influences on, voting behaviour, and, on the other hand, the growing impact of political issues. 'The rise of issue voting' (Nie *et al.* 1976) in fact became a growing pre-occupation of students of voting behaviour. Pamper (1975) concentrated on the *responsive* voter in America – the one who responds to issues. And a similar view of the British voter has become widely accepted. The authors of one study in the 1980s, for example, said:

> The portrait that emerges from our study of the voter today is of someone who is not simply conforming to his or her own past or following other people's examples, but makes up his own mind. While little interested in politics and fairly unsophisticated in his or her political thinking, the voter is nevertheless quite aware of the parties' major policy proposals and has views about the parties' ability or willingness to implement them; he also has fairly definite views on a variety of political issues, particularly those that have a bearing on his or her own life (Himmelweit *et al.* 1981).

Others have been more cautious, emphasising the *diversity* of influences on voting behaviour (Rose and McAllister 1986), but in one recent book on British and American voting behaviour which 'attempted to show students where the balance of scholarly opinion now lies', the author roundly proclaims 'a value-judgement which I believe the evidence justifies: that voters are not stupid. In this I share the views of V. O. Key' (McLean 1982).

What are the implications of these newer studies' findings? They certainly modify the challenge to traditional democratic theory that we have looked at; but whether they go far enough to 'reinstate' the theory is another matter. The point is that although the electorate is portrayed as more rational than it was by the earlier studies, the degree of rationality still falls far short of that assumed by radical democratic theory: there is no indication of the high level of political interest and the degree of detailed knowledge that radical theory assumes citizens to have. The gap between theory and reality remains, albeit reduced in extent. The differing interpretations of the significance of such a gap have already been indicated and we cannot assess them all here. But it is right that we should look at one of them now. This is the viewpoint – roughly speaking that of modern political science – according to which no such gap should exist: a viable theory of democracy must be realistic. From this viewpoint traditional democratic theory remains deficient. Does this mean, though, that democratic theory as such is deficient? Can alternative theories be formulated that are viable? The answer, according to some, is yes. Such alternatives are 'modern' theories of democracy, and it is to a brief consideration of these that we now turn.

Modern Democratic Theory

'Modern' theories of democracy are a mid-twentieth-century creation. They were developed by modern analysts to fit the realities of the political systems of modern democracies,[36] and thereby to rescue democratic theory by replacing what they saw as the discredited traditional theory.

There are, broadly speaking, two main varieties, although there is a significant overlap. The differences are quite important but, apart from any overlap in content, they share two common features. First, there is a full acknowledgement of those facts about modern democratic (or 'democratic') systems that were seen as undermining traditional theory. Indeed, it is these very facts that form, as it were, the bases of the modern theories. This leads to the second common feature: an identity of purpose. The aim in both types of theory is to show that the very things which, from a traditional perspective, were seen as undermining democracy are more properly to be seen as *elements of* democracy. This means explaining how a system characterised by such phenomena is nonetheless still a democracy. It also involves – though this is not always recognised – showing that the phenomena themselves are desirable rather than regrettable.

Space forbids more than a very brief sketch of these modern theories of democracy (a fuller picture can be gained by following up the references). The two main varieties are 'elitist' and 'pluralist' democratic theory.[37] Essentially, the former considers the issues posed by scale and complexity, elites and the studies of voting behaviour, whilst the latter has pressure groups as a main focus.

Elitist Democratic Theory

In elitist democratic theories the presence of elites is accepted – indeed welcomed – but, at the same time, their presence is reconciled with the existence of democracy. In such theories' model of democracy,[38] the system is run by elites, thus coping with the scale and complexity problems. But, so the argument runs, the system is nonetheless democratic for three main reasons. First, the elites are 'open': people may rise readily from the masses to become members. Second, elites alternate in power. Systems in which but one elite remains permanently in power are quite clearly *not* democracies. But these are quite different from systems in which there is a plurality of political elites, with elites moving in and out of power. Third, the moving in and out involves a competition of power; moreover – and crucially – the competition is for the people's votes. The system is a democracy because the electorate decides which elite is to hold power: 'the result of the competition between [elites] is democracy. And this is because the power of deciding between the competitors is in the hands of the *demos* – the onlooker who benefits from a quarrel between other people' (Sartori 1965). This central idea was summed up in the well-known definition of democracy given by the 'founding father' of elitist democratic theory, Joseph Schumpeter: 'the democratic method is that institutional arrangement for arriving at political decisions in which individuals acquire the power to decide by means of a competitive struggle for the people's vote' (Schumpeter 1976).[39] And, it should be added, through the electoral process, the people can remove elites from, as well as appoint them to, power. In this way the ultimate power is in the hands of the people. Indeed, the people make, and are entitled to make, the ultimate decisions; hence the system is a democracy (but see also the next paragraph).

We shall not attempt any assessment of elitist democratic theory here since this is effectively subsumed under the discussion of participatory theory – itself a critique of elitist democratic theory – in the next chapter. But there are two points which should be noted now. First, in order for the claim that it really *is* a theory of democracy to be substantiated, the people in appointing and removing elites must also be making the basic *policy* decisions. There is in fact some ambivalence in elitist democratic theory here, not least because the theory goes further than merely recognising the existence of elites and actually welcomes them for their superior decision-making capacity. For Schumpeter the voters should *not* make policy decisions at elections; rather, they should appoint elites to make these decisions for them: 'we reverse the roles of these two elements [as they occur in radical democratic theory] and make the deciding of issues by the electorate secondary to the election of the men who are to do the deciding' (Schumpeter, 1976); see also Miller (1983). But this is an extreme view, and most elitist democratic theorists impute at least a minimal policy-deciding role to the electorate, so that they are seen in broad terms as making the most basic or fundamental policy decisions. In short, the voters decide not only who shall have power but also, very broadly speaking, what they shall do with that power. Moreover, the electorate affect, and ultimately control, the policy of the ruling elite by their power of removal as well as by their power of appointment. The elite in power must always think of the next election, and adjust their policy decisions accordingly, if they wish to remain in power: they are 'guided by "the rule of anticipated reactions", that is, by the expectation of how the voters will react at the next elections' (Sartori 1965).

This brings us to the second point, which is that elitist democratic theory can quite properly be seen as fully realistic. Obviously it recognises the existence of elites but it is also in accord with studies of voting behaviour. As we saw just now, the more recent studies suggest that although they do not exhibit the kind of rationality required by radical theory, voters do in fact make just the kinds of broad and diffuse policy decisions – 'reactions' as well as forward-looking decisions – assumed in elitist democratic theory.

Pluralist Democratic Theory

Pluralist, like elitist, democratic theory transposes something which was held to undermine (radical) democracy into a *feature of* democracy. In pluralist theory this 'something' is the role of pressure groups as revealed by modern political science. Pluralist democratic theory is in fact, to a considerable extent, a democratic theory of pressure groups. It does, though, also tap and adapt a longer tradition of theory, a tradition which focuses on division and diversity within (the preferred kind of) society, the dispersal of power this involves and the contribution it makes to limiting the potentially dangerous power of a centralised state.

Pluralist theories of democracy are those in which the activities of groups are seen as operations on behalf of, and in some sense by, the people – so that the power of the people is manifested in the power of groups. Stated as simply as possible, the model typical of pluralist democratic theories can be outlined as follows. Elections, although important, do not properly express decisions by the people. The issues to be decided, and the various stands upon those issues, are too diffuse; above all there is a lack of correspondence between the multiplicity of electors' opinions and interests and the options available to vote on. This adds up to saying that no meaningful policy decision by the people is expressed at an election. Rather, the decisions of the people are expressed through the operations of pressure groups. This is because the groups effectively articulate the specific demands of their members and, in the model, all citizens are at least potentially members of pressure groups, or are catered for by them. Hence the actual views and interests of the electorate are precisely transmitted through the operations of pressure groups, and the outcome of the process is seen as a decision by all the people which has definite content.

In short, in this model the existence and operation of powerful pressure groups, far from undermining the liberal democratic process, actually constitute it. There are fundamental problems in this account which we cannot properly consider here (see Ricci (1971) for a useful discussion of the various criticisms of pluralist democratic theory). But there are some points we should note. First, a crucial weakness in pluralist democratic theory lies in its account of a general collective decision in terms of the pursuit of separate particular interests. The problems here parallel those of utilitarian democratic theory, although now the particular interests in question are those of groups rather than of individuals. An associated point is that pluralist democratic theory gets into some difficulties about the role of government and the state. The key point is that the theory seems to lead to the odd and troublesome conclusion that where actions by the government are generated independently of, and are perhaps opposed by, pressure groups, such actions are somehow illegitimate and undemocratic; this is odd and troublesome because it is normally held that the government has the distinctive and important function of promoting the public's interest in *contradistinction* to the demands of particular interests. A final feature to note about the pluralist model is its congruence with the notion of *liberal* democracy. Power is 'pluralised' – dispersed, or divided up, amongst many groups – and this ensures that there is not too much left in the hands of the government and liberty is thereby protected. This brings us to the final point. Critiques of pluralist democratic theory in particular often merge into critiques of liberal democratic theory in general, which we consider in the next chapter.

The typical or basic model of pluralist democratic theory is, in fact, something of an ideal type and there are important variations of it. One of these involves a greater emphasis on the electoral process and is really a combination of elements of both elitist and pluralist theory. Indeed, one of the best-known and most sophisticated of modern democratic theorists, Robert Dahl,[40] has been called a 'pluralist–elitist' democratic theorist. Theories of this hybrid type have two key features. First, the focus is not just on pressure groups, but on groups as such – and the way in which society is naturally divided into, and power is split among, them. Elites are seen as types of group, or as leading elements within groups. Elite competition tends to be assimilated to the pluralist scheme: elites are conceived as competing groups and power is accordingly viewed as being pluralised among them. But, second, this elite power process is also, to an extent, distinguished from – and modified by – the general group process. Elites win power through elections, but their exercise of such power is subject to, and modified by, the operations of pressure groups.

Consociational Democracy

Another variation on the basic model is provided by the idea and theory of consociational democracy (Lijphart 1968 and 1969). Here the general model of pluralist democratic theory is largely retained since the key feature remains the 'pluralisation' of power among various sections of society. But there are two main differences from the basic model.

First, the 'groups' concerned are not merely pressure groups; indeed they are not really 'groups' at all, but something more fundamental – segments of society. In fact a distinguishing feature of a consociational democracy is its existence where[41] society is deeply divided into various segments. These divisions are reflected in the political process in various ways, including the structure of the party system; and pressure-group activity on behalf of social segments is but one of them. The segments result from 'substantial cleavages in social structure in addition to those arising from socio-economic differences, cleavages founded on broad ideological and religious foundations' (McRae 1974, Introduction). Such foundations typically include linguistic and associated cultural differences. And here we should note a key aspect of the difference between the segments in consociational democracy and the typical groups in the basic pluralist model. In the basic model an important feature is the somewhat fluid and transient nature of the groups, with particular individuals belonging to many, and perhaps contrasting, groups. And particular groups have a variety of members, perhaps from many walks of life, with the same individuals sometimes turning up as members of various different groups. In the consociational model, on the other hand, the segments of society tend to be all-embracing so far as individuals are concerned: there is little or no intermixture of personnel and segments are stable blocks with permanent 'membership'. In short, the divisions of society are deep, permanent and significant. (There are, of course, gradations between these two ideal types, and many of the groups in systems to which pluralist theory's basic model is applied have a nature rather more solid and significant than the model suggests. Nonetheless the basic model's 'dilution' of group conflict, and the treatment of it as beneficial rather than threatening, remains an important feature of standard pluralist democratic theory.)

This brings us to the second difference between consociational and standard pluralist democratic theory. In standard theory, group demands are not regarded as posing a problem. On the contrary, as we have seen, the interaction of groups is held to constitute a decision by the people, which is seen as some kind of aggregate or synthesis of group demands. In the consociational model, though, sectional demands, and how to reconcile them, are a – indeed *the* – key problem.

Due to the fundamental nature of the sectional divisions and conflicts, demands cannot be simply aggregated or synthesised. In fact a very careful process of 'accommodation' is necessary. At times, indeed, it appears that consociational theory ceases to be about the nature of democratic decision making and becomes instead a theory about how such decision making remains possible in the face of grave difficulties. The *nature* of the decision making is taken as given, democratic theory proper being assumed to provide the necessary analysis. This is a reflection of the fact that consociational theory is seen mainly as 'empirical theory' concerned with explaining the functioning of actual political systems rather than as conceptual theory concerned with analysing the idea of a decision by the people. (The main 'empirical referents' of the theory – the 'classic' consociational democracies – are the political systems of The Netherlands, Belgium, Austria and Switzerland.)

Consociational theory does, nonetheless, at times also take on the role of democratic theory proper, providing an account of the nature of democratic decision making. Indeed, this is quite a sophisticated account, somewhat like Calhoun's theory of concurrent majorities mentioned in an earlier section of this chapter. In some ways it is rather better than the analyses found in standard pluralist theory and in discussions of majority decision making. In consociational democracy all important sectional demands have to be met. It follows that the only political decisions possible are those that go against no important demand and which will not therefore be vetoed by any section. In other words, whilst such decisions are not positively unanimous they do reflect a 'negative unanimity' or general consensus. Decision making of this type raises its own difficulties, though. These are chiefly to do with the difficulty of getting sufficient positive decisions in the face of blocking vetoes, which means that a small minority can block a large majority's wish to change the *status quo*. But at least there is a clear sense in which any positive decisions are by *all* those involved. And since, in consociational theory, the various 'sections' together comprise the whole society, a decision by all the sections is a decision by the whole people.[42] In fact it is possible to argue that there is a significant sense in which policies or actions which fail to alienate any section of society are ones that really are in the general interest – as distinct from standard pluralist theory's typical and suspect notion that the general interest is some kind of positive aggregation of particular sectional interests. We have here, indeed, some approximation to Rousseau's notion of the general will, where the genuine will of all the people is for that which is in the general interest.

Corporatism and Democratic Theory

Another, important variation of pluralist democratic theory is provided by corporatist theory. Whether 'variation' is the right description is debatable since corporatist analysis is often seen as an *attack on*, rather than as a variety of, pluralism; and 'corporatism' is frequently viewed as undermining, rather than as being a form taken by, liberal democracy. And for this reason corporatist theory is better regarded as a part of the critique of liberal democracy we look at in the next chapter. Nonetheless, it should be mentioned here because it does have some clear affinities with pluralist analysis and when appropriately interpreted and developed it can be said to yield a corporatist theory of democracy (Cawson 1983).

Corporatist theory is similar to pluralist theory in focusing on the extent to which power is 'pluralised' among various groups or sections. However, there are two important differences from standard pluralist theory.

First, power is not dispersed to the extent that it is in the pluralist model. And this is not just a matter of degree: there is a crucial intrinsic difference. A defining feature of 'corporatism'[43] is the extent to which interest groups – because their co-operation and collaboration is required by the modern interventionist state – become part of the centralised machinery of the state. The groups have a dual role of representing their members' interests and of being instruments of policy implementation – in a sense, arms of the state. They are then to a crucial extent, though *not* entirely, part of the power structure of the state. In standard pluralism, groups are autonomous organisations outside of the state – constituents of 'civil society'[44] – exerting pressure on it; in corporatism, groups are partially incorporated into the state and to that extent are no longer autonomous and dispersed centres of power.[45]

The second difference between corporatist and standard pluralist theory also concerns autonomy. In pluralist theory groups are conceived as voluntary associations, the object and reason for the formation of which is to promote objectives decided by individuals. Individuals form or join groups because they want certain objectives promoted, which may reflect an interest they discern themselves all to have. According to corporatist theory, groups are structured by external objective conditions – by the functions they perform in the economic and political system. Individuals find their situation in the economic and political system is structured in ways which *determine* their interests and actions. In pluralism a group 'takes its interest and derives its power from the individuals who comprise it. But for the functional group [of corporatist theory] the membership *takes its interest* from the function, and the power of the functional group in part derives from what are the objectives of state policy (Cawson 1983, italics in the original). This non-individualist basis of corporatism marks a crucial difference from standard pluralism. It illustrates the way in which standard pluralism falls within the basic individualism of traditional liberal democratic theory. The viability of such individualism, and its role in democratic theory, will be discussed in the next chapter.

Basic Features of Modern Democratic Theory

One final comment needs to be made before we leave modern democratic theory. We have seen that such theories are often said to be descriptive rather than prescriptive. However (and this is sometimes acknowledged by their proponents) modern theories are in fact prescriptive as well. Their models may seek to portray and to explain what actually exists, but those models are also pretty clearly recommended as the best type of political system. However, there is a further confusion which stems from the pre-occupation with descriptive analysis. This is a tendency to fall victim to the 'definitional fallacy' (see Chapter 1): because the theories' purpose is conceived as explaining the workings of actual democracies instead of abstract analysis, there is a tendency not to analyse the idea of democracy. Instead, it tends to be *taken for granted* that the systems being explained are democracies, without asking by what criteria they are counted as such. It follows from this that the theories tend to concern themselves with any salient aspects of the political systems concerned, without specifying whether they are characteristics of democracy. And this breeds considerable confusion regarding the nature of democracy, because it tells us little about it; rather as explanations, say, of the digestive systems of cats tell us little about the nature of cats.

We have looked at modern democratic theory in contradistinction to – as a replacement for – traditional liberal democratic theory. And yet there are crucial continuities and similarities. These are mainly to do with individualist assumptions. Despite the group orientation of modern theory, it is a group analysis which rests on an individualist foundation. We saw this just now when discussing the difference between corporatist and standard pluralist theory. The essential point is that the actions of groups are conceived and explained as the actions of individuals – i.e. the members, or key members, of the groups. And it is straightforwardly the case that those members constitute (and in an important sense themselves decide to constitute) the groups, rather than the groups being aspects or products of pre-existing social structures. In the end, then, even in group-oriented modern democratic theory 'decisions by the people' are seen as decisions by individuals. When we put this basic individualism together with modern theories' re-affirmation of liberal ideas about the limitation of the state, and dispersal of power away from it, we have a clear continuation of liberal individualism. This continuity is arguably more important than the differences with traditional theory: modern theory is essentially a variety of liberal democratic theory. And it is to critiques of liberal democratic theory as a whole that we now turn – the main target of which is liberal individualism.

Notes

1. In fact there is considerable scope for confusion regarding Rousseau's meaning here; indeed, very different interpretations are possible. Thus it can be argued that Rousseau, far from being a direct democrat, is actually in favour of an 'elective aristocracy', very similar to conventional forms of representative democracy today, in which those in government actually make most of the decisions – although for Rousseau such decisions have to be ratified by the people. And it is true that Rousseau in his own words rejects democracy as undesirable and/or impossible of realisation (Rousseau (1968), Book Three, Chapter 4). However, this is in the context of his distinction between the government and the sovereign, which is always the people. When Rousseau rejects 'democracy' he means he does not believe in government, i.e. *administration*, by the people (Rousseau (1968), Book Three, Chapters 2 and 3). This, however, is still compatible with his belief in *legislation*, i.e. basic political decision making, directly by the people. This distinction – or, rather, the failure to attend to it – accounts for a good deal of the confusion and controversy over Rousseau's meaning here.

Unfortunately, it does not account for all of it since there is another tendency in Rousseau (a) to enlarge the role of government beyond mere administration and (b) to regard legislation by the people as ratifying rather than proposing decisions (although that ratification by the people *is necessary* is still a point of fundamental importance). Part of the point here is that, to an important extent, Rousseau's conception of the people is a *juristic* notion, as compared to Anglo-American theory's empirical notion. A key associated idea is that the *legitimacy* laws obtain from being ratified by the people is what is important, rather than the content of laws being actually decided by the people. Nonetheless, this is to push only one aspect of Rousseau's theory and it remains true that the usual view is that Rousseau is a proponent of direct democracy. Part of the reason for this is the focus usually given to his best-known work, *The Social Contract*, in comparison to some of his other writings, where he departs from his stance in favour of direct democracy and against representation. In a very useful discussion, Fralin (1978, 1979) examines Rousseau's basic ambivalence regarding representation, and the changes in his ideas over time. See also Ryan (1983).

2. Birch (1972), in a lucid and concise analysis, argues the former, whilst Pitkin (1967) argues the latter. On representation see also Pennock and Chapman (1968).

3. One of the issues to be discussed later is the extent to which traditional democratic theory is always liberal democratic theory. However, when the context makes the meaning clear the terms 'democracy', 'democratic theory', etc. will often be used – as here – instead of the longer-winded 'liberal democracy', 'liberal democratic theory', etc.

4. Rousseau is something of an exception here. But then, as we shall see, there is a question about whether Rousseau really *is* a traditional *liberal* democratic theorist.

5. In fact Locke does specifically recognise the *possibility* of democracy as a legitimate form of government. A good characterisation of the ambiguity of Locke's thought with regard to democracy is given by Seliger: 'Locke did not favour the permanent establishment of democracy. But its recognition as a legitimate and workable form of government enabled him to justify his advocacy of the right of revolt' (Seliger 1968). For an argument to the effect that Locke's political theory *is* unambiguously democratic see Kendall (1941).

6. Whether or not J.S. Mill *should* be considered as a utilitarian is a controversial matter. At the very least, his is an importantly modified form of utilitarianism.

7. C.B. Macpherson sees J.S. Mill as important because he is a 'developmental theorist' (Macpherson 1977a). For rather a different view of Mill see Pateman (1970).

8. The 'greatest happiness principle' is central in utilitarianism: that which is right is that which produces the greatest happiness of the greatest number. And (according to critics) this can imply that an individual should be used as a means to the end of producing general happiness (or, at least, diminishing general unhappiness) – as when, say, dangerous

racial tension could be defused by the police charging *any* individual of the relevant colour (even though they know him to be innocent) in connection with the incident that gave rise to the tension. John Rawls is an important example of a theorist who criticises utilitarianism for subordinating justice for the individual to the general happiness (Rawls 1972, for example Chapter 1, Section 5). On utilitarianism see further below.

9. Jefferson is, of course, the author of the American Declaration of Independence. On his democratic thought see, for example, Padover (1946) and Koch (1964). Price was well known in his own day as an English supporter of the American and French Revolutions. He praised the French Revolution in a celebrated sermon, *The Love of Our Country*, which provoked Edmund Burke into replying with the even more celebrated *Reflections on the Revolution in France* (Burke 1968). On Price see, for example, Thomas (1959).

10. For an analysis and discussion of the concept of 'interests' see, for example, Barry (1965); Connolly (1972, 1983); Benditt, Oppenheim and Flathman (1975); and Oppenheim (1981).

11. Two points should be noted here. (1) Notions of interests and of their representation also play a part in widely varying political theories which are not democratic. (2) Such non-democratic theories focus typically on the interests of sections of society or groups, rather than on those of individuals (Birch 1972, Pitkin 1967). There are, though, also some varieties of *democratic* theory that focus on group interests: these are mainly modern theories (see Chapter 3), but some traditional theorists also have a similar focus – see the references to Madison and Calhoun below.

12. On utilitarianism, see for example Plamenatz (1958) and Smart and Williams (1973). On the utilitarian theory of democracy see Steintrager (1977), Lively and Rees (1978), Plamenatz (1973) Chapter 1, and Rosen (1983).

13. J.S. Mill also has such doubts; but, as we have just seen, he is still confident that the general interest will be pursued by the *wise* representatives – i.e. by the most enlightened representatives, who should hold the balance of power.

14. Within utilitarianism's original thoroughgoing individualism, the notion of *constituency* interests does not properly arise: it is *individuals* who have interests, rather than groups of individuals or entities such as constituencies.

15. For an extended discussion of utilitarianism in general, and of the relationship between the natural and the artificial identification of interests in particular, see Halevy (1954). There are, in fact, two very different arguments entangled here. First, there is the argument that whilst the 'invisible hand' works over a wide sphere, government is necessary in some, restricted, spheres. Second, there is the argument that there is no invisible hand, that individuals are always in mutually destructive competition and that government should not be narrowly confined to some restricted sphere.

16. See Pitkin (1967), especially pp. 203–5. Pitkin concludes that Bentham ends up with a view of representation like that of J.S. Mill and Burke.

17. On the doctrine of the mandate and the question of its validity see, for example, Birch (1964) pp. 116–22; Chapter 9 of this book contains a useful discussion of 'party democracy'. On democracy and political parties see also Ranney (1954), Ranney and Kendall (1956), Leiserson (1958), Duverger (1959), Rose (1974), Ware (1979).

18. For further discussion see, for example, Barry (1970).

19. There is not the space here to discuss Rousseau properly. He is an extremely important and controversial political philosopher, and is very important in the context of democratic theory. It is well worth reading further about him: see, for example, Shklar (1969), Hall (1973) and Grimsley (1983).

20. An important aspect of Rousseau's argument is that what might appear as being in an individual's interest (not having to give up time for jury service) may well not be so. And that which is for the common good may well be in his real, long-term (even if not his narrow, short-term) interests – living under a system of justice which is the better for having a jury system.

21. Besides the political systems of Britain and America the reference is also to other democracies (usually, but not always, English-speaking and members of the Commonwealth) whose structure and functioning have been heavily influenced by the British and/or American models. Examples are Australia, Canada, West Germany, New Zealand.

22. 'Idealism' with a capital 'I' refers not to an optimistic belief in the role of moral ideals in ordering life, but to the philosophical view – of which Plato is the originator and chief exponent – that ideas rather than matter constitute the ultimate reality.

23. For further discussion of neo-Idealist and citizenship theory see Holden (1974) and Thompson (1970).

24. As we shall see, this ambivalence is typified by the contrasts between Leninist theory, so important in one-party democracy, and Marx's own theory, which, in important senses, amounts to an espousal of some key liberal democratic values (Graham 1986, Chapters 9 and 10) – though it maintains that such values can be realised only through a revolutionary transformation of society.

25. Whether Lenin consciously made use of Continental democratic theory is another matter, although, for example, Harding comments (with reference to some of Lenin's arguments about the democratic role of revolutionary dictatorship) that, 'no doubt, Lenin had in mind the experience of France and the classic example of the French Revolution' (Harding 1983). And in Marx's original analysis it is said that 'we find a teleological variant of Rousseau's theory of the general will' (Levin 1983).

26. In its extreme form, in the last phase of Lenin's thought, the party remains as the true embodiment of the proletariat and its interest even where the masses, having been subverted by circumstances and become actively hostile to policies advancing the proletarian cause, in effect cease to be the proletariat (Harding 1983).

27. 'Model', instead of 'models' of democracy is used here mainly for the sake of simplification. It is, though, an error – unfortunately quite a common one – to assume that there *is* a single form of democracy presented in traditional theory.

28. Quotation marks are used here because, as we shall see, the question can arise of whether, in the light of these studies, the Western 'democracies' can properly be counted as democracies at all.

29. On political elites see, for example, Parry (1969).

30. The reference here is both to beliefs that political elites exist and to judgements that they are desirable. These can be disconnected: some condemn the existence of politcal elites, and others, including some elite theorists, describe their existence without (allegedly) passing judgement on them. In fact, however, in elitist theories the desirability as well as the existence of political elites is normally maintained.

31. On Pareto, Mosca and Michels see, for example, Meisel (1958 and 1965) and Lipset (1962); and on Weber see Held (1987), Chapter 5.

32. Questions about participation, other than voting, will be left on one side here, and will be taken up in the next two chapters. The main voting behaviour studies of this period were Lazarsfeld *et al.* (1968), Berelson *et al.* (1954), Milne and Mackenzie (1958) and Campbell *et al.* (1960). For further discussion of their significance see, for example, Burdick and Brodbeck (1959) and Holden (1974).

33. There is a vast literature on pressure groups, but useful introductions are: Alderman (1984), Ball (1986) and Schlozman (1986).

34. There are some tricky issues here, which are not always properly recognised. The point is that the same facts can hardly be said to demonstrate, at one and the same time, both the non-existence and the undesirability of radical democracy: if something is judged as undesirable, at least the possibility of its existence is surely presumed; at all events, it seems incoherent to contend that a factor which prevents something existing also makes that thing undesirable. The issues raised are quite complex, but one of the relevant points concerns the precise interpretation of certain 'facts': for example, is the nature and extent of voters' irrationality such that they are actually *incapable of making* political decisions; or is it that, whilst capable of making them they can only make them badly?

35. Daudt (1961) provides a particularly thorough re-examination of this kind. One of his central concerns was to demonstrate that voters who changed their minds from one election to another – and thus, in a sense, 'decided' the outcome – did have some political knowledge and did exhibit rational voting behaviour, at least to some degree. (The early voting behaviour studies suggested that, contrary to what was generally thought, these 'floating voters' were the most irrational of all.)

36. Perhaps one should write 'democracies'. It is very difficult to say anything here without begging important questions. An important issue, as we shall see, is whether in fact modern theories are not simply *assuming* what actually needs to be demonstrated, i.e. that those modern political systems commonly referred to as 'democracies' or 'liberal democracies' really are democracies.

37. As with most such labels, confusion can arise from vaguenesses and
     ambiguities. In the case of pluralist democratic theory, however, one
     should be particularly watchful. 'Pluralism', 'pluralist', etc. are terms
     that also have meanings more general than that involved in the use of
     the label 'pluralist democratic theory' to mark a distinction from elitist
     democratic theory. In a very general sense 'pluralist' distinguishes
     political systems which allow opposition to government – a *plurality* of
     viewpoints – to be expressed. In this sense 'pluralist' is roughly equiv-
     alent to 'liberal'.

38. There are complications – some of which are touched on later – arising
     from the fact that this *model* is itself very much built up from analyses of
     reality, that is to say analyses of actual political systems (above all the
     American system).

39. On elitist democratic theory, besides Schumpeter (1976) and Sartori
     (1965 and 1987) see, for example, Bachrach (1967), Parry (1969),
     Kariel (1970), Ricci (1971), Graham (1986), Held (1987).

40. R.A. Dahl is one of the most important of modern theorists and analysts
     of democracy. His main works are Dahl (1956, 1961, 1966, 1970, 1971,
     1982 and 1985), and there is a recent collection of his articles in Dahl
     (1986). Dahl (1956) was a seminal work and was not just limited to
     outlining a 'pluralist–elitist' theory of democracy. His conception of
     'polyarchy' – roughly a regime that is 'relatively (but incompletely)
     democratised' (Dahl 1971) – has become standard in analyses of politi-
     cal systems.

41. Unlike most theories of democracy, consociational theory is not so much
     an account of democracy as such, as an account of the form it takes in
     certain cases.

42. There is a problem here concerning the assumption that the expression
     of a sectional demand amounts to the same thing as a decision by all
     those 'in' that section in favour of that demand. But this is an underlying
     problem in pluralist theory and is not unique to consociational theory;
     it will be commented on later.

43. 'Corporatism' is here used to mean the features of a, or the type of,
     political system outlined in corporatist analysis (and such analysis also
     contends that the political systems of the Western democracies in fact
     are, or do have features, of this type).

44. The meaning of 'civil society' derives from Hegel's separation of the
     state (which stands above society and embodies rationality and moral-
     ity) and civil society (which is the area of private life and the pursuit of
     particular, especially economic, interests).

45. Even this is an oversimplification since corporatist analysis also focuses
     on the extent to which the state is *not* a monolithic organisation, precise-
     ly because of the extent to which its components have the character of
     dispersed power centres.

3
The Radical Critique of Liberal Democracy

3.1 General Nature of the Radical Critique

In this chapter we shall consider what can be called the radical critique of the theory and practice of liberal democracy. In fact two sorts of critique are brought together under this heading. Nonetheless, they share an important common theme that warrants the use of the unifying label; and, indeed, they are often interlinked. The connecting theme is the demand for radical change to existing ideas and/or practices in order really to achieve democracy. In other words, the basic argument is that liberal democrats are wrong in thinking that the ideas and practices to which they subscribe actually do bring about genuine democracy. It may be that practices do not actually realise liberal democratic ideals: that the Western 'liberal democracies', endorsed by liberal democrats, fail in fact to be democracies or properly to provide liberty. Or it may be that the ideas themselves are faulty; that the concepts, analyses and ideals of liberal democratic theories do not add up to a coherent or convincing picture of democracy or liberty. Or it may be a combination of both. But, whatever it is, in each case something radically different is required – be it a thoroughgoing change in social and political structures, or crucially different ideas, or both.

The radical critique, then, is not an attack on liberty or on democracy as such (unlike some of the arguments we shall be confronting in Chapter 4). Far from it; it is in fact an appeal for *more* liberty and democracy. What *is* attacked is the notion that liberty and democracy can be achieved by liberal democratic theory and practice.

Very broadly speaking, we can say that there are two main forms of radical critique. There are those which are concerned with the restructuring of political ideas and practices, and those which look to wholesale changes in society. Such changes include the underlying economic and other social structures, and not just the political aspects. There are connections and overlaps between the two categories; but there are also real issues, to do with the nature and significance of political activity in the functioning of society, that divide them. In the first category are the critiques developed by the theorists of participatory democracy, whilst the second category comprises the various forms of Marxist critique. (In each category there are in fact various forms of argument, among which there are significant differences as well as similarities. Nonetheless it is the overlaps and similarities that are most important, and, in the interests of clarity, we shall usually refer simply to the participatory critique and to the Marxist critique.)

3.2 The Participatory Critique

Before we look at its nature we might first see what issues have provoked the participatory critique of liberal democratic theory and practice. Broadly speaking there are four main reasons for looking to participatory alternatives to liberal democracy and its supporting ideas.

First, there is a quite widely held view that modern Western democracies are so vast and complex that the ordinary person cannot relate to such systems or have any meaningful influence on their governments (Pranger 1968, Ricci 1971). Apathy and disillusion are an outcome of this. This is a matter partly of the nature of modern society, but partly also of the sheer numbers of people in 'The Democratic Leviathan' (Dahl 1970). Bureaucracy, as a response to the organisational imperatives of modern society, is also seen as a threat to democracy that needs to be overcome (see, for example, Thompson (1983)).

Second, it is often argued that the liberal democracies do not, and (short of complete re-structuring) cannot, provide the kind of life they promise. It is sometimes the general quality of life that is at issue. Here the focus might be on such matters as pollution and the quality of the physical environment generally; or the imbalance between the paucity of public goods and the excess of private goods. Or the central concern might be with the dehumanisation of the work process or the poor quality of the cultural environment; and here there is an overlap with the Marxist critique. Sometimes it is the life of certain sections of society that is at issue. The general point here is that significant minorities, usually but not always ethnic minorities, are held to be excluded from the benefits enjoyed by more privileged groups; indeed, they are said not to have proper access to the democratic process. The liberal 'democracies' thereby fail to be properly democratic. Such arguments tend to merge into attacks which maintain that the actual inequalities, as opposed to formal equalities, in Western 'democracies' are too widespread and profound for them to be properly counted as democracies. Again, there is an overlap with the Marxist critique, but even a liberal democrat such as Dahl considers prevailing inequalities of political resources to be one of the most serious faults of Western democracies (Dahl 1970; see also Dahl 1985).

This brings us in fact to our third reason for the development of participatory critiques of liberal democracy. It is not just Marxists who are critical of the unequal distribution of power within liberal democratic societies. There are many, including Dahl, who still give primacy to political activity and structures but who nonetheless see the political sphere as subject to considerable influence. They see it as influenced by other aspects of society, in particular the organisation of industry and the economic structure generally. And such people argue that democracy is at best threatened, and at worst negated, by the inequalities inherent in the economies of Western democracies. However, the issues raised here – including those concerning 'industrial democracy' – are so heavily interrelated with the Marxist critique and its assessment that we shall consider them under that heading.

The fourth category of reasons for dissatisfaction with liberal democratic theory and practice are of a more theoretical kind. These include difficulties with providing a meaningful account of political obligation in the liberal democratic state – and the consequent serious implications for demonstrating and sustaining legitimacy – and philosophical problems connected with the justification of liberal democracy. They also include dissatisfaction with what liberal democratic assumptions imply for citizenship and the common good; and, underlying this, problems with the individualism of liberal democratic theory. We shall say something more about these topics when we look at the arguments supporting participatory theories of democracy.

Nature of the Participatory Critique

Let us turn now to the nature of the participatory critique itself. And first we should ask what is meant by 'participation', 'participatory theory', 'participatory democracy' and so on. 'Participation' means 'taking part in', and 'political participation' means 'taking part in politics or political decision making', but this does not get us very far. The important questions concern the nature and the extent of 'taking part'; and, of course, it is *popular* participation that is at issue, i.e. the ways in which the mass of the people take part in political decision making and the extent to which they do so.

There is a sense in which democracy necessarily involves participation. If the people make the ultimate political decisions they are necessarily taking part in political decision making: 'democracy involves popular participation by definition. It is always a question of how much participation . . . ' (Pennock 1979).[1] And indeed voting can be seen as a basic form of political participation. However, it is usually forms of participation over and above that of voting to which participatory theorists refer: indeed a central contention in such theories is that voting is not enough. This may not be simply a matter of quantity, in other words the failure of the mechanism of voting to transmit information about people's views in sufficient quantity or with sufficient frequency; it may be held that there is a *qualitative* failure as well. This can involve more than the contention that voting fails properly to convey the information in the way intended (Burnheim 1985, Chapter 3). It can also be argued that voting is 'an isolated, privatised act' inimical to the proper communal form of participatory activity; and, further, that it does not allow individuals autonomously to decide what views to express – and how – in a self-created activity. In liberal democratic states, indeed, voting is a fact of life that people have no choice but to accept (Pateman 1985).

What, then, is the 'something more' that is held to constitute (genuine) participation? This is best conceived in two related dimensions. On the one hand there are the kinds of activity involved. Here the central idea is that of positively *doing* things, as against passively choosing among options presented by others. Things such as joining political parties, engaging in their activities and speaking at political meetings are, then, typical examples of political participation. On the other hand there is the function performed by such activities. The broad function is that of playing a part in decision making, but just what this amounts to varies. At one extreme there is simply the eliciting of views – the views of the rank and file to whom the decisions will apply[2] – by those who will make the decisions. Here participation amounts to no more than a process of consultation. If the 'consultation' is in fact really used to gain acceptance of decisions *already taken* we might call this 'pseudo participation' (Pateman 1970). Genuine consultation, though, *precedes* the actual taking of decisions. And this merges into situations where even though the final power to decide rests elsewhere than with the rank and file, the views elicited actually have an influence on the decisions taken; this we can call 'partial participation' (Pateman 1970). At the other extreme there is equality of power in the decision-making process; here the rank-and-file membership all have an equal power with the leaders in determining the outcome of decisions. Indeed, here there really ceases to be a distinction between leaders and rank and file: *all* are equal members of the decision-making body. This can be called 'full participation' (Pateman 1970).

A participatory theorist is one who argues for more participation. And of course it is participatory theorists of democracy with whom we are concerned here: those who want more political participation by the people as the way of achieving proper – i.e. participatory – democracy within the state.[3] We shall see that such theorists often further argue that in order to achieve such a democracy there must also be participation in spheres like the work place, which a liberal would not count as 'political'.

Following on from our analysis of 'participation', we can say that a participatory democracy is one in which the basic determining decisions (and perhaps other decisions) are made by the people, actively participating in the political process. Just what this involves, and the extent to which it is full rather than partial participation or consultation, varies with different participatory theories. Some of these we shall touch on shortly.

Participatory Democracy and Liberal Democratic Theory

The participatory critique implies, of course, that participatory democracy and its theory are crucially different from liberal democratic theory and practice. But there is not a simple clash here – the difference is not unqualified. As we have already indicated, there is an overlap; to a significant extent there is a sharing of the ideals of liberty and democracy. In essence, then, what the participatory democrat argues is that liberty and democracy are not in fact realised in liberal democracy. 'The major devices by which liberal theory contrives to guarantee liberty while securing democracy . . . turn out neither to secure democracy nor to guarantee liberty' (Barber 1984). And the corollary and converse of this argument is that liberty and democracy are only secured in participatory democracy. The differences 'inside' the overlap thus remain crucial. They will be discussed at various points as we look at the pros and cons of participatory democracy, but, very broadly speaking, they involve three sorts of issue.

First, it has been argued that there is an underlying theoretical issue which gives rise to a fundamental, but largely unappreciated, difference between liberal democratic theory and practice and participatory theory. According to this argument it is only participatory theory that properly recognises and gives effect to the true liberal idea of voluntarism. The true idea involves individuals being conceived as *voluntary* members of a democratic community. This voluntarism, it is argued, was implicit in the origins of liberal democratic theory. It has, however, since been fatally obscured; and it is contradicted in the reality of the liberal democratic state (Pateman 1985).

Second, and deriving from Pateman's argument, there are differing accounts of what is necessary for it to be said that the people make the basic political decisions. Essentially liberal democrats say that universal suffrage and voting at regular free elections is sufficient. Participatory theorists, though, require active involvement by the people in policy formulation; and this may well involve elements of direct democracy, or at least radical 'democratisation' of the system of representation. A complication here concerns just what is included as liberal democratic theory. In the last chapter we included radical democratic theory. We saw, though, that there are important differences between radical and other liberal democratic theories, traditional as well as modern. Some might even *contrast* radical with liberal democratic theory. In the case of Continental democratic theory the relationship with liberal theory is even more ambivalent. And the key point here is that, with the emphasis on the positive, initiating role of the people, in radical and (even more) in Continental theory there are similarities with participatory theory. Indeed, to some extent participatory theory is inspired by, and is a modern manifestation of, radical and Continental theory. To that extent, then, it is an oversimplification to talk of a dichotomy between participatory and liberal democratic theory. In fact the division is clearest between participatory theory and conventional and modern varieties of liberal democratic theory. This is in fact the contrast that is usually drawn. Nonetheless, participatory theory is not simply a new version of radical and/or Continental theory. Apart from anything else key elements of participatory theory consist in contemporary responses to what is seen as the failure in the twentieth century of pre-existing democratic theory – radical and Continental as well as conventional and 'modern' theory.

The third kind of issue separating participatory and liberal democratic theory concerns notions of the individual and the community. Very roughly, participatory theory is 'communalist' ('social' or 'collectivist') in contrast to, and as a critique of, the individualism of liberal democratic theory. ('Communalism' and individualism are discussed further when we look at the Marxist critique.) To put it that baldly, though, is to over-simplify. And we can best explain this aspect of participatory theory by understanding the way in which this is an over-simplification.

In fact participatory theory combines both individualist and communalist perspectives: Pennock refers to 'the peculiar combination of the individualistic and the social . . . or "collectivistic" ' in theories of participatory democracy (Pennock 1979). And whilst participatory theory is a critique of liberal democratic theory, it does to an important extent also uphold liberal ideas as against Marxist analyses. There is indeed, at least in important varieties of participatory theory, a 'dissatisfaction with the heritage of political theory, liberal and

Marxist' (Held 1987). Perhaps the key point can best be summed up by saying that whilst participatory theory gives crucial importance to the value of community and to the extent to which individuals and their activities are social products, 'the participatory democrat is' nonetheless 'distinguished by his insistence that individuals remain not only distinct and various, but "open", spontaneous and fluid' (Pennock 1979). There is sometimes a 'convergence' from the other side as well. Not only does participatory theory have its individualist aspect but some varieties of liberal democratic theory have a communalist aspect – 'neo-Idealist' democratic theory and 'citizenship theory' should not be forgotten.

Another point of convergence between participatory and a form of liberal democratic theory might be seen in pluralist democratic theory. Here it is not the individualist/communalist distinction that is blurred,[4] so much as the distinctions involved in differing accounts of the nature of decisions by the people. The point is that on some interpretations, or in some forms, pluralist democratic theory may be construed as being about actively involving the people in policy formulation. Viewed in this way pluralist theory looks beyond passive voting at elections to the ways in which people become positively engaged in the policy formulating process through the positive political activity of the pressure groups of which they are members. It is true that critics of pluralist theory, amongst whom participatory theorists are prominent, see crucial fallacies in this sort of argument. The most important of these are said to involve the assumptions that the whole people are 'included' in pressure groups, and that their pursuit of group interests promotes the general interest and generates a 'will of the people'. But important counter-attacks in the name of 'pluralist participation' have also been made (Kelso 1978).

This comparison of participatory and liberal democracy shows us broadly what participatory democratic theory is. We can learn more by identifying the main participatory theorists and by looking at the main arguments for and against participatory democracy.

Participatory Theorists

Just who to include as the main participatory theorists could be a matter of some debate. But among contemporary theorists[5] let us follow David Held (Held 1987) in identifying three 'New Left' thinkers: Pateman (1970,1985), Macpherson (1977a) and Poulantzas (1980). Some of the main planks of their theories sum up central ideas involved in the commitment to participatory democracy. These include arguments about the insufficiency, although not the unimportance, of formal rights to secure freedom and equality in the face of the substantive inequalities of liberal democratic society. Also important is the idea that it is a fallacy to believe that the liberal democratic state is separated from, and is a neutral umpire with respect to, the processes and groups within 'civil society'; but it is held, too, that it is a fallacy to believe with Marxists that the state, and its power and structure, is unimportant, and that it is simply the manifestation of dominant social forces. It is consequently held that there is a need to democratise the state through participatory structures and processes. It is further contended that there is a need to democratise through participatory processes (a) structures which directly impinge on the state – above all political parties – and (b) other aspects of social life, particularly economic structures ('industrial democracy') (Held 1987).

In focusing on 'New Left' thinkers as leading participatory theorists we are again signifying the extent to which the participatory critique both overlaps with, and is also a reaction against, the Marxist critique. Indeed another way of looking at some, at least, of the participatory theories of this sort is to regard them as neo-Marxist critiques of liberal democracy which attempt to grapple with some of the failings of Marxist socialist analysis. Thus Pierson, writing of the type of theorising in which Poulantzas is a notable figure, says it is the 'seemingly intractable problem of how to defend existing and cherished liberties and democratic institutions and massively to extend the democratic control of society and personal autonomy, without lapsing into the 'statist' traps set by both traditional Leninism and traditional social democracy that could be said to summarise the agenda of recent democratic socialist theory' (Pierson 1986).

Arguments For Participatory Theory

Let us now move on to the pros and cons of participatory theory, beginning with the reasons for favouring participatory democracy. Some of these have already been indicated, but we should now bring these and others together to identify the main lines of argument in support of participatory democracy.

One sort of argument – or, more correctly, one aspect of some of the key arguments we are about to look at – concerns conceptions of the

relationship between 'civil society' and the state, or between economics and politics, or between the 'public' and the 'private' spheres.
These will be considered further when we come to the Marxist critique in the next section (this illustrates again that there are important
overlaps, as well as differences, between the participatory and Marxist critiques). But in essence there are two aspects of participatory
arguments relevant here.

First, there is the idea that 'democratisation of civil society' can and
should be achieved; and that this can overcome the negation of
political democracy by the social and economic power structure. Such
democratisation involves, principally, worker participation in industry, i.e. industrial or economic democracy.

Second, and more generally, participatory theory can involve a
radical critique of, and a means of overcoming, an artificial division
in the liberal democratic order to which liberal democratic theory is
blind, and which has profoundly undemocratic consequences. This
is the division between the social and political realms which breeds
and reflects corresponding and distorted conceptions of private and
public (Pateman 1985). In short, participatory democracy can itself
be conceived as transforming the structure of liberal bourgeois society
and bringing about human emancipation without – or instead of – the
revolutionary transformation which is essential according to the
Marxist analysis. (In fact this last statement, with its implication of a
single form of 'Marxist analysis', is something of an over-simplification, for several reasons. First, there are differences within classical
Marxism concerning the question of the form that the 'revolutionary
transformation' could take; and in particular whether it could consist
in the obtaining of power by the working masses through radical
participatory democratic control. Second, some participatory theorists, notably C. B. Macpherson, have what amounts to a type of
Marxist view of the necessity for a change in the structure of society
before participatory democracy can become possible – see Macpherson
(1977a) Chapter 5. For a discussion of whether Macpherson is a
Marxist see Svacek (1976); see also the discussion of Macpherson in
the next section of this chapter. Third, the idea of what a 'Marxist
analysis' is has become excessively attenuated. At the extreme, contemporary 'post-Marxist' analyses of socialism and democracy are at
times difficult to distinguish from mainstream liberal democratic, let
alone participatory, theory. Witness their emphases on pluralism; the
continuing need for the state, but at the same time the need to restrain

it in the interests of liberty; and the associated hostility towards attempts to replace 'forms of representative democracy by exclusively direct democracy [which] will issue in statism' (Pierson 1986).)

Returning to the main arguments in favour of participatory democracy we can say these fall into four broad categories: instrumental, developmental, communal and philosophical. We shall look briefly at each of these.

The instrumental arguments, though important, are not the most distinctive. They are essentially an adaptation of typical liberal democratic – in this case utilitarian – arguments. The central idea is that people protect their interests best by participating in the making of decisions that affect them. And it is held that a participatory democracy is the best way for people to protect their interests with respect to decisions by the state. This is really to agree with the objectives of those who focus on voting as *the* democratic mechanism, but to disagree with the idea that voting alone will achieve these objectives. People must get involved and actually make themselves heard and felt if they want their interests protected. Participation is not an end in itself, but is instrumental to achieving another end – the protection of interests. Or, to put the underlying point another way, rule by the people as utilitarians envisage it can be achieved only in a participatory democracy.

The developmental arguments, on the other hand, are distinctive. They really derive from Rousseau and they are essentially foreign to Anglo-American theory. (However, the variety of Anglo-American theory and the blurring of categories should be remembered. We should recall, for example, that John Stuart Mill uses developmental as well as instrumental arguments in the (albeit qualified) role he gives to participation in his theory. And we should remember that in neo-Idealist and citizenship theory, which really overlap with participatory theories, key 'developmental ideas' play a very important role.)

The central idea is that participation is valuable in itself and not, as in the instrumental arguments, just as a means to another end. It is valuable in that it develops the individual and his capacities. Rather as taking part in sport, and not just spectating, develops one's physical capacities, so taking part in political activity develops one's mental and spiritual capacities. At bottom this is to re-assert the view of man expressed in Aristotle's famous dictum that 'man is by nature a political animal' (Aristotle 1981): the view, essentially, that man

needs to engage in politics, with all that it involves in human interaction, rational discourse and the exercise of autonomy, in order to
develop into a fully human being. But this basic notion is filled out
with a more specific account of the educative function of
participation, where 'education' is used in a wide sense to cover the
development of responsible, individual social and political action.
One important aspect of this is said to be that political participation
itself increases people's confidence in their ability to participate efficiently and meaningfully in politics: participation increases their sense
of 'political efficacy'.

The communal arguments are in part extensions of these developmental arguments. It is held that an important aspect of how individuals are developed and educated by the experience of political
participation is the way in which this teaches them about the nature
and importance of the community and of their place within it. This
is valuable in various ways but above all it integrates the individual
into the community. This has a dual aspect. On the one hand it
benefits individuals, for example by giving them a true perspective on
the communal aspect of life and how to relate to other individuals and
their claims. On the other hand it develops and strengthens the
community itself: the individual's subjective perceptions of, and com-
mitments to, the community are at the same time objective bonds
which bind the community together; and to strengthen the former is
at the same time to develop the latter. Participation, then, strengthens
the community and the individual's attachment to it.

An important implication of this with regard to political participation is that it increases the state's 'legitimacy' by strengthening
individuals' attachment to the political community. But the state's
legitimacy is also increased by political participation because of what
this means in terms of individuals' involvement in the making of the
decisions carried out by the state. In a participatory democracy there
is a real sense in which individuals can feel that the government's
decisions are *their* decisions, and should therefore be accepted. This
strengthening of legitimacy is particularly important in view of the
'legitimation crisis' that is said to be afflicting the liberal democratic
state (Habermas 1976); for a useful summary see Held (1987) Chapter 7. Another significant aspect of the way participatory democracy
can increase legitimacy is by means of the more coherent account it
can be said to provide of political obligation. In her very important
book on the liberal democratic theory of political obligation, Carole

Pateman discusses the difficulties of providing a coherent account of political obligation in the liberal democratic state and argues that a satisfactory account can only be given in a participatory democracy (Pateman 1985).

This brings us to the fourth category of arguments for participatory democracy – the 'philosophical'. These relate to basic theoretical issues and contend that only in participatory democracy can they be satisfactorily resolved. In essence they are those posed by the individualism of liberal democratic theory. Arguably, fundamental theoretical difficulties are intrinsic to this individualism. These are central to the Marxist critique, and we shall be looking at this in the next section. But participatory theory, too, confronts some of these issues. At the risk of over-simplifying complex matters we could say that whereas Marxists see liberal democratic theory's individualism as an irredeemable fault, participatory theorists wish to preserve vital aspects of it and to overcome the faults it has in liberal democratic theory.[6] Pateman's discussion of political obligation can be seen in this light. She argues that the incoherence of the liberal democratic account of political obligation is part and parcel of the impossibility of giving a voluntarist account of the liberal democratic state – one that would accord with certain of liberal democratic theory's individualist premises. Only participatory theory, she argues, can adequately combine the idea of being obligated to obey the state with the idea of voluntarily undertaking such obligations. Participation fills the vacuum between the individual and the liberal democratic state by actively engaging individual citizens in the process by which it is run; and in a proper participatory democracy *all* adults would be engaged. In this way there is a genuine sense in which they can all feel they have individually contributed to, and are committed to upholding, the state's decisions (Pateman 1985). Participation, then, is seen as giving the fundamental nexus between the community and the individual (which is unrecognised by liberal democratic theorists), and the connection between the individual and the state, a rational and volitional character which generates or allows a genuine form of individual autonomy. This is to be contrasted with the bogus autonomy which, Pateman argues, characterises the liberal democratic state.

Another, very interesting, 'philosophical' argument has recently been put forward by Botwinick (Botwinick 1985). This, too, is a participatory response to theoretical problems within liberal

democratic theory that arise, in part, from individualism. In this case
the focus is on the nominalism and radical scepticism and relativism to
which liberal individualism gives rise. Botwinick's argument has to be
carefully read to be properly understood, but the key idea is that with
an individualist analysis of social reality there are no 'supra-
individual supports for knowledge and belief'. This involves a radical
relativism such that in a society of 'epistemological equals' there is no
warrant for the view of any person or group of people, including a
majority, to prevail over that of anyone else. The only way out of the
problem this poses for political decision making is for all individuals
to be involved in reaching a consensus, via political participation.
Where all views have equal validity, only a genuine consensus can
have moral and political authority and only a participatory democracy can generate such a consensus. And again, the argument is that
participatory theory rescues rather than opposes liberal democratic
theory: 'liberal democratic theory rests upon an historically unresol-
ved paradox which has prevented political theorists from recognising
the radical participatory implications inherent in classical democratic
theory' (Botwinick 1985).

Arguments Against Participatory Theory

There are, then, strong arguments in favour of participatory democracy. But what of the counter-arguments? Let us try and indicate
briefly the form that they take. Although there is a considerable
overlap they can for convenience be divided into those that question
the feasibility of participatory democracy and those that question its
desirability. We can leave an assessment of the 'philosophical' issues
until we consider individualism again in the light of the Marxist
critique.

Arguments challenging the feasibility of participatory democracy
broadly take two forms: those that focus on people's political behaviour and motivations, and those that consider features of the 'logic'
of the situation within which political behaviour occurs.

The main burden of the arguments that focus on political behaviour is that the mass of the people do not have the inclination or the
capacity to engage in the kind of political activity favoured by participatory theorists. We came across this sort of argument before when
we looked at studies of voting behaviour in the last chapter. And as
we saw then, any attempt to assess it raises fundamental issues. In the

case of participatory theory there is an added dimension of difficulty: such theory sets out to challenge and go beyond the status quo so that the status of any empirical evidence about how and why people now behave is itself subject to radical doubt. For example, if people in existing political systems do not have the capacity or interest to participate in politics this, participationists argue, is precisely because in those systems they do not have a chance to participate properly. It is the experience of participation that breeds the capacity and interest to participate effectively.

The 'situational' arguments against the feasibility of participatory democracy are more varied, but their common theme is the impossibility of participatory democracy in the face of the scale and complexity of modern society. The very factors which, as we saw earlier, have provoked a demand by some for participatory democracy are seen by others as making it impossible. And we should notice here that the issues, arguments and counter-arguments again parallel those involved in the appraisal of the critique of radical democratic theory by the 'modern democratic theorists'. For example, on the one hand what is seen as the inevitability of elite rule is regarded as excluding the possibility of participatory democracy. On the other hand it is argued that radical social and political changes should be made which will prevent elite rule by establishing, or making possible the establishment of, participatory procedures and processes. Here we have again the same difficulty in assessing the empirical 'evidence', since it is that very evidence which is itself in question. However this time there is a difference. Before, radical democratic theory was being challenged by factors beyond its cognisance, as it were; whereas participatory theory, although challenged by those same factors, is itself also a self-conscious counter-attack upon them.

This counter-attack has various features, but one of the main themes is a countering of the problems of scale and complexity with arguments for breaking down the size of political and social units. Such arguments still recognise the inevitability of *some* overall political organisation for large-scale modern society, even if this is only for 'co-ordination'. But the question is, how is this to be combined with the existence of small political units? Solutions offered to this problem vary from loose, federal and usually multi-stage combinations of political units, to the development of important, though subordinate, roles for 'community' political organisations within the existing type of national institutional framework. There are important difficulties with proposals of this sort, however, which are admirably discussed by Dahl (Dahl 1970). For example, what does 'co-ordination' amount to? If it is actually to be effective, will national co-ordination bodies be different from existing national states in any important respects? And if power *is* radically devolved to smaller units, this may bring the intended benefits of meaningful participation (as the individual is no longer swamped by sheer numbers), but at what cost? The smaller the unit, the less power it has to achieve what people want done in the modern world – control of pollution and unemployment, for example. The smaller the unit, the more the individual can participate; but the fewer or the less important are the matters in which that participation can occur.

We should notice here that the desire for smaller political units as a way of making participation more meaningful is closely connected with a hankering after direct democracy. Direct involvement by the individual in the actual decision-making body is seen as the most authentic form of political participation. Here there is a difference again between modern participatory theory and radical democratic theory (although Rousseau in this, as in other ways, can be seen as a direct progenitor of contemporary participatory theory). Radical theory saw representation as the solution to the problem of scale and the impossibility of direct democracy. Participatory theory, though, is in part a hostile response to the actual experience of representative 'democracy': 'representation destroys participation and citizenship . . . representative democracy is as paradoxical an oxymoron as our language has produced; its confused and failing practice make this ever more obvious' (Barber 1984).[7]

Direct democracy is clearly feasible where the unit is small enough, the New England town meeting for example. But are small units themselves feasible? This is, of course, directly the point at issue. As we noted in the last chapter there is a growing interest in modern communications technology as a way of making direct democracy possible in large political units. But, as we indicated before, it is doubtful whether the kind of 'participation' possible would have the same quality as participation in a face-to-face meeting. Sheer numbers of participants and the qualitative difference between actual discussions and 'electronic interaction' are crucial factors. Nonetheless, there are those who see communications technology as very important here (Margolis 1979; McLean 1986). At the very least it could be seen as offering an improvement on that more traditional mechanism for achieving some form of direct participation in modern states, the referendum (on referendums see Butler and Ranney (1980)).

Judgement about the feasibility of participatory democracy must depend, in part at least, on one's judgement about its desirability. Apart from anything else (and in fact the reasons go further than this) if participatory democracy is regarded as desirable, the difficulties in the way of its realisation will be seen as obstacles to be overcome. Whereas if it is viewed as undesirable, such obstacles will be taken as crucial additional arguments for not seeking to achieve it, and indeed as sufficiently demonstrating that it is not feasible. So let us now see what sorts of argument can lie behind the contention that participatory democracy is undesirable.

One of these illustrates another dimension of the overlap. Part of the facts-of-political-behaviour argument against the feasibility of participatory democracy was that people do not have the wish to participate more fully in politics. And it is reasonable to argue that it would be undesirable to have a system which required from people that which they do not wish to do. Either they would in some way be compelled to participate, which would seem to be clearly undesirable; or else decision making would be left in the hands of those who did wish to participate. In this latter case participatory systems would run the danger of becoming systems of minority rule rather than democracies, since it would be only a minority who would be interested. Moreover, it would probably be unrestrained minority rule since a guiding idea of participatory 'democracy' – derived from Continental theory – is that the popular will should be unrestrained. The minority of activists, like the vanguard party of one-party 'democracy', would be conceived as expressing and implementing the general will. Moreover, since the activists would probably be extremists, it is likely that the end result of participatory 'democracy' would be totalitarian rule by a minority of extremists – a vanguard state in fact.

Compare all this with the liberal democratic idea of representative government. This involves a system of defined and delimited governmental functions being performed by those who, having the inclination for the political life, are appointed and made accountable by popular election. This provides for a combination of popular, responsible and delimited decision making.

As before, using and drawing conclusions from empirical 'evidence' about people's present political behaviour and inclinations may be dismissed as beside the point by participationists. Nevertheless, one need not couch the anti-participationist argument in terms of evidence about what people's motives (presently) are, so much as in terms of what it is reasonable to expect of people, even in new circumstances. And in this connection it is noteworthy that the prominent participatory theorist C. B. Macpherson says that 'the price of participation' should not be 'a greater degree of activity than the average person can reasonably be expected to contribute' (Macpherson 1966). (He is referring here to the possibility of democratic one-party systems, but the general point remains valid.)

But even supposing, or even when, more people do wish to participate to a greater extent, this itself would be undesirable, argue the anti-participationists. One of the key arguments is that participation by large numbers in the decision-making process clogs and slows that process and generally makes it thoroughly inefficient. The objections involved here clearly overlap considerably with the 'sheer numbers' objection against the *feasibility* of participatory democracy; and some of the same considerations and participatory responses apply. It should also be noticed that it is by no means clear that assessing this argument is simply a matter of weighing the value of efficiency against other values held to be realised by participation. It can be argued that, in some ways at least, popular participation itself *increases* efficiency by mobilising the knowledge latent and dispersed in the community. This is very similar to one of the traditional justifications of democracy as such, against the claims of rule by experts, which we shall look at in the next chapter. (On this, and other aspects of the pros and cons of participatory democracy, there is a very useful discussion in Lucas (1976).)

Another form of argument against too much participation has connections with one of the arguments about the threat posed to liberty by equality that we looked at in Chapter 1. This dwells not so much on the clogging up of the system as its general breakdown – a breakdown followed by a totalitarian takeover (this overlaps with the argument that participation leads to a totalitarian takeover by extremist minorities). Mass political activity is here regarded as too frenetic, as overloading the decision-making system and as leading to instability and a collapse into totalitarianism. 'The collapse of the Weimar Republic, with its high rates of mass participation, into Fascism, and the post-war establishment of totalitarian regimes based on mass participation, albeit participation backed by intimidation and coercion, underlay the tendency for "participation" to become linked to the concept of totalitarianism rather than that of democracy' (Pateman 1970). Again, empirical evidence from political sociologists has been used to back up an anti-participatory argument. Voting-behaviour studies found not only that most electors were normally uninterested in politics, but also that the uninterested majority should not be raised out of their apathy since they tended to have non-demo-cratic or authoritarian attitudes.

Critics of participatory theory, then, turn the participationists' case on its head. That case, it will be remembered, can be summed up by saying that only participatory democracy can realise the values and objectives of liberal democratic theory. The critics, on the other hand, say the opposite: participatory democracy – or rather the attempt to realise it – leads to results that are neither democratic nor liberal.

Today, it is true, it is fashionable to worry more about the threat to democracy and liberty from the 'top' than from the mass: that is to say, the threat posed by the 'overloading' of the liberal democratic state and/or the crisis in its legitimacy (the latter being a problem to which participatory democracy may be seen as a partial solution). However, the worries about the dangers of over-emphasising partici-pation and unlimited democracy remain valid. Even as sympathetic a commentator as David Held thinks participatory theorists remain vulnerable to the criticism that they 'have attempted to resolve prematurely' complex matters involving liberty 'by allowing demo-cracy to prevail over all other considerations' and have not asked whether there should 'be limits on the power of the *demos*' (Held 1987).

This renewed concern with traditional liberal worries about in-dividual freedom is also a hallmark of some recent Marxist or neo-Marxist theorising (which in any case, as we have already seen, tends to converge with participatory theory). But before looking at this we must first understand the basic features of Marxist critiques of liberal democracy. And it is to these that we now turn.

3.3 The Marxist Critique

Before outlining 'the Marxist critique' of the theory and practice of liberal democracy, two important points must be made. First, Marx's thought is profound and wide ranging. Moreover, the commentaries on, and studies of, this thought are voluminous. They also include differing expositions on many controversial points of interpretation. This means that it is often difficult, or impossible, to say definitively exactly what Marx's ideas are. Added to this, and to a considerable extent arising from it, amongst the followers of Marx there have been proponents or adherents of some very different theories, all claiming to be Marxist. Indeed, there have been, and are, some very different brands of Marxism. The upshot of all this is that it is often misleading, to say the least, to talk of *the* Marxist line on anything – the theory and practice of liberal democracy not excepted. And in fact, as already mentioned, there is currently something of a convergence between some varieties of what might be called Marxist theory – 'post-Marxism' – and liberal democratic theory. All this having been said, however, it still makes good sense to talk of 'the Marxist critique' of liberal democracy. This is because there are some very important points and arguments which, despite all these differences, the various theories and interpretations have in common. And in any case, where the differences are crucial these can be pointed out.

The second point is that for reasons of space there will be no attempt to give an exposition of Marxist ideas.[8] The previous paragraph, in fact, shows how unwieldy such an exposition would be. Here we will simply indicate some of the main lines of argument in – and the most important of the issues that arise from – Marxist analyses that relate to liberal democratic theory and practice.

We have talked of the Marxist critique of the theory and the practice of liberal democracy. And, up to a point, it does fall into two parts, or has two aspects, i.e. the critique of the theory and the critique of the practice. Even though this is true only up to a point, since the two are so heavily interrelated, it still provides a useful way to organise the discussion. And we shall begin with the critique of the practice.

The Critique of Liberal Democratic Practice

This part of the critique is in a sense less fundamental. To a significant extent it consists in showing that the practice does not accord with liberal democratic theory's account of it. The critique of the theory, though, in a sense goes one step further and contends that the theory is faulty in the first place. (We should remember, however, not to push the notion of a split of this kind too far, since there is so much of an overlap. For example, it can be held that the defectiveness of liberal democratic theory's conceptions is one of the reasons for their failure to be realised in practice.)

The central argument in the 'critique of practice' starts from the association of 'liberal democracy' with capitalism: liberal democracy – or what liberal democrats maintain is such – occurs where there is a capitalist system. But such a system, it is argued, actually prevents the realisation of liberal democracy. Capitalism, contrary to what liberal democrats suppose, makes it impossible for liberal democracy to exist. 'For Marx and Engels the reality of liberal democracy appeared systematically to curtail its pretentions' (Levin 1983). What actually exists is said to be a sham democracy that Marxists frequently call 'bourgeois democracy'.

An important aspect of Marxist criticisms here is a moral one – that liberal democrats are blind or insensitive to the inhuman nature of capitalism, to the inhumanity of the conditions it imposes on the mass of the people. The implication is that a political system that allows this to happen cannot in fact be one which promotes liberty or is controlled by the people. But this is not just left as an implication, and the nub of the critique consists in explicit argumentation to the effect that freedom and democracy do not in fact exist in bourgeois 'democracy'.

Freedom – genuine freedom – is said not to exist; only 'formal' freedom. This is basically due to the inequalities that characterise capitalist society, so that the position of the proletarian 'wage slave' is in fact one of lack of freedom, despite possession of the same civil liberties and political freedoms as the bourgeoisie. 'In its implementation abstract freedom emerges as bourgeois freedom. Seek for the content behind the form and this freedom reduces itself to private property and free trade. It is not men who are set free but capital' (Levin 1983). Or, as Pierson puts it, writing of the noted Marxist, Rosa Luxemburg (1871–1919): 'like Marx, [she] sought to develop an analysis which would reveal bourgeois democracy's "hard kernel of social inequality and lack of freedom hidden under the sweet shell of formal freedom and equality" ' (Pierson 1986). There is also another, and rather different, argument about the lack of freedom in capitalist systems – and therefore in liberal democracy. This Marxist argument is not always focused upon, and its significance is rather different because it shows that *all* are unfree, 'proletarians and capitalists alike'.

Their lack of freedom consists 'in their domination by an economic system . . . which has its own laws and logic' (Gray 1986a).

Democracy, too, is said not to exist. This is because, it is argued, the mass of the people are not in fact in control. The underlying thesis here derives from Marx's class analysis, according to which the class that controls the means of production dominates society. Under capitalism this class is the bourgeoisie; and so it is the bourgeoisie – the capitalists – and not the mass of the people, who have power in bourgeois 'democracy'. This basic thesis, though, is subject to a number of elucidations and interpretations. And these have given rise to some controversies within Marxism which, besides being important in themselves, are of considerable significance in assessing the nature and validity of the Marxist critique of liberal democracy. These interpretations and controversies concern the meaning – and mode of exercising – 'domination', and the role of the state in this.

Most typically this domination has been conceived as an exercise of power: the bourgeoisie is viewed as a ruling class which exercises power over society. (That is, in so far as *any* group exercises power. At another level it is often held to be a key Marxist argument that society is subject to historical laws so that the scope for purposive control of society is severely limited. However, this too is a focus for controversy and subject to radically differing interpretations.)

This exercise of power can in part be conceived as the 'direct' exercise of economic power by the individual, or individual groups of, controllers of economic enterprises. But this merges into, and may well require, the exercise of power over society as a whole by those controllers acting collectively as a ruling class (i.e. it may well be that such actions by the ruling class are required to maintain the system of 'individual' exercises of 'direct' economic power). And it is especially through or by means of the state that the ruling class is conceived to act. This is taken as an aspect of the basic Marxist thesis that the state is only part of the 'superstructure' of society and, as such, it does not control, but merely reflects, the underlying economic structure. But just how this occurs, and how it is that it occurs when the institutions of liberal democracy apparently give control of the state to the mass of the people, are some of the key issues in the interpretations and controversies just mentioned. There have always been differences within Marxist thought on these matters but the issues have been revived lately as interest in the whole question of the Marxist view of the nature and role of the state has been revived

(Benjamin and Elkin 1985).

Traditionally the prevalent idea has been that the state is the *instrument* of the ruling class. This received its best-known expression in the famous statement in *The Communist Manifesto* that 'the executive of the modern state is but a committee for managing the common affairs of the whole bourgeoisie'. A well-known modern formulation is to be found in Miliband (1969).

It may be that the bourgeoisie actually and directly control the state machine, by providing the personnel who staff the governmental machinery; or it may be that they indirectly control the state by using, or threatening to use, their economic power to block policies which would threaten their interests; or it may be a combination of both. In the first case it has to be explained how it is that contested elections and universal suffrage do not place the control of the state in the hands of the mass of the people. Again there are two rather different kinds of argument here, both of which may be used. On the one hand it may be contended that the elected politicians do not actually control the governmental machine. They are merely figureheads who are in fact manipulated and/or blocked by the bureaucracy, which is under bourgeois control. On the other hand it may be argued that so-called free elections do not in fact express the will of the people, so that the elected politicians are not, after all, the agents of the popular will: the state remains in the hands of the ruling class. This might be a matter of *de facto* restriction of choice at elections, so that there is no option which would offer the voters a radical, 'anti-capitalist' policy. Or it may (or may also) be that the ruling class, by controlling the mass media and the education system for example, can mould public opinion in such a way that there are no 'anti-capitalist' views to be expressed. In this case elections simply 'echo back' the ideas or 'ideology' of the ruling class and leave them undisturbed in their control of the state.

The argument that public opinion may be moulded by control of the instruments of communication and socialisation can merge into different kinds of argument, which we shall consider in a moment. These maintain that it is the effects or requirements of the system, rather than the deliberate or conscious exercise of power, which promote the bourgeois cause. The contention is that the whole social-isation process imbues the mass of the people with a pro-capitalist outlook. This sort of argument may extend to the contention that not only ideas but also desires are the result of indoctrination or socialisation, and that 'false needs' are created (Marcuse 1968). But whether it is needs or ideas, and whether it is an exercise of power or a result of the system, the outcome is the same: the electorate are the victims of 'false consciousness' and unable to express an authentic will of their own.

This idea is of profound importance in – and in assessing the validity of – the Marxist critique of liberal democracy, and we shall be returning to it later. It also overlaps with a key idea of Gramsci's. Antonio Gramsci (1891–1937), one of the founders of the Italian Communist party, 'is probably the most original political writer among the post-Lenin generation of Communists' (Kolakowski 1978).

According to his conception of hegemony, the ruling class secure their power not so much by the use of the state as by control of society's intellectual life – and therefore of the people's ideas – by purely cultural means. 'The privileged classes . . . secured a position of hegemony in the intellectual as well as the political sphere; they subjugated the others by this means, and intellectual supremacy was a precondition of political rule' (Kolakowski 1978).

As Gramsci's analysis shows, the Marxist idea of domination by a ruling class need not centre on control of the state by that class. Moreover, Marxist analysis often acknowledges that the state is not necessarily directly and closely controlled by a ruling class and may well act 'autonomously' to some extent. And it may even be that at times the state will act against the short-run interests of capitalists. This idea of the 'relative autonomy' of the state has lately been of increasing importance in Marxist theory.

The idea of relative autonomy points to, and can be a part of, another and rather different form of Marxist analysis. Here bourgeois domination of society is seen not so much as an exercise of power by a ruling class as a matter of the system operating to the benefit of the bourgeoisie, or, one might say, in the interests of capitalists. (It might be more accurate to say 'in the interests of capitalism'; or, if this is thought to be circular, one might talk of the system operating 'in such a way as to maintain its capitalist character'. The presumption would be, of course, that it is only capitalists who benefit from capitalism; however, as we shall see, one of the liberal democratic responses to the Marxist critique is to question this presumption.)[9] The argument might be in terms of 'structural determination', where the state is seen as constrained by the structure and functions of the capitalist system, including the international capitalist system, to pursue only policies that benefit capitalists. Or the argument might focus on the nature of the state itself, and the way it functions, in capitalist society. Here the essential argument is not so much that the state is *constrained* by something outside itself – the capitalist system – as that the state in capitalist society *is itself* necessarily of such a nature that it 'naturally' promotes the interests of capitalists. For example, its revenue and the criterion by which its performance will be judged, could both be said to involve the successful operation of the capitalist economy. Such an argument might be developed in terms not just of the nature of the state but also of the *regime* in which the state is embedded (Elkin 1985). (For further excellent, recent analyses of the nature and role of the state in capitalist societies see also Benjamin and Duvall (1985) and Braybrooke (1985).)

In either case – structural determination or the necessary role of the state – there can be recognition that there is a sense in which the state is popularly controlled. That is to say, the idea is that *within the area of manoeuvre left to the state* its actions can be broadly decided by the people through the electoral process. But this area of manoeuvre is so constricted that the interests of capitalists cannot, fundamentally, be harmed. To the extent that liberal democrats could accept this analysis the issues between them and the Marxist critics would then become: (a) the extent to which it is true that the state's room for manoeuvre *is* limited by being bound to pursue the essential interests of capitalists, and (b) the extent to which pursuit of the interests of capitalists is against the wishes and interests of the mass of the people (an issue already referred to and one which will be taken up again later). By contrast the other issues we were concerned with just now centred not on whether the state can *serve* the people, but on whether it is *controlled by* them.

The focus on the role rather than the control of the state, and the argument that this role is to a crucial extent determined, brings us back to the underlying Marxist theory of the determination of the political superstructure by the economic basis of society. And in fact in Marx's earlier works we find a still more general and 'theoretical' argument about the dependence of the state upon society (see, for example, Pierson (1986) Chapter 1). It will be remembered, indeed, that we earlier deferred a consideration of the more theoretical or 'philosophical' aspects of the Marxist critique; and it is to this that we should now turn.

The Critique of Liberal Democratic Theory

The arguments here are concerned not so much with reality being out of accord with liberal democratic theory, as with fundamental faults in the theory itself.

One of liberal democratic theory's main faults according to Marxists is the mirror image, as it were, of the key faults discerned in the practice of liberal democracy. The basic reason given for the practice being faulty was that the structure of society, in particular the economic structure, prevents the liberal democratic state from operating in the way liberal democrats suppose it does. The mirror image is the blindness of liberal democratic theory to this: its failure to recognise the importance and effects of the structure of society, particularly the economic structure. An aspect of this blindness is said to be the insistence in liberal democratic theory that the state is separate from the private sphere of civil society; and that precisely because of this separateness it can act as a neutral 'umpire' and regulate society in an impartial, disinterested manner. This, says the Marxist, fails to recognise that the state reflects civil society. And in particular, of course, the arguments we have just looked at contend that, far from being impartial, the state reflects and promotes the interest of the dominant class.

Associated with this blindness, the Marxist contends that there is a false conceptualisation of social and political, private and public. Basically he argues that the liberal democrat wrongly conceives there to be a clear distinction between the political and other spheres of life.[10] Likewise the liberal democrat wrongly discerns a clear division between public and private aspects of life, and this enables him (mistakenly) to elevate what he conceives as private life and regard it as the most important sphere. (Perhaps it would be more accurate to talk of the liberal drawing the distinction in the wrong place – very much the wrong place, though. Few Marxists would dispute the importance – as distinct from the supreme importance – of private life; but they would have a *very* different, and a much narrower, conception of private life.)

These misconceptions are important in themselves; but, in this context, their particular importance lies in the implications they have for the possibilities and forms of democracy. Liberal democratic theory, according to the Marxist, wrongly conceives popular control to be just a matter of the people controlling political institutions, the state. This mistaken idea is a part of the simple failure to see the influence of the economic structure. But it is compounded by the misconception that there is a separate sphere, the political, and that it is only here that popular control is necessary – or, indeed, desirable. In fact another liberal democratic misconception is said to be the liberal idea that the scope of state decisions should be restricted to a 'public sphere' and not invade the 'private sphere'. This goes along with the misconception about the liberal democratic state being a neutral umpire adjudicating in a public sphere, and ignores the fact that it is already structuring private life (to the advantage of the bourgeoisie and the disadvantage of the mass of the people). Because of these misconceptions, the Marxist argues, liberal democratic theory fails properly to conceptualise, and comprehend what is necessary for, control by the people. The Marxist alternative – the Marxist account of the conceptualisations and practices that are necessary for genuine democracy – we shall come back to shortly.

Behind this kind of criticism of liberal democratic conceptualisations of the nature and significance of key social and political processes lies what is perhaps the most fundamental part of the Marxist critique of liberal democratic theory: the critique of individualism. We have already remarked, in various places, that individualism is a key characteristic of liberal democratic theory. And it is time now to draw these points together; to see just what is postulated and assumed in liberal democratic theory and to look at the way in which Marxist theory calls it into question.

The issue is actually a little more complex than at first appears. It is easy to assume – and it often is assumed – that it is a matter of a straightforward clash: individualism on the one side and the Marxist critique of this on the other. But, because of the complexity of the notion of individualism and the richness of Marxist theory, this is not really the position. The best way, though, to clarify matters a little is to start with the over-simplified, and commonly assumed, account and then see how this has to modified. In this account what we described in Chapter 2 as 'ontological individualism' is taken as central to liberal democratic theory. Marxist theory is then seen as mounting a fundamental attack on this. This attack has two inter-related aspects.

First, there is a rejection of what is seen as an outcome of ontological individualism, the blindness to the reality and value of 'community'. Liberal democrats, it is held, are unable to perceive the existence –

and are therefore unable to appreciate the value – of community because ontological individualism involves seeing social collectivities merely as collections of individuals. (In fact this is an over-simplification since liberal democratic theory – even if we exclude Continental theory – includes, as we have seen, neo-Idealism and citizenship theories where the reality and value of community is clearly important: compare Tucker (1980) who includes A. D. Lindsay amongst 'liberal humanists'. It is even arguable that John Stuart Mill's thought at times recognises community. However, as a statement about the rest of Anglo-American democratic theory it is true enough to make it important.)

We cannot here go into the very important idea of community. Suffice it to say that from classical Greece onwards there has been a tradition of thought in which the community that individuals inhabit is seen as having, in an important sense, a reality of its own – quite apart from the individuals who inhabit it at a particular time. In this sort of conception the focus is on such things as institutions, customs, traditions, language and, more generally, culture. Indeed, before the growth of individualist ideas in early modern times, the notion that individuals could be conceived as separate from the character they had as part of a society or community did not really make sense. And, to an extent because individuals gain their character from the community they inhabit, community is seen as having very great moral worth. It is the community (or the properly ordered community) that develops an individual's capacities, gives a sense of belonging and identity, and provides the focus for motivation and activity. Liberal democratic theory, it is argued, being blind to all this is unable properly to evaluate social and political activity. In particular it fails, on the one hand, to see the true inhumanity and 'alienation' that the capitalist system involves; and on the other hand it is unable to give a proper account of a collectivity, and hence of a collective – a democratic – decision.

As we have just indicated, Marx was not the first exponent of a communalist perspective. But he was particularly important in turning this perspective, as a critique, on liberal democratic theory. Although to some extent he was using and developing Rousseau's and Hegel's thought here, Marx added his own ideas and, what is more, combined these with the other aspects of his wholesale and fundamental critique of liberal democratic theory and practice.

The second aspect of the challenge to ontological individualism is a direct attack. Here the target is the very notion that society is composed only of individuals, and that its character is determined by the characteristics of those constituent individuals. A variety of telling arguments derive from communalist theory, and receive their most penetrating development from Marx. There are perhaps two main ones. First, that 'man is not an abstract being squatting outside the world' (Marx 1844, quoted in Lukes 1973). Rather, he takes his character from his historical and social context. Individuals, that is to say, are social beings and their character and behaviour are, to a crucial extent, the product of their particular social environment. The second main argument is that social phenomena are not explicable simply as the product of the character and (at any rate the intentional) behaviour of individuals. Rather, social structures have, in a crucial sense, an existence of their own; and, indeed, they structure the behaviour of individuals. (Consider, say, the Indian caste system, the market and, more generally still, language.)

These arguments raise profound and complex issues in political and social theory. In unravelling them one would need to look more carefully at the conception of 'ontological individualism', and perhaps 'unpack' it into component features. In particular, it would be helpful to distinguish between the idea of what Lukes calls the 'abstract individual' and 'methodological individualism' (Lukes 1973). Our purpose here, however, is not to engage in a full analysis of individualism, so much as to focus on issues crucial to an understanding and appraisal of liberal democratic theory. One key issue – and perhaps the most fundamental – that arises is this. If the character and behaviour of individuals are the product of their social environment, can (or to what extent can) we say that they are making decisions of their own, expressing their own will? Similarly, can we say that the people make their own decisions – that there is any such thing as an authentic will of the people? This connects up with the kind of Marxist critique of liberal democratic practice we have already looked at, that sees the people as the victims of false consciousness. We shall come back to this issue at the end of the chapter, when we attempt to assess the Marxist critique.

Another issue that arises concerns the relationship between ontological and what we earlier called 'moral' individualism. The liberal democratic assumption is that there is a tight connection between the two so that the latter is dependent on the former. In other words, the assumption is that the proper kind of moral importance can be given to the individual only if individuals are seen to be independent entities rather than social products which are merely pieces of the social fabric. Here the Marxist critique is turned back against itself, as it were. For the liberal democrat the Marxist arguments issue forth in, or imply, unacceptable moral conclusions.

Again, though, it is necessary to look more carefully at the notions of individualism involved, and matters are not so straightforward as at first appears. It may well be that any close relationships here, involving the values of moral individualism, are with only some of the components of ontological individualism. Or, to put the point another way, it is arguable that these values can be held without subscribing to all that is included in ontological individualism. In particular, it can argued that a commitment to 'respecting persons, to maintaining and enhancing their autonomy, privacy and self-development . . . does not . . . imply the adoption of . . . the abstract conception of the individual' (Lukes 1973). But this is more than a hypothetical argument: the point is that Marxism – despite what its critics might say – does subscribe to these values. 'There can be little dispute over whether Marx was an individualist, for he places great value on the achievement of autonomy' (Tucker 1980). And arguably most Marxists, with the possible exception of Lenin and Mao, are individualists in this sense.

This brings us back to the point that there is not a straightforward clash between individualism, seen as a distinctive feature of liberal democratic theory, on one side, and Marxism on the other. In fact the Marxist critique can be seen not so much as an attack on the values of individualism as an attack on the theory and practice of liberal democracy for not implementing them. Again, then, the criticism of liberal democracy is not of its ideals but of its failure to realise (or worse its negation of) them. 'Marx's individualism goes further than that of most liberals' and 'his critique of liberalism arises out of his claim that the prevailing conditions in liberal society actually serve to frustrate our efforts to be self-directing' (Tucker 1980). Marx, then, does not 'reprimand liberal philosophers . . . for failing to articulate the true nature of these ideas [true human autonomy, true political liberty and equality]; rather, he is concerned that they do not see how difficult it is for these goals to be realised under capitalist relations of production' (Tucker 1980).

Possessive Individualism

Marxists, then, are not critics of individualism as such. But it must be remembered that they are, as already pointed out, fundamentally critical of an aspect of ontological individualism. They completely reject 'abstract individualism' – that is to say they reject the idea of the abstract individual, the idea of man as 'an abstract being squatting outside the world'. And we shall come back to this. It can also be said that Marxists are critics of what is, in a sense, a 'perverted' variety of moral individualism. And this *is* held to be distinctive of liberal democratic theory because of that theory's association with capitalist society. This is what C. B. Macpherson calls 'possessive individualism' (Macpherson 1962). Briefly, this consists in the idea 'that each person is the sole *proprietor* of his own person and capacities, and that each person has an infinite desire to *appropriate* resources (human as well as natural)' (Levine 1981). This involves a sanctification of the idea of private property and its accumulation that leads to the iniquities of capitalist society. And it is also said to involve the invalid assumption 'that individuals owe nothing to society for the skills which they acquire when they are trained to accomplish sophisticated tasks' (Tucker 1980).

Whether 'possessive individualism' is, in fact, a central feature of liberal democratic theory is arguable. First, there is the 'liberal humanist' or neo-Idealist strand to be remembered. In fact Macpherson does explicitly recognise the different nature of some liberal democratic theory: neo-Idealist and citizenship theory. He regards J. S. Mill as a major figure in this category of 'developmental democracy' (Macpherson 1977a). Indeed, Macpherson's aim is to separate 'out the developmental from the possessive elements of liberal individualism' (Lukes 1979) and incorporate the former into a 'non-market' theory of liberal democracy. However, he thinks J. S. Mill's theory was also contaminated with Benthamite assumptions,[11] and that both he and the later neo-Idealist and citizenship theorists failed to come to grips with the class nature of capitalist society. And in any event, Macpherson argues, it was purely possessive individualist theories that came to predominate in twentieth-century liberal democracy. This, though, is surely an over-simplification.

Even if it is not, there is a second argument to consider: it is actually doubtful whether, *pace* Macpherson, utilitarian varieties of liberal democratic theory can properly be regarded as embodying possessive individualism. As Tucker points out, utilitarians have generally defended the principle of preserving an area of individual freedom similar to that sanctified by natural rights theorists (pre-eminently Locke) and which 'possessive individualists regard as a principle of justice' from which an entitlement to accumulate property follows. But utilitarians 'have done so only because they were convinced by the argument that human happiness will be maximised by a policy which allows people to do what they choose. They certainly have not regarded the principle as a natural entitlement which can be claimed regardless of the social consequences which might be thought to follow' (Tucker 1980). And, where necessary, utilitarians would justify state interference in what possessive individualists would regard as areas of sanctified individual liberty: such state action could be justified if it were to produce a greater sum total of happiness.

Nonetheless, Macpherson's argument has been influential. And it is true that it is a plausible interpretation of the implications of the natural rights strand in liberal democratic theory – which is, after all, a major strand. Macpherson's critique here is broadly Marxist. And his general stance towards liberal democracy is very similar to Marx's, as interpreted above: 'he places himself among "those who accept and would promote the normative values that were read into the liberal-democratic society and state by J. S. Mill and the nineteenth and twentieth century idealist theorists, but who reject the present liberal-democratic society and state as having failed to live up to those values, or as being incapable of realising them"' (Lukes 1979, quoting Macpherson 1977b). However, as we have already remarked, Macpherson is not, perhaps, 'fully' a Marxist since he does not subscribe to a Marxist account of what is necessary to transform capitalist society. This is associated with what can be argued is his 'failure' to free himself from ontological individualism in his criticism of liberal theory's possessive individualism: he does not complete 'his penetrating critique of its possessiveness' with 'an abandonment of its individualism' (Lukes 1979). Macpherson, in fact (and this is part of the reason for his importance), straddles the Marxist–liberal democratic divide. 'Remaining faithful to the truth of the central maxim of liberal-democratic theory which affirms self-realisation as an end in itself, while drawing inspiration from the Marxian critique of capitalism, Macpherson proceeds to reform liberal-democratic theory. His [theory is a] synthesis of the two traditions, liberal democratic and Marxian' (Kontos 1979, Preface).

It will be remembered, indeed, that Macpherson was earlier

identified as a leading participatory theorist. And it might be taken as a characteristic feature of participatory theory that it combines a radical critique of the actuality of liberal democracy (perhaps, but not necessarily, Marxist inspired) with a commitment to its fundamental ideas and to working within its framework to reform it. But although its ambivalence to ontological individualism and its commitment to working within the framework of liberal democracy perhaps makes it importantly different from Marxist theory, there are also important overlaps. Apart from the particular case of Macpherson and the convergence we have already noted between 'post-Marxist' thought and non-Marxist democratic theory, there are in Marx's own thought important elements of participatory democratic theory which we should now consider.

Marxist Democratic Theory

After the revolution, control is in the hands of the mass of the people – the proletariat. And Marx envisages that control being exercised by processes and mechanisms of a sort that would be approved by participatory democrats. In particular he focuses on the Paris Commune as a model, where all officials were elected by universal suffrage 'responsible and revocable at short terms'. The commune was to serve as a model for the rest of France where the 'commune was to be the political form of even the smallest country hamlet . . . The rural communes . . . were to administer their common affairs by an assembly of delegates . . . and these district assemblies were again to send deputies to the National Delegation in Paris, each delegate to be at any time revocable and bound by the *mandat impératif* (formal instructions) of his constituents' (Marx 1970, quoted in Held 1987).

Marx, in fact, has a theory of democracy; although, as in the case of participatory theory, it is not a theory of *liberal* democracy: boundaries are not drawn round the sphere of public activity to protect a wide sphere of individual, private activity. In the Marxist critique of liberal democracy that we have been looking at it is not democracy that is criticised but its non-realisation. So Marx's theory includes an account of what this democracy is that ought to be realised. We mention this here to indicate the full range and character of the critique of liberal democracy, although as a *political* theory, over and above the social theory and philosophy, Marxism is widely held to be deficient. As such it may be considered to have little to contribute in the way of a theory about the institutions and processes of democracy. Nonetheless, it raises some quite complicated questions concerning the fundamental ideas embodied in democracy, and the way in which Marx's account of it fits into his underlying social theory; and we shall briefly indicate one or two important points (for further analysis of Marxist democratic ideas see, for example, Levin (1983), Pierson (1986) and Graham (1986)).

To begin with, it is not entirely clear how far Marx's theory of democracy is a theory about the character of the transitional phase, and how far about the eventual communist society in which the state has withered away. In the latter case, complex issues arise concerning the conception of the state and its relationship to the conception of democracy. The usual, and certainly the liberal democrat's, view would be that democracy is *a form of* state. However, apart from the apparent Marxist view that true democracy may require the absence (in at least some sense) of the state, it has recently been argued from a non-Marxist standpoint that the state is unnecessary and that 'a democratic state is a dialectical contradiction' (Burnheim 1985). There is also the anarchist tradition which is not unlike aspects of Marxism at times. Here again there is an ambivalence between on the one hand treating democracy as a form of the rejected state, and on the other hand seeing stateless anarchist society as the most perfect (or the only true) form of democracy. William Godwin (1756–1836) is the key figure here. But as radical a theorist as Carole Pateman regards the state – albeit a reformed state – as necessary to democracy (Pateman 1985; Chapter 7 contains an illuminating discussion of anarchism and democracy). And certainly in this book we have treated democracy as a form of state.

We should, though, now return to the uncertainties in Marx about the *stage* at which democracy will exist. These uncertainties are troublesome in understanding Marx; and they have been the source of a deep ambivalence, and endless controversy, within subsequent Marxist theory. (And this is apart from, or superimposed on, controversies concerning whether the proletarian takeover, which ushers in the transitional phase, could itself be effected by democratic means. On both types of controversy see Pierson (1986).) In particular, such uncertainty has intermeshed with arguments about the difficulty of getting a proletariat imbued with false consciousness to see its own interests. This double ambivalence has generated doubt about whether the transitional phase should itself be democratic or whether it should be seen purely as a necessary step towards true democracy. Or perhaps there can be some amalgam of the two via the notion of the real will, as against the apparent will, of the proletariat. We have already seen how the theory of 'people's democracy' grew out of Lenin's interpretation of Marx here. And we should at this point remember that Lenin's views on democracy can be seen as crucially different from those of Marx. In essence the two crucial points are these. First, Marx is more concerned with characterising the communist society as democracy whilst Lenin is pre-occupied with the business of getting there. Second, despite some oscillations in Lenin's view, Marx is unlike Lenin in also seeing the transitional phase as democratic in a sense that a participatory democrat would endorse, principally because the proletariat themselves are conceived by Marx as developing a revolutionary consciousness.

These differences have too often been obscured because 'the terrible fate which befell Marx was that he was Leninised' (Graham 1986). And because of this fact liberal democrats have, on the whole, paid less attention than they should have done to what Marxism says about democracy. The iniquities of Leninism tend to be viewed as self-evident; and with this the whole of Marxism is frequently dismissed by liberal democrats. In fact, though, as we have just seen the Marxist critique of liberal democracy is profound and cannot be ignored.

Assessment of the Marxist Critique

What, then, are we to make of this critique? This is obviously a large and complex question and in the space available we can only sketch in an answer by making a few points about some of the more salient issues.

Let us start with what we called the critique of practice. Leaving aside for the moment arguments about an exercise of power by a ruling class, let us look first at the more general line of argument to the effect that the system operates in the interests of capitalists.

There are powerful arguments here and, although it might be possible to take issue with them to some degree, let us accept their cogency. But let us also be clear about just what it is that is being accepted. It is accepted, then, that the system operates in the interests of capitalists; but the crucial point is that this does not of itself imply that it operates *against* the interests of the mass of the people. Or, rather, it is only an accompanying theory about the nature of capitalism that implies this. So a crucial issue then becomes the validity or otherwise of this theory. Marxist critics of liberal democracy naturally take the validity of this accompanying theory for granted. It never occurs to them, *at this point*, that it can be challenged. The question of this challenge we must leave hanging in the air for the moment, for the point to get clear here is this. *If* it is the case that capitalism is in the interests not just of capitalists, but also the whole people, then a demonstration that the system operates in favour of capitalists does not, *of itself*, show the system to be necessarily undemocratic. And if the system not only operates in the interests of the whole people, but the people (because of this) subjectively approve of the system, then there is every reason to call it democratic – assuming, of course, that the other necessary conditions of a democracy (free elections and so on) are present.

To go a bit deeper, it must be acknowledged that the above argument rests on the assumption that *if* the people ceased to approve of the system then they could change it – through the mechanisms of liberal democracy. Or, to put the point another way, the assumption is that the approval of the people is a necessary condition for the continuance of the system. This raises the issues that we left on one side just now, concerning the power structure within the system, and we shall come back to these in a moment. One of the arguments relating to those issues was that the people are the victims of false consciousness. And this argument is also a direct challenge to the point we are trying to establish at the moment. That is to say, if the people approve of capitalism only because of their false consciousness, then we are back to square one: the people's approval would then be one of the mechanisms by which the system maintains itself and would not be an authentic expression of their own will. Again, we shall come back to this shortly.

Let us now return to the argument that, whether or not the system itself is biased against them, power within the system is not exercised by the people but by a ruling class. We have not the space to go into the essentially 'empirical question' of whether, or to what extent, in the various Western political systems, government has failed to respond to electoral decisions when they go against the interests of those who hold economic power. Nor, similarly, can we go into whether government, attempting to respond to such decisions, has been blocked by that economic power. It will merely be dogmatically asserted that the evidence does not seem to bear out the proposition that electoral decisions have been systematically flouted in this way. (See Turner (1986) for a recent argument to the effect that the working class, for example, *can* use the political institutions of liberal democracy to promote their interests.)

In any case, the more theoretically interesting, and the more fundamental, arguments to consider are those that we left on one side a short while ago. These maintain that the electorate is unable to make 'anti-capitalist' decisions in the first place. The most basic argument here is that 'pro-capitalist' views are produced by controlling or moulding public opinion. This is an aspect of the 'false consciousness' argument. The idea of the deliberate control of opinion is importantly different from the notion of 'automatic' socialisation. And both are different from the idea of being subjected to 'cultural hegemony' or the ideology of the ruling class. Nonetheless, there is a significant overlap, and we shall deal with the control-of-public-opinion argument as part of a general assessment of the common element in all these arguments. (Again we shall not attempt an assessment of empirical evidence – evidence about the control of the media in different countries, the processes of socialisation and so on. Rather we shall concentrate on the theoretical question of whether it is plausible to argue that people's views *can* be completely determined in this way.) Moreover, the issues here link up with some of those raised by the Marxist critique of abstract individualism.

The critical part of the common element is that the ideas individuals have are not generated by themselves but are in some way externally induced in them. The question of the validity of this notion is of profound importance in assessing the viability of liberal democratic theory and practice; and we shall come back to it shortly when we look again at the Marxist critique of individualism, where some of the issues raised are the same, or are directly relevant.

Even if we reject the Marxist argument that the people are not in control of political decision making in capitalist society we are still left with other important criticisms. There are still the arguments about the inequalities and injustices of capitalist society, and the lack of real freedom behind the 'formal' freedom provided by the liberal democratic state.

Broadly speaking there are three forms of counter-argument with which to defend liberal democracy here. The first largely overlaps

with the contention above that the liberal democratic state *can* be used
by the people for their own ends. It is to the effect that *if* the people
wanted to change the system to rid themselves of its alleged iniquities
then they could in fact do so (and to the extent that they do not do
so then these 'iniquities' are not regarded as such by the people). This
is the argument of 'social democracy' and 'reformism'. There are
many issues here but the key ones for our purpose have already been
covered in considering whether the people can in fact use the liberal
democratic state for their own ends.

The second form of argument provides, as it were, the reasons why
the people do not want to change the capitalist system. In other
words, we have here justifications of those features of the system that
are alleged to be iniquitous. These include the arguments of perhaps
the best-known of recent liberal political philosophers, John Rawls
(Rawls 1972 and 1985) and Robert Nozick (Nozick 1974). Both hold
that what a Marxist would call 'formal' freedom is profoundly important and that its significance is not negated by inequalities, provided
that those inequalities benefit the least well-off (Rawls)[12] or that they
result only from holdings to which people are entitled (Nozick). We
cannot here get into a discussion of the issues raised; there is in fact a
burgeoning literature in this whole area. (For a useful survey of this,
and other aspects of the debate about the application of liberal values,
see Gray (1986b).) We must stick to what the people can do rather
than why they should – or should not – do it. Nonetheless, *that*
justifications of this kind exist is relevant to an argument put forward
a little earlier. This was to the effect that the validity of aspects of the
Marxist critique turns on the assumption that capitalism is not in the
interests of the people. And though we cannot enter into an assessment of rival arguments about the justice, or otherwise, of capitalism,
the very fact that rival arguments exist shows that there is an issue to
be settled. It is not, therefore, indisputably the case that capitalism
goes against the interests of the people (further relevant points are
taken up below when we consider capitalism and democracy generally). Moreover, a democrat would argue that it is the people who
should settle the issue.

The third form of argument, which is perhaps the most important
and convincing, is rather different in that it half accepts the Marxist
case. Here it is acknowledged that there is a great deal wrong with the
capitalist system, but that it can be put right without a total transformation of the system. In particular the economic inequalities, and

accompanying injustices and lack of freedom, can be remedied without changing the structure of the liberal democratic state and the
market system. This can be done by changing the economic power
structure itself in such a way as to give control of capital to the mass
of the workers, rather than to just a few managers and owners: in
other words a system of industrial democracy.

Industrial Democracy

This subject is large and controversial. Many questions arise concerning what exactly is meant by 'industrial democracy', its feasibility and
its desirability. There are many objections to be overcome in defending a system of industrial democracy, workers' control or economic
democracy; and there are many difficulties, both theoretical and
practical, in the way of instituting and running such a system. Many
of these – and other theoretical and empirical issues – are lucidly
discussed in an excellent recent book by R. A. Dahl (Dahl 1985; see
also Dahl 1970) which also contains a useful survey of the relevant
literature. Aware as he is of all these issues, Dahl is nonetheless firmly
in favour of economic democracy. In fact he builds up an extremely
strong case for it. Here, though, we shall simply point to one or two
of the more important issues involved.

The general idea behind economic democracy, as Dahl sees it, is to
provide an 'alternative to corporate capitalism' which strengthens
'political equality without sacrificing liberty'. Arguably, then, it re-
tains key virtues of a liberal democratic and capitalist system without
its main defects. And this is a crucial point: economic democracy (at
least of the type Dahl is talking about)[13] constitutes a modification,
not a complete rejection, of capitalism. The free market and the profit
motive are retained but the control of economic enterprises is changed
so that the mass of the workers, rather than just a few dominant
people and groups, are in charge. Another way of putting the central
point is to say that we have here the free market without the iniquities
that a certain rendering of the notion of private property gives to it
(see further below). In a lucid and devastating analysis, Dahl shows
the mistake in thinking that corporate capitalism – private ownership
of (sometimes vast) corporations – can be derived from the notion of
private property rights (Dahl 1985).

Another important point is that economic democracy is a central
element in most participatory theories of democracy (Pateman 1970).

Participatory theory, it will be remembered, wants society as a whole to be firmly under the control of the people (to the extent, indeed, that *liberal* democrats see some dangers here). And we referred earlier to the idea that such control properly involves control of economic structures. This clearly connects up with socialist ideas, but where it differs from (at least traditional mainstream) socialism is in the stress on direct democratic control of industry. This is to be contrasted with the notion of control of industry by the state, albeit a democratic state (see also note 13). It further connects up with those aspects of the Marxist critique which decry the nature of the distinctions liberal democratic theory draws between political and social, public and private. Part of the participatory theorists' case, roughly speaking, is that the structures, processes and activities in what the liberal democrat wrongly regards as the separate sphere of social and private – particularly economic – life ('civil society'), have just as much to do with determining the nature of collective existence as do those in the sphere that the liberal democrat marks off as the 'political'. As we saw earlier, this idea that there are, in effect, political power structures outside the liberal democrat's restricted vision of the 'formal' political realm, is linked with a critique which sees the public realm as much wider than the liberal democrat supposes. (Dahl, however, does not really push his theory in this direction: his remains a liberal democratic theory, albeit one that has strong affinities with participatory theory.) Here again we see the overlap between the participatory and Marxist critiques. But, unlike the Marxist, the participatory democrat argues that these bogus divisions of liberal democracy can be overcome by democratisation of the economic, as well as the formally political, power structures; and this can be done without – or rather, instead of – a wholesale transformation of the system.

Discussion of key liberal democratic concepts brings us again to the Marxist critique of liberal democratic *theory*. In assessing this we shall focus on just one aspect: the critical analysis of the idea of the abstract individual. This is not so much because other issues are unimportant as because, arguably, they are not really relevant to a critique of liberal democratic theory as such. That is to say they properly figure in critiques not of liberal democrat theory in general, but of some of its varieties, albeit important ones. The criticisms concerning blindness to the importance of community, for example, are not applicable to the 'liberal-humanist' varieties (which perhaps include J. S. Mill as well as neo-Idealist and citizenship theories). Nor are the criticisms of possessive individualism. Moreover, as we also saw, these are not really applicable to utilitarian theory either.

This is not to deny that these criticisms are important. Nor is it to deny that what are perhaps the dominant varieties of liberal democratic theory, in the Anglo-American world at least, are those that suffer from these criticisms. For example, the kind of individualism which is the corollary of the blindness to community, lands most accounts of collective decision making in the kind of mess we referred to in the Appendix to Chapter 1. However, the 'answer' to such criticisms lies within the spectrum of liberal democratic theory itself: neo-Idealist theory has an important contribution to make in this way. What we need to do here is to focus on that aspect of the Marxist critique that applies to *all* varieties of liberal democratic theory. And this is the critique of abstract individualism. This applies to liberal humanism as much as to varieties that are individualist in other ways as well (it even applies, as we saw, to Macpherson's participatory theory).

Critique of Individualism Pushed Too Far

It seems to me that the nub of the argument in defence of liberal democratic theory here is this. It should be acknowledged that the criticism of abstract individualism has much force and that liberal democratic theory is largely guilty of not seeing this, but that the critique in the end fails because it tries to prove too much.

The fundamental point is that, although overall the notion of the abstract individual *is* faulty, still it has at its very core a conception that is valid. And whilst it is true that liberal democratic theory in its usual formulations can be faulted for containing the full, defective conception, it must nonetheless be endorsed for incorporating the valid core conception. Moreover, this conception is crucial to any theory of democracy.

The faults in abstract individualism are indeed those we focused on as part of the Marxist critique. Man does not 'squat outside the world'. Individuals are in the social world: they are social beings in the sense that their characters and behaviour are to a very large extent a product of their social environment. Moreover, to an extent that liberal democratic theory does not recognise, individuals' lives, as well as their characteristics, are social. Their behaviour consists in the part they play in the various *social* practices in which they are enmeshed, and can only be understood as such (just as the behaviour of an individual playing cricket must be understood not by analysing him as an individual but only by understanding cricket).

However, this line of argument can be pushed too far. Despite the extent to which individuals are social beings, and activity is social rather than purely individual, there is also a crucial and irreducible extent to which individuals are independent of their social environment and their activity is voluntary. This has several aspects, or can be expressed in several ways.

First, to say that individuals are 'socially constituted' does not imply that they are socially *determined*. They can still be separate autonomous beings with human capacities that are innate and not the product of their social environment.[14] And this connects up with moral individualism – which the critics of liberal democracy theory also wish to uphold here. Indeed, it may be that a proper recognition of the social constitution of individuals, rather than the blindness of abstract individualism, is necessary for a proper connection to be made. Lukes expresses all this very well when he says:

> the principle of respect for persons requires . . . that we regard and act towards individuals in their concrete specificity, that we take full account of their specific aims and purposes and of their own definitions of their (social) situations. And . . . that we see them as the (actually or potentially) autonomous sources of decisions and choices . . . Respecting them as *persons* . . . involves the kind of understanding of both their social and individual aspects which the abstract view of them precludes. For, on the one hand, such respect requires us to take account of them as social selves – moulded and constituted by their societies – whose achievement of, and potential for, autonomy, whose valued activities and involvements and whose potentialities are, in large, socially determined and specific to their particular social contexts. On the other hand, it requires us to see each of them as an actually or potentially autonomous centre of choice (rather than a bundle composed of a certain range of wants, motives, purposes, interests, etc.), able to choose between, and on occasion transcend, socially-given activities and involvements, and to develop his or her respective potentialities in the available forms sanctioned by the culture – which is both a structural constraint and a determinant of individuality (Lukes 1973).

Pateman makes similar or complementary points in arguing that a voluntarist understanding of politics is not incompatible with, and indeed requires, a recognition of the faults of abstract individualism. Abstract individualists – because they see all social practices as 'external' to, and as constraints upon, the individual – necessarily see obligations as limitations on individual autonomy. (And thoroughgoing 'communalists' are no better because they are liable to interpret social constitution as social determination.) It is only by a *proper* appreciation of the ways in which individual life is a social phenomenon that one can really see where autonomy lies. Pateman argues that 'if individuals are separated from their social relationships . . . it is then impossible to give due weight to the fact that individuals are, at one and the same time, both superior to and bound by their rules, rights and obligations' (Pateman 1985). Individuals cannot 'escape' social life, which is constituted by such practices; but individuals can *decide* which obligations to enter into. Again, it 'is true that no one comes into the world fully mature, free and equal and free from all social ties, but it is only abstract individualists who argue as if they do. The fact that humans are social creatures, born into a network of social relationships, is the foundation for, not a barrier against, the construction of a democratic association' (Pateman 1985).

Another aspect of this argument about the way in which the case against abstract individualism overshoots itself can be put in terms of a false deduction of particular conclusions from a general proposition. There is, in fact, very often an invalid move from the proposition that individuals are socially constituted to the conclusion that they are fully constituted by the *particular* social environment that they inhabit. Socialisation theories tend generally to commit this fallacy because, in their empirical particularity, they necessarily focus mainly on the mechanisms of particular societies. But Marxist arguments are especially prone to this because they are enmeshed in a general theory, the polemical purpose of which is precisely to show the particular effects of a *particular kind* of society – capitalist society – on individuals. (The full story is more complex, however, since the implications and assumptions of Marxist conceptions of the nature and role of the individual in the future communist society are very different – see the discussion of Marxist individualism above. However, Marxist analyses of capitalist society do have a tendency to over-simplify and fall foul of this fallacy.)

Another way of making the point that 'social construction' does not equal 'social determination' concerns the status of individuals' own thinking. It can be argued, again, that the notion that individuals' ideas are always socially *determined* is an argument that goes too far. In fact, as we shall see, it is incoherent. This is crucial because the notion must be refuted if democracy is to be possible at all. Meanwhile the task of the liberal democrat must be to show that individuals'

thinking is not socially determined in capitalist society (Holden 1983).
This connects up with the issue raised by the false consciousness and
cultural hegemony arguments that we looked at earlier.

If people's ideas are induced in them by – are simply a product of
– their socio-cultural environment then there is a crucial sense in
which their thoughts, and hence any decisions they make, are not
their own.[15] (In fact there are various complications here, but this
statement remains valid; see Holden (1983).) It follows that there
cannot be any real decisions by the people – no authentic will of the
people – but only a processing of people's cultural milieu, rather as
prisms refract but do not generate light. If there cannot be decisions
by the people, there can be no democracy. And this is not just a
'theoretical' point (albeit a momentous one): any such invalidation of
the notion of decision making by the people can have fateful practical
consequences. If the views the people express are not really their own
then no particular importance attaches to the 'will of the people'. And
indeed, as in Leninist vanguard theory, the view is justified that the
expressed will of the people should be ignored in favour of 'objective'
assessments of their real interests. In practice this can mean that the
expressed wishes of the people can be ignored in favour of anything
rulers wish to do, and we end up by justifying pernicious forms of
tyranny, as in Stalinist Russia.

Of course, simply showing the unfortunate consequences of the
people's ideas being socially determined does not in itself prove that
they are not (although it may cause us to ponder the matter very
carefully instead of easily accepting the notion). To go into all the
issues involved would demand a book in itself and we shall focus on
just one point, arguably the most fundamental. This arises from the
relativism which is a corollary of the notion that ideas are socially
determined. It is a general point but it crucially undermines any
attempt to show that the voters' ideas are socially determined in the
particular case of the existing liberal democracies. To cut short a
somewhat complex argument (Holden 1983) the key element is this.
Any particular argument that ideas are determined in a certain sort
of way, or that the ideas of a particular group or historical period are
determined in a certain way, implicitly rests heavily on the notion
that *all* ideas are socially determined. And this underlying and crucial
pre-supposition is simply taken for granted. But as we have already
suggested, this notion is, arguably, incoherent. And if this is so, any
particular argument about social determination collapses because a

key part of its foundation crumbles away.

The argument that the notion of all ideas being socially determined is incoherent, turns on a central issue. This is that ideas which are socially determined do not express truths, any more than nightmares caused by indigestion express truths about the digestive system. Thus the contents of ideas which are socially determined – or, more precisely, the statements in which these contents are expressed – are not true; and, conversely, ideas expressed by statements which are true, have not been socially determined (although they, or their occurrence, may well have been subject to social influence: the point is that only the social *determination* of ideas is antithetical to their being true).[16] Hence to say that all ideas are socially determined is to say that no statements are true. We then come up against the paradox that it is self-defeating, or incoherent, to say that *all* statements are untrue since that statement itself must be untrue. This knocks on the head the idea that *all* statements are untrue, and thereby destroys the notion that all ideas are socially determined. But besides destroying, in this negative way, a crucial prop to arguments that particular (sets of) ideas are socially determined, it also does so in a 'positive' sense, because it 'lets in' the conception of true ideas. And to say the least it is extremely difficult to see how the contention that some ideas are held *because* they are true can then be resisted. Indeed, another way of putting this argument is to say that if ideas are true then their existence, and their presence in people's minds, has been explained – or at least a crucial part of the explanation has been given – without bringing in social determination (who would invoke social determination to explain, say, why people fear war or famine?)

Marxist arguments that people's ideas in capitalist societies, and hence in liberal democracies, are socially determined thus loses its main support – for, to repeat, powerful support is derived from the pre-supposition that *all* ideas are socially determined. But, more than this, we can see how the particular Marxist arguments can be challenged. We have already looked at this line of reasoning, but to bring the threads together let us say again that it is at least, at the very least, arguable that the beliefs of the people in capitalist liberal democracies are true or valid.[17] But, as we have just seen, to the extent that this is the case we have the reason, or one of the key reasons, why they hold these beliefs. And, conversely, Marxist explanations in terms of partisan socialisation, ideology of the ruling class, or cultural hegemony are thereby rendered redundant. It should be noticed that the contention is not that such 'Marxist explanations' are *never* valid, but rather that frequently they are not; in any case they should be scrutinised with a great deal more rigour than is usual. Moreover, as was previously suggested, the democratic response to the difficulty of deciding which ideas are valid – and hence not socially determined – is to let the matter be decided by the people themselves. Another way of putting this is to say it must be recognised that popular opinion should be treated as valid. It might be objected there is a circle here that is impossible to break out of: if people's ideas are invalid then they will not themselves be able to see this. But, again, there is no getting away from the fact that whether there *is* a circle is problematic, i.e. deciding what ideas *are* valid remains fundamentally problematical. Given this is the case, the argument that it is popular opinion which is valid – or should be treated as valid – at the very least should not be ruled out. And a traditional justification for democracy is that there are good reasons for treating popular opinion as valid (see the next chapter).

A final reason for objecting that the emphasis on the social character of individuals and their activity – which is proper enough in itself – can be pushed too far, involves another form of concern with the 'anti-voluntarist' implications of social explanations of individual minds. This time the focus is on the notion of decision making. A democracy is a political system in which the basic determining decisions are made by the people. But this idea of a decision has individualist implications. Part of the very concept of 'a decision' is the notion of an *act* of a human mind. Such an act can only take place 'within' an individual: only an individual (or an individual's mind) can act. Indeed, only an individual has a mind. True, individual minds are crucially influenced – structured even – by their sociocultural context, subject to the limitations implied by our social determination of ideas argument. But the notion of minds *acting* has irreducibly individualist implications. A collective decision can be conceived only in terms of a combination of individual decisions; so the notion of a decision by the people also has irreducibly individualist implications.

It is true, as we have seen, that there are fundamental problems in the way of interpreting a collective decision as a combination of individual decisions. And it may be that overly individualist mainstream Anglo-American democratic theory, with its focus on preferences, has to be modified along the lines of a neo-Idealist theory, so that the shaping effect of interaction, the communal context and individuals' views of the common interest are given proper weight. However, though such a process of integrating views may be a necessary condition for the making of decisions by the people, it does not itself constitute the making of such decisions.

As before, we should beware of assuming that simply showing its unfortunate consequence in itself disproves the existence of social determination. In this case the unfortunate consequence would be the non-existence of decisions by the people, and the aspect of (alleged) social determination would be that implying that individuals are passive transmitters of socio-cultural influences rather than decision-makers. But again, it should at least cause us to ponder carefully. Having pondered, it is true that it is difficult to claim that one comes up with a definite, final answer. Apart from anything else we are here entrapped in the venerable free-will versus determinism controversy. Nonetheless, it is arguable that one's own experience amply demonstrates the absurdity of supposing that individuals are not decision-makers.

3.4 Liberal Democracy and Capitalism

In considering the Marxist critique of liberal democracy two assumptions have remained largely unquestioned. These are that there is a special connection between liberal democracy and capitalism;[18] and that this connection is problematic for liberal democracy. We ought now to query the validity of these assumptions.

The two are in fact intermeshed to a considerable extent. Whether, and in what ways, capitalism is (or is not) regarded as problematic for liberal democracy depends to no small degree on the way in which they are seen to be connected. That there *is* a connection is strongly suggested by the empirical evidence: overwhelmingly, liberal democracies exist in capitalist societies (the converse, however, is not true: there are, and have been, plenty of capitalist societies that do not have liberal democratic political systems). However, whether or not there are exceptions is not simple to determine. This depends on such things as the definitions of the terms involved and interpretations of the nature of particular societies and political systems.

A matter of special interest, to which we shall refer also in the next chapter, is the question of the existence of liberal democracy in Third World developing countries. And also what are to count as examples of liberal democracy in the Third World, and whether, where they occur, the associated societies are 'capitalist', are obvious points of contention. Another obviously important issue is whether, even if all occurrences of liberal democracy have so far been in capitalist societies, future occurrences might be in a different socio-economic context. And this ties up with aspects of the preceding discussion since it could be argued that at least some participatory theorists and Marxists are in favour of 'true' liberal democracy which could exist only in a non-capitalist system. C. B. Macpherson certainly sees his argument this way. (All these theorists are in favour of 'true' democracy; the only point which can be at issue here is whether the system they favour is meant to be, or can properly be called, *liberal* democracy.) But it is not just radical critics who regard liberal democracy as possible in non-capitalist contexts. Even Schumpeter, who maintains there is 'a natural affinity between capitalism and democracy', thinks 'it is also true that democracy can survive and even thrive in a socialist state' (Coe and Wilber 1985).

But let us assume that liberal democracy does occur only in broadly speaking capitalist systems. (The qualification 'broadly speaking' is inserted here because, as we shall see, one important issue concerns the definition of 'capitalism' and whether a market system is necessarily capitalist.) The reasons for this connection are partly historical and contingent. But there are, arguably, also inherent connections between liberal democracy and capitalism. A good part of the Marxist critique, indeed, assumes or argues exactly this. But the opposite sort of case is also commonly argued: that there are inherent connections between liberal democracy and capitalism such that capitalism is a necessary condition (or, at the very least, highly favourable) for liberal democracy.[19] It may be said that 'both systems are based on the belief that freedom of individual choice will result in socially desirable outcomes . . . A capitalist market economy relies on the maximising decisions of individual consumers and producers to achieve an efficient allocation of resources. A democratic political system relies on the decision of individual voters[20] to achieve the proper resolution of political disputes. In both cases power is widely dispersed. Thus each system reinforces the other' (Coe and Wilber 1985). See also Usher (1981), but note the critical analysis by Berg (1986).

It should be realised that the connection discerned is specifically with *liberal* democracy. That is to say, capitalism is seen as being inherently connected not just with democratic control – via the notion of consumer/voter sovereignty – but also with freedom. Even an author who insists there 'are all sorts of limits to political toleration that the state imposes for the sake of economic order' in capitalist liberal democracies, nonetheless points out 'the one grimly unshiftable fact that must make all socialists pause: "There is one striking generalisation that can be extracted from the otherwise indeterminate history of democracy. It is that political freedom in modern times . . . has only appeared in capitalist states . . ."' (Ryan 1986, quoting Heilbroner 1985).

Now, it may be that there are compelling arguments here. But it may also be that the radical critics are nonetheless right – as Heilbroner's qualifications suggest – in stressing the illiberal and anti-democratic implications of the power structure of corporate capitalism. As we have already seen this is, essentially, the position now taken by Dahl (Dahl 1985), in contrast to his earlier stance (Dahl 1956). Charles Lindblom, a fellow exponent of 'neo-pluralism' (McLennan 1984, Held 1987), graphically expresses the viewpoint in these words: private corporations are 'disproportionately powerful . . . the large private corporation fits oddly into democratic theory and vision. Indeed, it does not fit' (Lindblom 1977).

Whether this concession to the radical critique amounts to admitting that capitalism and liberal democracy are, after all, antithetical, depends partly on one's definition of capitalism – in particular, is it equivalent only to 'corporate capitalism' in the sense indicated by Dahl? But this definitional question is less interesting than the underlying point that an inherent connection can be seen between *the market* and liberal democracy. In other words, the key connection discerned concerns that aspect of capitalism referred to as 'the market'; so the contention is that if capitalism is divested of its structure of corporate power it remains closely connected, and perhaps is a necessary condition for, democracy.[21] (However whether Lindblom is arguing this, or its contrary, is another matter. It is not entirely clear whether the essence of his argument is that corporations are inherently favoured by the market, at the expense of democracy, or whether it is the market itself that is the culprit. Besides Lindblom (1977) see Lindblom (1982) and Elkin (1982). There is a similar issue in interpreting Levine's argument about freedom and its tensions with capitalism and the market (Levine 1981, Chapter 9).)

The relationships between democracy and the market constitute a large, important and complex subject in its own right, not least because it overlaps with fields in political economy which are also large, important and complex in their own right – such as the relationship between the state and the market in individualist economic analysis and, indeed, the whole field of public choice analysis. All we can do here is point to a few of the key issues.

As just indicated, the organising assumption at issue is that, broadly speaking, the relationship between the market and liberal democracy is the same as that which 'pro-capitalist' democrats see as obtaining between capitalism and democracy. In other words, the assumption is that there are inherent connections between the market system of distribution and exchange and liberal democracy, provided that units of production are internally democratised. Another crucial assumption, also one attacked by latter-day Marxists, is that we are dealing with a *genuine* market system. In other words the proviso is that the market is not rigged or dominated by a few disproportionately powerful enterprises, as in 'monopoly capitalism'.

Points that could be made against this assumption of inherent connections between the market and liberal democracy would centre on the allegation that a market system, with its intrinsic competitiveness and pursuit of private gain, is destructive of the kind of community which can be seen as necessary for democracy. As against this, though, it can be pointed out that (a) 'private' gain and the pursuit of profit have a different significance in a non-(corporate) capitalist market, and (b) some kind of market system is necessary even in overtly communal systems. And this point about the sheer efficiency of the market is of crucial importance. It is noteworthy that even as radical a critic of orthodox liberal democracy as Burnheim, who is by no means wholly in favour of the market, still sees it as having a vital role (Burnheim 1985, Chapter 4).

On the positive side, then, one of the main factors is efficiency – not least, efficiency in generating outcomes from myriads of individual decisions.[22] This is a factor which is stressed by Hayek and Friedman, who also focus on the connection between liberty and the free market (Hayek 1960, 1976, 1982; Friedman 1962). And if one were to try and summarise the connections between liberty and the free market, the following would be the main points on which to focus. The free market can be seen as necessary to preserving liberty, since it disperses decision making and therefore power. But it can also be seen *as* a key liberty, or system of liberties.[23] The important ideas here are that crucial individual liberties are necessary for, or presumed by, the operation of a free market, that freedom of trade is itself an important liberty and, more generally, that the whole notion of *laissez faire* can be seen in terms of the most extensive form of liberty possible. Moreover, the market provides for – and enlarges in the most practicable way – freedom of choice. This last point can be extended into 'positive' or 'developmental' ideas of liberty since it can be argued that freedom of choice is a necessary condition for self-development. Indeed, this can be pushed further, since it can be argued that ' "self-development" . . . may essentially require, market incentives and competitive striving. Thus many contemporary liberal thinkers, among them John Rawls and Robert Nozick, argue (in different ways) for *both* a market system based on incentives and a Humboldtian/Millian[24] vision of the maximal development of human personality' (Lukes 1979). And it should not be forgotton that material prosperity, even though it may not figure directly in characterisations of 'self-development', *is* a necessary condition for it. Here we come back to the efficiency of the market, and what is argued to be its indispensable role in providing material prosperity. (We might also recall that Marx himself saw capitalism as necessary for the material development without which the eventual communist society could not exist.) In all these ways, the market could be said to be strongly connected with *liberal* democracy. And we should remember here that the market operating in the context of 'economic' or 'industrial' democracy is perfectly compatible with many forms of, or ideas about, participatory democracy.

Having now discussed a particular kind of defence of liberal democracy we shall turn, in the next chapter, to the general question of the justification of liberal democracy.

Notes

1. A full statement of the point would be a little more complex. A key element in the participatory critique is that the liberal democrat's account of democracy is faulty, and that what is assumed to be ultimate decision making by the people is really not such – precisely because there is not enough participation by the mass of the people in the decision process. Perhaps the point is better made by saying that a genuine democracy necessarily involves participation, and by allowing that there are different accounts of what a 'genuine' democracy is.

2. The term 'rank and file' is used because the idea of participation is applied in various contexts – for instance in industry, as we shall see, 'rank and file' means the workforce. With regard to participation in a democratic state, of course, it means the mass of the people or the people as a whole.

3. There are really two arguments here (though they are not necessarily always clearly distinguished): that participatory democracy is the best, or the only worthwhile, form of democracy; and that a system is not a democracy at all unless it is a participatory democracy.

4. Although less frequently, pluralist theory is also sometimes seen as 'bridging' the individualist/communalist divide. Here the individual is seen as being integrated into the total community via membership of ('partial') groups. This is a perspective that derives ultimately from Hegel (Pateman 1985).

5. Forerunners include, as we have seen, traditional democratic theorists. Above all it is the Continental theorist, Rousseau, who is crucial (Pateman 1970). Within Anglo-American traditional theory it is, interestingly enough, not a radical theorist but John Stuart Mill who is most important. Though Pateman argues that there are inconsistencies between the 'participatory' and other aspects of Mill's theory (Pateman 1970), Thompson (1976) disputes this, one reason being Mill's focus on the importance of participation in *local* government. In the early twentieth century G.D.H. Cole was an important participatory theorist, and in his thought there is an extensive overlap between participatory theory and an early form of pluralist theory (Pateman 1970).

6. This *is* an over-simplification since, as we shall see, the place of individualism in Marxist theory is complex and controversial, and on some interpretations Marx was committed to individualism. However, the dominant view – and the one most influential in Marxist confrontations with liberal democratic theory – is that Marxism involves a fundamental critique of liberal individualism (although, as we shall see, what is meant by 'individualism' here needs specification).

7. The significantly different radical approach of Burnheim should also be noticed here. He, too, despairs of representation as it exists in the liberal democratic state, and indeed goes so far as to argue for the dissolution of the state; but instead of looking to direct participation he argues for a system of 'statistical representation', with selection of representatives by lot, on functionally defined, autonomous decision-making bodies (Burnheim 1985).

8. For a useful, lucid account of some of the main currents of Marxist thought, and their relation to ideas about democracy in particular, see Pierson (1986). See also Levin (1983). For an introduction to the thought of Marx see, for example, Elster (1985).

9. Of course, from a Marxist viewpoint, there is an important sense in which there can be nothing which benefits capitalism or capitalists in the long-run – for in the long-run capitalism is doomed to extinction. However, the run may be very long indeed, and the nature of the present system and who benefits from it remain matters of profound importance.

10. Even this may be a misleading way of putting it. Arguably there is an important sense in which liberal democrats do not properly conceptualise a *public* sphere at all, but rather an arena in which private activities that impinge on each other are played out and dealt with. Pateman characterises voting in liberal democracies in this way: 'formally, individuals act as citizens or political actors when they vote; substantively, they are still concerned with private affairs. At election time individuals put on what Marx called their "political lion skin" of citizenship, but underneath they act as before' (Pateman 1985).

11. Not only was J. S. Mill's thinking 'contaminated' in this way, but, according to Macpherson, it was necessarily so: 'In the nineteenth-century economy of scarcity' possessive market ideas and developmental ideas 'were, rightly, seen as necessarily linked together: the only way to free all individuals to "use and develop their human capacities fully" was "through the productivity of free enterprise capitalism"' (Lukes 1979, quoting Macpherson 1977a). In the modern world, though, a post-scarcity form of liberal democracy is possible (this seemed more plausible in the 1960s and 1970s than it does today).

12. One of the main justifications of capitalism has always been that by raising the general level of prosperity more than any other system, even those who benefit least are better off than they would be under any other system.

13. If developed in a different way, economic democracy can become part of a socialist theory – cf. the guild socialism of G.D.H. Cole (Pateman 1970; Glass 1966). But it is instructive that mainstream 'state socialists' have always been uneasy about industrial democracy precisely because of the extent to which it implies something other than state planning for the overall allocation of resources, and there is a very strong tendency for this 'something other' to be the market.

14. There is a fundamental issue of social and political theory involved in, or lying behind, those being considered here: whether there is a constant or identifiable 'human nature'; and, if so, what it is.

15. The notion that individuals' ideas are determined in this way is widely based. There are theories of socialisation in modern sociology and political science, there is the sociology of knowledge and behind this the historicist tradition which feeds into – and which Marx combines with – ideas about the nature and role of ideology (see, for example, Benewick *et al.* (1973)).

16. Fundamental issues are, of course, raised here, which we cannot go into. The extent to which rationality and criteria of validity and truth can be viewed as transcending socio-cultural contexts and influences are matters which are deeply controversial and are the subject of much sociophilosophical analysis. The very important work of Habermas can be called in aid of the general line taken here; for a useful and illuminating introduction to Habermas see Bernstein (1985).

17. Ideas which are not actually true may nonetheless be 'valid' in the sense of being 'rationally acceptable'. As such, it is arguable that they have the same status in this context as true ideas (Holden 1983).

18. Strictly speaking, in order to avoid question-begging we should say that

the connection is between *systems that are called* liberal democracies, and capitalism. However, the interests of clarity make it desirable to avoid such circumlocutions and either the proviso can be taken as read, or we can accept that the preceding argument has sufficiently demonstrated that democracy *can* exist in a capitalist society.

19. It is possible to see connections running the other way as well, but it is difficult to see these as inherent since, as we have said, few would dispute that capitalism can exist under non-liberal democratic systems.

20. There is, indeed, a literature on the 'economic theory of democracy', which seeks to analyse the voter-attracting behaviour of political parties on the model of the consumer-attracting behaviour of producers. This really began with Downs (1957); for a critical review of some of this work see Barry (1970) and for a later review Aranson (1981), Chapter 7. One important sector of this literature is a branch of political economy specifically concerned with developing a theory of democracy in which the democratic process is seen as the analogue of the market, with elections viewed as exchange mechanisms in which the currency is votes and the commodity is political power. Especially important here is Buchanan and Tullock (1962); for comment, besides Barry (1970), see for example Cornford (1972).

21. Many, including Marxists, would argue that this kind of separation cannot be made and that a market system necessarily leads to, or is accompanied by, concentration of ownership of resources. For a Marxist, also, there are other 'capitalist evils' connected with alienation and the exchange relationship which are rooted in the market system as such. We cannot enter here into a discussion of these issues; but it does seem that many of them are defused when control of economic enterprises, instead of being vested in a few managers or owners, is put into the hands of the mass of the workers. There is, in fact, an increasing interest in non-capitalist forms of the market, as the current concern (both in the East and the West) with 'market socialism' and 'the social market' testifies (see, for example, Sartori (1987) 14.4).

22. This, of course, is to bypass the whole question of the nature of public goods – and the way collective decisions about them are generated from the decisions of individuals – which so exercises public-choice theorists. However, there are two key points which remain valid. First, where it is private goods that are desired, the market is very efficient at providing them; and this is because the market mechanism copes efficiently with the interplay of the myriads of individual decisions relating to private goods. Second, because the market does this efficiently it leaves channels freer for coping with collective decision making about public goods.

23. It is the 'negative sense' of liberty to which reference is being made here, but as the text shows, there are also implications in terms of 'positive' conceptions as well.

24. The reference here is to Wilhelm von Humboldt (1767–1835) (Humboldt 1969) and to John Stuart Mill (Mill 1982).

4
The
Justification of
Liberal
Democracy

In this chapter we are concerned with the question of how liberal democracy is to be justified. Or, to put the emphasis slightly differently, the question is whether, and if so why, liberal democracy is a good system of government. In fact the question is usually put in the 'stronger' form of asking whether, and why, liberal democracy is the *best* system of government.

4.1 Questions About the Justification of Liberal Democracy

Before we address the question directly there are two preliminary issues to be cleared out of the way. These arise from considering what 'justification' consists in, and what precisely is to be justified.

The main point about the first issue is that the nature of justification is a controversial matter. This is a large subject, but the most important thing as far as we are concerned is that some would deny that justification as such is possible at all. Someone might, for example, *prefer* liberal democracy to other systems of government, but this would be a matter of subjective preference rather than objective, rational justification. This view was especially prevalent in Anglo-American thought and had its main bases in fundamental assumptions or positions in philosophy and social analysis. In brief, it was held that value judgements – especially moral judgements – could not be 'validated' or proved correct in any sense. And in particular they could not be scientifically validated, a position dubbed 'scientific value relativism' (Brecht 1967).

All this, of course, left the justification of democracy in a sorry mess.[1] However, the situation has changed somewhat over the last two decades. There are several reasons for this, but perhaps two stand out. First, there have been developments in philosophy, including the philosophy of science, which question the notion of a significant divide between objective science on the one hand and moral judgement on the other. Arguably, an implication of such developments is that moral judgements can be rationally defended, at least to the extent that scientific theories can be. (According to some extreme interpretations, though, even scientific theory cannot, properly speaking, be rationally defended. This has, paradoxically, bolstered the moral relativism earlier derived mainly from the very scientific value relativism now being attacked. But there is another paradox: as we shall see below, this relativism has itself become part of a justification of liberal democracy!) Second, developments in the political world – among the most important being the Vietnam War and the traumas of American politics in the 1960s – have destroyed the post-war complacency about liberal democracy. The case for liberal democracy now needs to be made and can no longer be taken for granted.

But this brings us on to the second preliminary issue: just what is it that we are seeking to justify? For an important point to remember here is that liberal democracy itself is to be justified and not something that *fails to be* liberal democracy. Critics of complacent liberal democrats have in fact often been developing the kind of critique we looked at in the last chapter. That is to say they have been attacking the American and other Western political systems for failing to realise the liberal democratic ideal, for failing to embody the idea or model of liberal democracy in practice. But it is with the justification of the model itself that we are concerned in this chapter and not with systems that fail to embody it.[2] Having said this, though, we should also recognise that the 'failure arguments' tend to flow over into attacks on the liberal democratic model itself. We saw this in the case of Leninism and the idea of one-party democracy. And even participatory theory was seen to have a certain ambivalence or blindness about the idea of needing checks upon popular power, which could be construed as a rejection of a key element in the liberal democratic model.

The justification of liberal democracy – the liberal democratic model – thus requires a double aspect. It needs to be justified against traditional attacks from the 'right', to the effect that the people should not have the power it ascribes to them. But it also needs to be justified against attacks from the 'left', to the effect that this power is given insufficient scope.

But we now come to another point that arises in settling what exactly is to be justified. In Chapter 2 we saw that there were many different theories and models of democracy. It is arguable, indeed, that in the face of such diversity we should not seek a justification of democracy, or *the* model of democracy, as such. Rather we should focus on justifying *a* form, or *a* model, of democracy (Nelson 1980). And though we are here crucially reducing the amount of diversity by concerning ourselves specifically with *liberal* democracy, the amount we are left with is still very significant. Nonetheless, there are common elements in this diversity: these are the very elements by virtue of which the single label liberal democracy is appropriate and which figure in the definition given in Chapter 1. In other words it makes significant sense – very significant sense – to talk of a general model of liberal democracy here, and to ask about the justification simply of 'liberal democracy'. This is not just a point about definition. The more important point, or implication, is that there are good reasons for favouring a governmental system of a certain general form – and this form corresponds with the general model of liberal democracy. This can perhaps be better appreciated by focusing on the importance assigned by these reasons to the difference between this general form and others that are held to be *un*desirable.

There are, though, a couple of partial qualifications to be made to this notion of an overall justification of a general model. First, one of the types of justification referred to below does not apply to all forms of liberal democracy. This is the 'developmental' justification which is held to apply specifically to participatory democracy. We referred just now to the ambivalence of participatory theory, and it may be that this is not to be counted as a justification of liberal democracy at all, since participatory democracy is sometimes seen as a *contrasting* form of democracy. But this is to over-simplify the subtle relationship between participatory and 'orthodox' liberal democracy; and it should also be remembered that the developmental justification can apply to indisputably liberal democratic theories such as John Stuart Mill's. Even so it is absolutely clear that there is one type of liberal democratic theory in respect of which this form of justification is not applicable. This is elitist democratic theory, which is explicitly criticised by participatory theorists for rejecting the developmental idea. Elitist democratic theory is also explicitly *defended* by its advocates for rejecting more than the very minimum of participation – i.e. voting. Indeed, it is by virtue of this that participationists see elitist 'democratic' theory as ceasing to be a democratic theory at all.

The second partial qualification to the notion that we shall be considering justifications of a general model, concerns the characterisation of that model as *liberal* democracy. Traditional justifications often tend to be of democracy as such, and whether the democracy spoken of is (or is intended to be) necessarily liberal democracy may not be clear. But at least the application of such justifications to specifically liberal democracy is not ruled out, and we shall treat them as having this application. And anyway, part of the case for liberal democracy that informs this book is that genuine democracy must necessarily have key features of the liberal democratic model. One type of traditional justification, though, must be looked at a little differently. This is where democracy is favoured because it ensures liberty. As a justification of *democracy* this has substantive content, and its validity can be debated (in fact many of the issues discussed in Chapter 1 would come up again). But as a 'justification' of *liberal* democracy it is merely tautologous.

4.2 Justifications of Liberal Democracy

Having cleared the ground it is time now to sketch in the main types of justification of liberal democracy. (Referring back to the previous remarks about the nature of justification, we shall not be attempting to analyse the logical form these take; but at least looking at their substance will illustrate this form.)

Starting with justifications against the 'challenge from the right', there are a number of different types of argument in support of liberal democracy. It is, though, fruitful to group them into three categories. These focus respectively on the underlying principles, the inherent virtues and the beneficial results of liberal democracy. From another perspective one might divide justifications into those which contend that in order to be legitimate government must take the form of liberal democracy and those which contend that the actual substance of government in a system of this form has merit. However, there is a great deal of overlap between the reasoning in the latter case and the reasons for ascribing legitimacy, and it becomes confusing to try and keep them separate. We shall therefore stick to our threefold categorisation.

Underlying Principles

Let us look first at the 'underlying principles' category. Here liberal democracy is seen as giving expression to fundamental moral principles, and as the way of ensuring or facilitating their operation. These principles may in turn be based on fundamental theoretical or philosophical analyses of the nature of man and reality. We might call these 'philosophical' justifications.

An important type in this category is the 'Christian justification' of liberal democracy. Key theorists are Jacques Maritain and Reinhold Niebuhr (see, for example, Maritain (1945) and Schram (1976)). In fact to treat this as a single type is to over-simplify and merge together different arguments. Nonetheless there are important common elements. Perhaps the best way of characterising the Christian justification is by saying that it consists in a religious expression of, or provides a religious underpinning for, moral principles typically seen as the bases for liberal democracy (and which we shall look at in a moment). For the Christian, it can be argued then, these principles, which other theorists regard as secular, have their proper expression or foundation in Christianity. The principles in question are primarily those of equality and liberty, so important in 'philosophical' justifications of liberal democracy (see below), although other important principles and ideas can be involved as well.[3] The Christian underpinning or expression is chiefly concerned with the dignity of man and the equal status of individuals in the sight of God. More generally still, we see here a religious foundation for the liberal democrat's belief in the supreme worth of the individual. And ultimately, perhaps, it is only a Christian conception of the individual that really secures individualism from its critics: even the minimal individualism that we saw in the last chapter was necessary for liberal democratic theory may be vulnerable to the kind of fundamental (but not specifically Marxist) critique of liberal individualism advanced by, for example, Sandel (1982). A flavour of the Christian justification is given by Maritain's approving quotation from a speech by an American Vice-President, Henry A. Wallace, in 1942: 'The Idea of Freedom . . . is derived from the Bible with its extraordinary emphasis on the dignity of the individual. Democracy is the only true political expression of Christianity' (Maritain 1945).

A secular equivalent of the transcendental foundation for the belief in the individual provided by Christianity is to be found in the philosophy of Kant, although it is specifically attacked by Sandel (1982). As in the case of the Christian justification this can be developed into a justification of liberal democracy. It is true that Kant is in no straightforward way a liberal democrat. In fact his position is rather complex and can, perhaps, be best summed up as involving a belief in government by those who are representatives of, but who are not necessarily answerable to, the people (Williams 1983). Nonetheless his underlying philosophy gives an account of the human individual in which autonomy and respect for persons is of supreme importance. His distinctive pronouncement on the moral importance of individuals is that people should never be treated 'simply as a means, but always at the same time as an end' (Kant 1964). And he is usually counted as a liberal philosopher. Moreover, what is perhaps the most comprehensive recent justification of liberal democracy, John Rawls' *A Theory of Justice*, can be seen as an application of Kantian philosophy (Rawls (1972), Section 40; Rawls (1980); Darwall (1976); Williams (1983); but see Höffe (1984)). There will be no attempt to summarise Rawls' justification of democracy here, other than to say that the conclusion that liberal democracy is the appropriate form of government for free and equal individuals is derived from the idea that this is the form of government to which entirely free, equal and rational individuals would agree. (The literature on Rawls is now very considerable but the following may be mentioned: Barry (1973), Daniels (1975), Wolff (1977), Tucker (1980) Chapters 7 and 8.) They would agree to it because it satisfies principles of justice. These principles give priority to the maintenance of equal basic liberties. At another level, then, Rawls provides a version of justifications of liberal democracy in terms of equality and liberty, and these we shall now indicate.

Such justifications ascribe fundamental importance to the principles of equality and liberty and seek to show that liberal democracy is necessary for their realisation – and is to be valued because of this. We have already discussed the connection between democracy and the principles of equality and liberty (Chapter 1) and hence we have looked at some of the ways in which liberal democracy can be said to realise these principles. Only one or two further remarks need to be made here.

These stem from the observation that if a case for liberal democracy is to be made because it realises these principles, any such justification will also have to show why the principles themselves are to be valued. In the Christian and Kantian cases this was a major part of the justification. But what other sorts of reasoning are there?

An aspect of the background to the recent intellectual difficulties regarding the nature of justification, mentioned earlier, was the notion that it is impossible to validate basic principles. This impaired recent (but 'pre-Rawlsian') justifications of democracy. One such apparently impaired justification in terms of equality is lucidly presented in Cohen (1971). He takes the view that the validity of the basic principle cannot be demonstrated. This principle is the contention that people are in an important and basic sense equal. (In an earlier idiom this would have been a 'self-evident truth': 'We hold these truths to be self-evident, that all men are created equal' – American Declaration of Independence, 1776.) In fact, though, he provides persuasive argumentation in its support. Democratic decision making, he contends, is necessary to give an equal say to all individuals. And the provision of an equal say is, in turn, necessary to give proper recognition to the basic equality of all men, deriving from an essential quality they all have beneath their undeniable differences.

Justifications that focus on liberal democracy as the means of protecting and promoting liberty have, apart from the Christian and Kantian foundations already mentioned, three main bases. These are the ideas of natural law and natural rights and the classic defence of individual liberty given by John Stuart Mill in *On Liberty* (Mill 1982).

A natural law justification is given by Hallowell (Hallowell 1954) in which he connects natural law, liberty and equality. He argues that the natural law tradition stemming from Cicero (106–43 BC), and transmitted to the modern world via Christianity, shows people are equal in their capacity to reason and thereby to determine right from wrong. Freedom requires that they all should know and will the good; and this in turn requires that they all should share in the control of government.

We saw in Chapter 1 how democracy – although some see it as threatening individual liberty – can be regarded, and valued, as the form of government which will secure areas of individual liberty. (And the notion of *liberal* democracy can be seen either as expressing the idea of an automatic connection between liberty and democracy, or as a modification of democracy needed in order, on occasion, to protect individual liberty against democracy.) Natural rights theories and Mill's defence of liberty are accounts of why there ought to be areas of individual liberty, where individuals are free from governmental interference. It will be remembered that although the accounts are different, the areas of individual liberty sanctified are broadly similar (Chapter 1); and that the natural rights justification of democracy given classical expression (by implication at least) in Locke's *Second Treatise* was embodied in Paine's *Rights of Man* and in the American Constitution. John Stuart Mill, on the other hand, although ultimately a believer in democracy, is very worried about the propensity for individual liberty to be threatened by it. His defence of democracy rests more centrally on utilitarian and developmental grounds.

But it remains true that one of the most widely held justifications of democracy (which can find expression by stressing the notion of *liberal* democracy) is to the effect that democracy is desirable because it preserves freedom. As Hallowell puts it:

> When we talk today about the preservation of democracy, what most of us, I think, are concerned about is the preservation of freedom. We realise that democratic forms and institutions find their essential and ultimate meaning in the preservation and enlargement of human freedom. They are not ends in themselves but means to an ultimate end. They are not identical with freedom but the means through which freedom may find its best political expression (Hallowell 1954).

Inherent Virtues

Let us turn now to the 'inherent virtues' justifications. These are justifications which centre on the value of the liberal democratic process itself, in contrast to those in the third category which focus on the value of the results obtained by, the outcomes of, that process (though there is not always a clear division between the two).

One of the most important of these is the 'developmental justification': the argument that democracy is to be valued because it develops the potential of the individuals involved to become fully rounded human beings. As we have seen, this is essentially an argument connected with participatory theories of democracy; for it is political participation that develops those engaged in it (see the remarks above about the admissibility of this as a justification of liberal democracy).

The main ideas, including those that connect individual development with integration with the community, were covered in the discussion of participatory democracy in the last chapter.[4] One interesting argument which we mentioned but did not consider in depth, however, is that developed recently by Botwinick (Botwinick 1985). He argues that there is a radical scepticism and relativism involved in the individualism of liberal democratic theory, such that the possibility of objective validation of belief is denied: 'supra-individual supports for knowledge and belief are knocked out'. This causes deep problems that cannot be resolved by theorising. The only answer is political: since there is no *theoretical* basis for agreement amongst individuals they must reach a consensus by *action* – political action. This can be done only by political participation. One of the problems to be solved is that 'the fact that we are all as it were epistemological equals [implies] industrial and governmental power cannot legitimately be invoked in furtherance of any particular individual's conception of the good unless that conception has managed to attract to itself what we might call a participatory consensus'. The other problem is that scepticism (or relativism) is self-defeating (as we noted in the last chapter when we saw that relativism was implied by the notion that ideas are socially determined). Now, Botwinick continues, it is important to understand the relativist thesis, the importance of its consequences and how to cope with them. But this cannot be done theoretically since, because it is self-defeating, the relativist thesis cannot be stated. It can only be done practically:

> If skepticism can only be shown, or intuitively perceived, but not stated, then perhaps the way out of this dilemma is to create a participatory society in which epistemological equals interact with each other in fashioning the institutions and decisions that affect their lives. If the philosophical quandaries pointing towards skepticism and yet

inhibiting a consistent formulation from being put forward are indeed irresoluble, then in this negative, indirect sense we will have provided an objective ground for political participation.

Besides those that focus on participation there are other justifications which can be classed as valuing the liberal democratic process itself. One such is that the democratic process is the best way of managing conflict. Liberal democracy allows the sources of conflict to be expressed – thereby acting as a safety valve. But besides allowing disagreement and dissent, it defuses their consequences by providing and 'ceremonialising' processes of conflict resolution. 'The ultimate claim of a democratic government to authority is that it permits dissent and survives it' (Frankel 1962, quoted in Cohen 1972). But besides *managing* conflict, liberal democracy can be said to reduce or minimise it, at least if the democracy in question is not in the process of breaking down. The argument is that such things as freedom of discussion, freedom of association and the opportunity to attempt to convert people to one's own point of view tend to lessen frustration and thereby to minimise violent conflict. They also facilitate peaceful change. But, above all, the electoral mechanism provides a peaceful solution to one of the key problems of modern political systems: the problem of succession. A significant justification of democracy, then, is that it provides for an orderly succession of rulers.

Another set of arguments in the 'inherent virtues' category comes back again to scepticism (although this time they are not just linked to participatory theory and apply generally to liberal democracy as such). One of these is called by Wollheim 'the completely sceptical argument for democracy':

> According to this argument, it is impossible for anyone to discover what is the right course of action for the community, or where the true interests of its inhabitants reside. From this it follows that everyone in the community should be allowed to do what he wants to do as far as is socially possible. The only society in which this can happen is the one in which everyone has some control in the government: therefore Democracy is favored' (Wollheim 1958).

The Relativist Justification

A variation of this kind of justification is one to the effect that relativism implies democracy. If it is the case that there are no absolute standards of right and wrong, then, it is argued, all viewpoints are equally valid and ought to have an equal chance to compete and to be adopted as public policy. That is to say, in the absence of absolute standards the only criterion left by which to decide which policy ought to be chosen is popularity: that policy should be adopted which can attract the most votes.

Superficially, this form of justification may seem convincing. However, it is fundamentally misconceived. At a crucial point the argument contends that the absence of absolute standards implies the non-existence of moral judgements; yet this is denied by the very judgement asserted by the argument itself. Indeed, the whole argument is self-contradictory: a moral judgement asserting that democracy ought to obtain is derived from what amounts to a contention that no moral judgements can be made.

The so-called 'relativist justification' of liberal democracy is, then, fundamentally flawed (in fact Botwinick's argument in this context is much more convincing). However, this defective 'relativist justification' has, in fact, been extraordinarily influential. This is partly because it connects up with the liberal value of tolerance. But it is also because it 'made a virtue of necessity'. As we indicated earlier, moral relativism left the intellectual defence of democracy in a sorry mess; but, paradoxically, via the relativist justification the cause of this mess became itself the justification of democracy! (See the brilliant survey and analysis in Purcell (1973); for an excellent short analysis, see Spragens (1973) pp. 95–9; Thorson (1962) provides an explicit and lucid example of the relativist justification – but its very lucidity serves to expose its central weakness.)

Another argument in favour of democracy that we should mention is, to an extent, a combination of the previous two. Even if the relativism argument is mistaken, it can still be acknowledged that democracy might be said to cope well with the existence of a diversity of values. Within certain limits, it allows for the expression of, and influence upon policy by, many different viewpoints. In this way, it could be argued, dangerous frustrations are avoided. And here we come back to the justification indicated earlier: that liberal democracy minimises conflict. If it is presumed that in modern societies there is likely to be a substantial diversity of values and interests, and there is much to support such a view, then a justification can be formulated to the effect that democracy is the only system of government likely to be viable in modern society. Wollheim includes another dimension when he writes of the argument that:

under modern conditions [democracy] is the only working possibility. No member of an emancipated industrial society will put up with political tutelage. He insists on having a fair chance of influencing the government in accordance with his own desires and ideas; and by a 'fair' chance he means a chance 'as good as the next man's'. This argument was succinctly summarised in the nineteenth century by the conservative James Fitzjames Stephen who said that in Democracy we count heads to avoid breaking them; and it remains today one of the best arguments in favor of democracy on account of its extreme economy (Wollheim 1958).

This is surely an excellent argument for liberal democracy, quite apart from any virtue of 'economy'! And it complements another argument which we can put under the heading of the inherent value of the liberal democratic process, albeit in a negative sort of way. The argument just indicated is of the form: even if democracy has nothing else to commend it, it is at least likely to work. The justification complemented by it adds that democracy is at least better than other systems of government. This was exemplified in Winston Churchill's remark in the House of Commons in 1947 that 'It has been said that democracy is the worst form of government except all those other forms that have been tried from time to time.'

Beneficial Results

The final category of arguments was justifications of liberal democracy in terms of its beneficial results or outcomes. The key point in some of the most commonly cited of these arguments is that a democracy allows the opinions of the 'common man' to prevail. From the Greeks onwards one of the reasons traditionally given for regarding this as a good thing is the contention that 'true opinion on political and moral matters is the privilege of the common man. Accordingly, power in a community should reside with him: and this it does only in a democracy. Hence the superiority of democracy' (Wollheim 1958). Variations on this theme have included the idea that 'true opinion' is the possession of a majority of people, even if not of all of them, and that therefore the majority should rule. Another variant is the argument that wisdom is scattered throughout the community, and hence that wise policies can be obtained only by tapping as much of it as possible in the decision-making process. This can only be done – or, at least, it is only practicable to do this – by involving everyone in the decision-making process. A stronger form of this argument is the one developed by Aristotle to the effect that, although each individual may be deficient in the qualities necessary for political decision making, the people collectively are not deficient in this way: they are, indeed, better endowed than any 'experts', since the *combined* qualities of all the individuals add up to a far from deficient totality (Aristotle 1981).

Whether or not such contentions about the 'true opinion' or the wisdom of (many or all) ordinary people are valid is a matter about which there has been dispute down the ages. Indeed, it has been one of the main issues upon which 'right-wing' critics of democracy focus.

It might be objected that it is one thing to accept that the common man has a certain amount of wisdom – or common sense – but quite another to accept that he has greater wisdom than those who might be specially trained or otherwise specially qualified to rule. Or, to put it another way, it might be said that the common man is not devoid of wisdom, but that he does not possess 'true opinion'. From Plato onwards, a powerful stream of thought has asserted that the common man is insufficiently qualified to rule (see, for example, Spitz (1965)). But here we must bring in the main argument that has been adduced in support of the view that the opinion of the common man should prevail.

In its 'strongest form', this additional argument is the one especially associated with utilitarian democratic theory. This is the idea that whether or not common men – or all individuals – are wiser than the select few (or one) in some absolute sense, it is at least the case that each individual knows his or her own interest better than anyone else. And a specifically utilitarian justification of democracy builds on this conception to reach the conclusion that a democracy is the best system of government, since it secures the greatest happiness of the greatest number. (Individuals achieve happiness by pursuing their interests; democracy is the system of government in which it is assured that the interests of all, or a majority of, individuals – 'the people' – will be pursued; therefore democracy secures the greatest happiness of the greatest number.) Now, as we have seen before, there are great difficulties that stand in the way of a theory of democracy in terms of self-interest alone. And this greatly complicates – if not entirely frustrates – any attempt at a straightforward utilitarian justification of democracy. But it can be argued that a more sophisticated justification, which focuses on individuals' judgements about what is in the common interest, can overlap with utilitarian theory. In any case there is an important core to the argument from individuals being the best judges of their own interests that remains valid. This is simply the notion that whatever else goes into the making of communal decisions, in the end such decisions are only justifiable if the mass of the people judge their experiences of them to be acceptable. And a democracy provides the means whereby the mass of the people can effectively overturn policies that they find unacceptable.

This type of argument has been developed by Lindsay (Lindsay 1943) from an argument of Aristotle's and is stated in terms of a 'shoe-pinching' analogy: only the wearer (the people) knows where the shoe pinches (the effect of governmental policies). As Lindsay points out, this idea is quite compatible with fairly 'elitist conceptions' of democracy (although this is not his terminology). The 'expert' could be said to propose and the mass dispose: the shoemaker makes the shoes and the people decide whether to accept them or call for others, and perhaps for other shoemakers, according to whether they pinch or not. This is, indeed, a powerful argument for liberal democracy.

Significance of the Justifications

These arguments for liberal democracy against 'right-wing' attacks add up to a powerful, convincing justification. They are perhaps not very often focused upon in the developed world because here criticisms from the 'right' are so seldom heard now. But they have often been voiced in the past. Moreover, these arguments are very relevant to those parts of the world where military *coups* are frequent, justifications of which often make use of such criticisms of democracy. We are talking mainly here of the Third World, about which we shall have more to say in a moment, but it should not be forgotten that quite recently there were military or authoritarian dictatorships in Europe: Spain, Portugal and Greece.

Also not so long ago, Europe was the scene of the greatest challenge to liberal democracy – the triumph of totalitarian dictatorship in Nazi Germany and Fascist Italy. These were in effect right-wing (in our sense as well as the usual one) challenges to democracy, although their own rhetoric, it might be said, was more similar to 'left-wing' criticism. In fact the main target of criticism was the specifically liberal element in liberal democracy, both the ideas about restricting the state and the underlying liberal individualism. In this respect, Fascist criticism of liberal democracy had important affinities with Leninist criticism. And of course many would argue that in terms of the totalitarian challenge to liberal democracy Leninist-Stalinist Russia was on a par with the Fascist dictatorships. This brings us back to the challenge from the 'left' to liberal democracy. It might be disputed whether Leninist criticism and the theory and practice of people's democracy really amount to 'left-wing criticism' in the sense defined earlier. But it is certainly true that elements of the Marxist critique, with which Leninism is connected (even if perversely), fall into this category.

Defending the Other Flank

In fact, as we said earlier, the radical critique generally oscillates between accusing liberal democracy of not realising its ideals and attacking those ideals themselves. It is the latter that constitutes the 'left-wing' attack. More implicit than explicit, it amounts essentially to the contention that liberal democratic ideas about defending individual liberty involve unacceptable – undemocratic – limitations on the power of the people. It might be said that the founding father of this line of criticism is Rousseau. And this harks back to the difficulties encountered in deciding whether Continental theory should be counted as liberal democratic theory. But the modern radical critique of liberal democracy is more pointed because it has the actual experience of the (alleged) deficiencies of the theory and practice of liberal democracy on which to sharpen itself.

There are two main sorts of justification in the face of this kind of attack. These are reiterations of traditional arguments in liberal democratic theory, but they are none the worse for that. First, there is the stress on the importance of individual liberty in the classical liberal, 'negative' sense. Areas of individual life should be preserved from regulation by the state, or invasion by the community, even, or perhaps especially, where the state or community in question is fully democratic. Many of the issues here have already been discussed and we cannot go over them again. But the essence of the matter is the strength of the case for protecting areas of purely individual autonomy – areas of life within which each individual decides what activities to pursue; moreover, these are areas of private life and such activities can legitimately include those which fulfil purely individual, as distinct from communal, objectives. It is true that the validity and extent of such private areas continues to be much debated by critics of liberalism. But it is worth recalling Held's remark, quoted in the last chapter, concerning the necessity for 'discussion about the desirable limits of collective regulation . . . *if* the model of participatory democracy is to be adequately defended. Such an engagement might well have to concede more to the liberal tradition than has hitherto been allowed by left-wing thinkers' (Held 1987).

The second form of justification here focuses on practical consequences of ideas and theories. The main point is that the liberal democratic idea emphasises certain sorts of institution and process as a way of both expressing and limiting the popular will. Above all, there is the stress on the importance of free, competitive, contested elections. And theories involving critiques of the liberal democratic model tend to issue forth in systems that dispense with free, contested elections. The results are nearly always undesirable and can be disastrous. Neither Hitler nor Stalin would have remained in power if he had had to face his people in free elections (it is true that Hitler came to power by winning an election, but he subsequently abolished them). A knockdown justification of liberal democracy remains that it prevents tyranny because the people can – through peaceful, constitutional means – kick the rascals out. And this is a justification against 'left-wing' as well as 'right-wing' attacks because, as Leninist-Stalinist theory and practice so graphically illustrates, it is theories about the need for the supremacy of popular power that are most likely to lead to pernicious tyrannies.

There is, then, a powerful and convincing justification of liberal democracy against attacks from both the left and right. It is true that there remain compelling left-wing criticisms of liberal democracy. Carole Pateman's book (Pateman 1985), for example, is profound and important. When all is said and done, however, the attacks that are most convincing are those that criticise the liberal democratic state for not realising the liberal democratic ideal. The ideal – the liberal democratic model itself – is to be rescued or 'retrieved' rather than attacked. This is true of both Pateman and Macpherson. To be sure, both do mount critiques of liberal democratic theory as well as practice. But, essentially, these amount to attacks on misconceptions which prevent orthodox liberal democratic theorists from comprehending the true nature of the liberal democratic ideal – the authentic liberal democratic model. Again, the model itself is acclaimed rather than attacked.

4.3 Justification of Liberal Democracy in the Third World

Finally, before we leave the justification of liberal democracy, we should ask about its generality. Does the desirability of the liberal democratic model extend generally across space and time? In particular does it extend to the developing countries of the Third World?

The point here is that it is frequently argued that liberal democracy is the best form of government for the developed world,[5] but not for the Third World. J.S. Mill uses a similar argument when he says that although representative government is the ideal form of polity it is not necessarily suitable for underdeveloped societies (Mill 1912, Chapter 4). Again, John Rawls argues that until a certain level of wealth has been attained in a society, his principles of justice do not fully apply (Rawls 1972).

Economic underdevelopment is the most frequently cited reason for the inapplicability of the liberal democratic model to the Third World. The argument is that the first priority is the alleviation of grinding poverty, and only then can the 'luxury' of liberal democracy be afforded. Having sufficient to eat is more important than liberty and self-government. But it is not just the economic argument that is cited. Almost as important is the contention that the historical and cultural backgrounds in the countries of the Third World are very different, and are unsuitable for liberal democracy.[6] Arguments here tend to merge into those in favour of the 'underdeveloped variant' of non-liberal democracy, where it is maintained that the economic, historical and cultural characteristics of Third World countries imply the need for 'one-party democracy'.

To state properly and assess all these arguments, and the issues they raise, would require a lengthy analysis which is beyond our scope. (For a useful and stimulating debate, which covers many of the issues, see Nehru and Morris-Jones (1980); see also Niebuhr and Sigmund (1969) and Thakur (1982).) However, there are three important points which ought to be made here.

The first is that liberal democracies *do* exist in the Third World.

Part of the unsuitability argument is that the significant absence of liberal democracy from, demonstrates its unsuitability for, the Third World. This contention is further strengthened by the fact of the breakdown of liberal democracy in many of the countries formerly in the British Empire, which had inherited the system from the British on independence. However, liberal democracy has persisted all along, in some instances, with the massive example of India being most notable.[7] Moreover, liberal democracy is now making something of a comeback in the Third World: the cases of Argentina and the Phillipines illustrate that there is a significant move in this direction.[8]

Second, the superficially plausible argument that poverty and desperate economic conditions require regimes which are not liberal democratic is, to say the least, disputable. Besides Morris-Jones' reply to Nehru (Nehru and Morris-Jones 1980) see, for example, Frohock and Sylvan (1983) who argue that liberty, instead of being impossible or an unaffordable luxury in such economic conditions, is in fact a first condition for an increase in economic well-being.

The third point leads on from this. It can be convincingly argued that one of the reasons why liberal democracy is necessary for, rather than an obstacle to, the alleviation of poverty is precisely that popular pressure on rulers prevents them pursuing policies detrimental to the mass of the people (Frohock and Sylvan 1983). Thus the general arguments for the desirability of liberal democracy that we have already looked at, far from being inapplicable to the Third World, can be said to have especial relevance for it. And since it is in the Third World that whether or not to have liberal democracy is actually a live issue, it is here that the arguments for liberal democracy should be most forcefully put and most carefully attended to.

Notes

1. On this subject see further Holden (1974) Chapter 8, and Thorson (1962).
2. Strictly speaking, to avoid begging a key question, one should say 'systems that fail to embody the model, but without pre-judging the question of whether the Western systems labelled "liberal democracies" are ones which fail to embody the model'. And we should remember that in the last chapter we were concerned to rebut arguments contending that Western liberal democracies failed in this way.

3. A good example of the relationship between a fuller statement of what from one viewpoint can be regarded as secular principles of liberal democracy, and their Christian foundation, is provided by Maritain's idea of the 'democratic charter'. For an illuminating and comprehensive discussion see Howell (1986).

4. It should also be remembered that participatory democracy can be justified in terms of its beneficial results (see the previous chapter).

5. There is no problem in saying this about the 'first world'. But in the case of the 'second world' there can be complications: all liberal democrats hold that liberal democracy is better than people's 'democracy'; but whether, or how, the 'conversion' of communist countries should be attempted is another matter.

6. There is a considerable overlap between propositions about the conditions suitable for liberal democracy (those whose presence is necessary for liberal democracy to be a desirable system of government) and about the necessary conditions for liberal democracy (those whose presence is necessary for liberal democracy to *exist*). The question of liberal democracy's necessary conditions is an important subject in its own right, with a large literature. For one of the best analyses see Dahl (1971).

7. It is true that in 1975 Mrs Gandhi imposed the Emergency in India and suspended elections. But equally notable were the facts that the Emergency came to an end, and that when it did so Mrs Gandhi was thrown out of power at a free election.

8. For a recent in-depth analysis of the existence of and prospects for liberal democracy in the Third World, see Diamond *et al.* (1988).

Conclusion

The main conclusion I would wish to draw from our discussion of liberal democracy concerns its importance. To understand liberal democracy is to understand why it is important, and that it should be defended.

The reasons for supporting liberal democracy were outlined in the last chapter. It was suggested there that these are convincing reasons. And it is surely the case that when such reasons are rejected it is usually only because of misunderstandings about liberal democracy. In conclusion, then, let us recapitulate some points and finally dispose of some misunderstandings.

First, we have seen that when the liberal democratic model is criticised it is often because it is mistakenly conceived. In particular, overly individualist versions of it have been (in many ways rightly) castigated. But the mistake is to assume that such versions are *the*, general, model of liberal democracy and to overlook the other ways in which it can be, and has been, stated. Not only have Locke, Paine, James Mill, Bentham and Schumpeter contributed to liberal democratic theory, but so also have John Stuart Mill, Lindsay and Barker. The shortcomings in the former strand of theory – in its over-emphasis on the negative concept of liberty, and in its accounts of human activity and collective decision making – are rectified by the insights of the latter.

Second, we must distinguish clearly between theory and practice. A recurring theme has been the extent to which (especially 'left-wing') attacks on liberal democracy have been criticisms of actual political systems, *called* liberal democracies. The systems have been criticised for departing from the liberal democratic model, rather than the model itself (or at least approved versions of it) being attacked. It is important to understand this and to appreciate that the model remains unscathed in such cases.

We have seen that there is a good deal in the criticisms of liberal democratic systems in practice; what perhaps have not been sufficiently stressed are the arguments in defence of the practice as well as the model. Western political systems labelled liberal democracies to a large extent *do* embody the model, and are thereby correctly labelled. To be sure, reforms are needed; and in particular it could well be that the kind of 'economic democracy' advocated by Dahl has much to commend it. The fact remains, though, that in these systems the people make the basic determining decisions, and the systems are thereby democracies. Pateman's criticisms are penetrating, but their main force is in questioning the 'voluntarist' character of liberal democracies. To this extent it may be that some of their liberal credentials are put in doubt. But only some: the civil liberties and the freedoms associated with free elections exist and are of supreme importance; and their importance is increasingly acknowledged even by 'left-wing' critics.

Moreover, even to the extent that it can be argued that the systems labelled liberal democracies do not fully embody the liberal democratic model, they are nevertheless still better than other systems. The fact of contested elections is in itself of overwhelming importance – whatever the wider interpretation given of the systems in which they occur. The positive way of bringing this out is to say that the fact of being able peacefully to remove rulers is of tremendous importance. The negative way of highlighting the point is to remember how those who, and theories which, denigrate the importance of contested elections contribute to the establishment and/or maintenance of tyrannical regimes.

In stressing the importance of liberal democracy, then, it is the relevant Western political systems as well as the model to which we are referring. Both deserve and require our commitment.

Bibliography

Abrams, M. and Rose, R. (1960) *Must Labour Lose?*, Penguin.

Alderman, G. (1984) *Pressure Groups and Government in Great Britain*, Longman.

Aranson, P.H. (1981) *American Government: Strategy and Choice*, Little, Brown.

Aristotle (1981) *The Politics*, Penguin.

Arrow, K.J. (1963) *Social Choice and Individual Values* (2nd edn), John Wiley.

Ashcraft, R. (1986) *Revolutionary Politics and Locke's 'Two Treatises of Government'*, Princeton University Press.

Bachrach, P. (1967) *The Theory of Democratic Elitism*, Little, Brown.

Baldwin, T. (1984) 'MacCallum and the Two Concepts of Freedom', *Ratio*, vol. 26, no. 2 (December), pp. 125–42.

Ball, A.R. (1986) *Pressure Politics in Industrial Societies: A Comparative Introduction*, Macmillan.

Barber, B.R. (1984) *Strong Democracy: Participatory Politics for a New Age*, University of California Press.

Barker, E. (1942) *Reflections on Government*, Oxford University Press.

Barry, B. (1965) *Political Argument*, Routledge & Kegan Paul.

Barry, B. (1970) *Sociologists, Economists and Democracy*, Collier-Macmillan.

Barry, B.M. (1973) *The Liberal Theory of Justice*, Oxford University Press (Clarendon Press).

Benditt, T.M., Oppenheim, F.E. and Flathman, R.E. (1975) contributions to 'A Symposium on Interest', *Political Theory*, vol. 3, no. 3 (August), pp. 245–87.

Benewick, R., Berki, R.N., and Parekh, B. (1973) *Knowledge and Belief in Politics*, Allen & Unwin.

Benjamin, R. and Duvall, R. (1985) 'The Capitalist State in Context', in Benjamin and Elkin (1985).

Benjamin, R. and Elkin, S.L. (eds) (1985) *The Democratic State*, University Press of Kansas.

Berelson, H., Lazarsfeld, P.F. and McPhee, W.N. (1954) *Voting*, University of Chicago Press.

Berg, E. (1965) *Democracy and the Majority Principle*, Scandinavian University Books.

Berg, E. (1986) 'The Proof of Capitalism: Usher's Celebration of the Status Quo', *Political Studies*, vol. 34, no. 1 (March), pp. 99–119.

Berlin, I. (1969) *Four Essays on Liberty*, Oxford University Press.

Bernstein, R.J. (1985) 'Introduction', in Bernstein R.J. (ed.), *Habermas and Modernity*, Polity Press.

Birch, A.H. (1964) *Representative and Responsible Government*, Allen & Unwin.

Birch, A.H. (1972) *Representation*, Macmillan.

Black, D. (1963) *Theory of Committees and Elections* (2nd edn), Cambridge University Press.

Bottomore, T.B. (ed.) (1963) *Karl Marx, Early Writings*, C.A. Watts.

Botwinick, A. (1985) *Wittgenstein, Skepticism and Political Participation: An Essay in the Epistemology of Democratic Theory*, University Press of America.

Bramsted, E.K. and Melhuish, K.J. (eds) (1978) *Western Liberalism*, Longman.

Braybrooke, D. (1985) 'Contemporary Marxism on the Autonomy, Efficacy and Legitimacy of the Capitalist State', in Benjamin and Elkin (1985).

Brecht, A. (1967) *Political Theory* (2nd edn), Princeton University Press.

Buchanan, J.M. and Tullock, G. (1962) *The Calculus of Consent*, University of Michigan Press.

Burdick, E. and Brodbeck, A.J. (1959) *American Voting Behaviour*, Free Press.

Burke, E. (1861) 'Thoughts on the Present Discontents', in *The Works of Edmund Burke*, Bohn's British Classics.

Burke, E. (1949) *Burke's Politics* (ed. J.S.H. Ross and P. Levack), Knopf.

Burke, E. (1968) *Reflections on the Revolution in France* (ed. Connor Cruise O'Brien), Penguin.

Burnheim, J. (1985) *Is Democracy Possible?*, Polity Press.

Butler, D. and Ranney, A. (eds) (1980) *Referendums*, American Enterprise Institute.

Calhoun, J.C. (1851) 'A Disquisition on Government', in Cralle, R.K. (ed.), *The Works of John C. Calhoun*, published under the direction of the General Assembly of the State of South Carolina.

Campbell, A., Converse, P.E., Miller, W.E., and Stokes, D.E. (1960) *The American Voter*, Wiley.

Campbell, T. *et al.* (eds) (1986) *Human Rights: From Rhetoric to Reality*, Blackwell.

Cawson, A. (1983) 'Functional Representation and Democratic Politics: Towards a Corporatist Democracy?', in Duncan (1983).

Charvet, J. (1981) *A Critique of Freedom and Equality*, Cambridge University Press.

Christophersen, J.A. (1966) *The Meaning of 'Democracy'*, Universitetsforlaget.

Coe, R.D. and Wilber, C.K. (1985) 'Schumpeter Revisited: An Overview', *Capitalism and Democracy: Schumpeter Revisited*, University of Notre Dame Press.

Cohen, C. (1971) *Democracy*, University of Georgia Press.

Cohen, C. (ed.) (1972) *Communism, Fascism and Democracy: The Theoretical Foundations* (2nd edn), Random House.

Connolly, W.E. (1972) 'On "Interests" in Politics', *Politics and Society*, vol. 2, pp. 459–77.

Connolly, W.E. (1983) *The Terms of Political Discourse* (2nd edn), Martin Robertson.

Cornford, J. (1972) 'The Political Theory of Scarcity' in Laslett, P., Runciman, W.G., and Skinner, Q. (eds) *Philosophy, Politics and Society* (Fourth Series), Blackwell.

Cranston, M. (1967) *Freedom: A New Analysis* (3rd edn), Longman.

Dahl, R.A. (1956) *A Preface to Democratic Theory*, University of Chicago Press.

Dahl, R.A. (1961) *Who Governs? Democracy and Power in an American City*, Yale University Press.

Dahl, R.A. (1966) *Political Oppositions in Western Democracies*, Yale University Press.

Dahl, R.A. (1970) *After the Revolution?*, Yale University Press.

Dahl, R.A. (1971) *Polyarchy: Participation and Opposition*, Yale University Press.

Dahl, R.A. (1982) *Dilemmas of Pluralist Democracy*, Yale University Press.

Dahl, R.A. (1985) *A Preface to Economic Democracy*, Polity Press.

Dahl, R.A. (1986) *Democracy, Liberty, Equality*, Norwegian University Press.

Dahl, R.A. and Tufte, R. (1973) *Size and Democracy*, Stanford University Press.

Daniels, N. (ed.) (1975) *Reading Rawls: Critical Studies of Rawls' Theory of Justice*, Blackwell.

Darwall, S. (1976) 'A Defense of the Kantian Interpretation', *Ethics*, vol. 86, no. 2 (January), pp. 164–70.

Daudt, H. (1961) *Floating Voters and the Floating Vote*, H.E. Stenfertkrose, N.V.

Davies, J.K. (1978) *Democracy and Classical Greece*, Fontana.

D'Entreves, A.P. (1967) *Natural Law*, Hutchinson.

Diamond, L., Ling, J. and Lipset, S.M. (1988) *Democracy in Developing Countries* (4 volumes), Adamantine Press.

Downs, A. (1957) *An Economic Theory of Democracy*, Harper & Row.

Duncan, G. (ed.) (1983) *Democratic Theory and Practice*, Cambridge University Press.

Duncan, G. and Lukes, S. (1963) 'The New Democracy', *Political Studies*, vol. 11, no. 2 (June), pp. 156–71. Reprinted as 'Democracy Restated', in Kariel (1970).

Duverger, M. (1959) *Political Parties* (2nd edn), Methuen and John Wiley.

Dworkin, R. (1978a) *Taking Rights Seriously* (2nd edn), Duckworth.

Dworkin, R. (1978b) 'Liberalism', in Hampshire, S. (ed.) *Public and Private Morality*, Cambridge University Press.

Elkin, S.L. (1982) 'Markets and Politics in Liberal Democracy', *Ethics*, vol. 92, no. 4 (July), pp. 720–32.

Elkin, S.L. (1985) 'Pluralism in Its Place: State and Regime in Liberal Democracy', in Benjamin and Elkin (1985).

Elster, J. (1985) *An Introduction to Karl Marx*, Cambridge University Press.

Elster, J. and Hylland, A. (1986) *The Foundations of Social Choice Theory*, Cambridge University Press.

Finley, M.I. (1973) *Democracy Ancient and Modern*, Rutgers University Press.

Finnis, J.M. (1980) *Natural Law and Natural Rights*, Oxford University Press.

Fralin, R. (1978) 'The Evolution of Rousseau's View of Representative Government', *Political Theory*, vol. 6, no. 4 (November), pp. 517–36.

Fralin, R. (1979) *Rousseau and Representation*, Columbia University Press.

Frankel, C. (1962) *The Democratic Prospect*, Harper & Row.

Friedman, M. (1962) *Capitalism and Freedom*, University of Chicago Press.

Frohock, F.M. and Sylvan, D.J. (1983) 'Liberty, Economics and Evidence', *Political Studies*, vol. 31, no. 4 (December), pp. 541–55.

Gallie, W.B. (1955) 'Essentially Contested Concepts', *Proceedings of the Aristotelian Society*, vol. 56, pp. 167–98.

Glass, S.T. (1966) *The Responsible Society*, Longman.

Gooch, G.P. (1954) *English Democratic Ideas in the Seventeenth Century*, Cambridge University Press.

Graham, K. (1986) *The Battle of Democracy*, Wheatsheaf Books.

Gray, J. (1983) *Mill on Liberty: A Defence*, Routledge & Kegan Paul.

Gray, J. (1986a) 'Marxian Freedom, Individual Liberty and the End of Alienation', in Paul *et al.* (1986).

Gray, J. (1986b) *Liberalism*, Open University Press.

Grimsley, R. (1983) *Jean-Jacques Rousseau*, Harvester.

Habermas, J. (1976) *Legitimation Crisis*, Heinemann.

Halevy, E. (1954) *The Growth of Philosophical Radicalism*, Faber.

Hall, J.C. (1973) *Rousseau: An Introduction to His Political Philosophy*, Cambridge University Press.

Hallowell, J.H. (1954) *The Moral Foundations of Democracy*, University of Chicago Press.

Harding, N. (1983) *Lenin's Political Thought* (paperback edition in one volume) Macmillan.

Hayek, F.A. (1960) *The Constitution of Liberty*, Routledge & Kegan Paul.

Hayek, F.A. (1976) *The Road to Serfdom*, Routledge & Kegan Paul.

Hayek, F.A. (1978) *New Studies in Philosophy, Politics, Economics and the History of Ideas*, Routledge & Kegan Paul.

Hayek, F.A. (1982) *Law, Legislation and Liberty*, vol. 3, Routledge & Kegan Paul.

Heilbroner, R.L. (1985) *The Nature and Logic of Capitalism*, Norton.

Held, D. (1987) *Models of Democracy*, Polity Press.

Held, D. and Pollitt, C. (eds) (1986) *New Forms of Democracy*, Sage.

Himmelweit, H.T., Humphries, P., Jaeger, M. and Katz, M. (1981) *How Voters Decide*, Academic Press.

Hinsley, F.H. (1986) *Sovereignty* (2nd edn), Cambridge University Press.

Höffe, O. (1984) 'Is Rawls' Theory of Justice Really Kantian?', *Ratio*, vol. 26, no. 2 (December), pp. 103–24.

Holden, B. (1974) *The Nature of Democracy*, Nelson and Barnes & Noble.

Holden, B. (1983) 'Liberal Democracy and the Social Determination of Ideas', in Pennock and Chapman (1983).

Howell, C. (1986) *Secular Faith and the Democratic Charter in Jacques Maritain's Political Philosophy*, unpublished Ph.D. thesis, University of Reading.

Humboldt, W. von (1969) *The Limits of State Action* (ed. J.W. Burrow), Cambridge University Press.

Jones, A.H.M. (1964) *Athenian Democracy*, Blackwell.

Jones, P. (1988) 'Intense Preferences, Strong Beliefs and Democratic Decision-Making', *Political Studies*, vol. 36, no. 1 (March), pp. 7–29.

Kainz, H.P. (1984) *Democracy East and West*, Macmillan.

Kamenka, K. and Tay, A.E-S. (eds) (1978) *Human Rights*, Edward Arnold.

Kant, I. (1964) *Groundwork of the Metaphysic of Morals* (trans. H.J. Paton), Harper & Row.

Kariel, H.S. (ed.) (1970) *Frontiers of Democratic Theory*, Random House.

Kase, F.J. (1968) *People's Democracy*, A.W. Sijthoff.

Kelso, A.W. (1978) *American Democratic Theory: Pluralism and Its Critics*, Greenwood Press.

Kendall, W. (1941) *John Locke and the Doctrine of Majority Rule*, University of Illinois Press.

Kendall, W. and Carey, G.W. (1968) 'The "Intensity" Problem and Democratic Theory', *American Political Science Review*, vol. 62, pp. 5–24. Reprinted in *Kendall Contra Mundum* (1971), Arlington House.

Key, V.O. (1966) *The Responsible Electorate*, Harvard University Press.

Koch, A. (1964) *The Philosophy of Thomas Jefferson*, Quadrangle.

Kolakowski, L. (1978) *Main Currents of Marxism*, vol. 3, Oxford University Press.

Kontos, A. (ed.) (1979) *Powers, Possessions, and Freedom: Essays in Honour of C.B. Macpherson*, University of Toronto Press.

Lazarsfeld, P.F., Berelson, B. and Gaudet, H. (1968) *The People's Choice* (3rd edn), Columbia University Press.

Leiserson, A. (1958) *Parties and Politics*, Knopf.

Lenin, V.I. (1960) 'State and Revolution', in *The Essential Left*, Allen & Unwin. (*State and Revolution* was originally published in 1917.)

Levin, M. (1983) 'Marxism and Democratic Theory', in Duncan (1983).

Levine, A. (1981) *Liberal Democracy: A Critique of its Theory*, Columbia University Press.

Lijphart, A. (1968) 'Typologies of Democratic Systems', *Comparative Politics*, vol. 1, pp. 17–35.

Lijphart, A. (1969) 'Consociational Democracy', *World Politics*, vol. 21, pp. 207–25. Reprinted in McRae (1974).

Lindblom, C.E. (1977) *Politics and Markets*, Basic Books.

Lindblom, C.E. (1982) 'The Market as Prison', *The Journal of Politics*, vol. 14, no. 2 (May), pp. 324–36.

Lindsay, A.D. (1935) *The Essentials of Democracy* (2nd edn), Oxford University Press.

Lindsay, A.D. (1943) *The Modern Democratic State*, Oxford University Press.

Lipset, S.M. (1962) 'Introduction', in Michels, R. *Political Parties: A Sociological Study of the Oligarchical Tendencies of Modern Democracies*, Collier Books.

Lively, J. (1975) *Democracy*, Blackwell.

Lively, J. and Rees, J. (eds) (1978) *Utilitarian Logic and Politics: James Mill's 'Essay on Government', Macaulay's Critique and the Ensuing Debate*, Oxford University Press (Clarendon Press).

Lomasky, L.E. (1987) *Rights Persons and the Moral Community*, Oxford University Press.

Lucas, J.R. (1976) *Democracy and Participation*, Penguin.

Lukes, S. (1973) *Individualism*, Blackwell.

Lukes, S. (1979) 'The Real and Ideal Worlds of Democracy', in Kontos (1979).

Maas, A. (1966) 'Foreword', in Key (1966).

MacCallum, G.C. (1972) 'Negative and Positive Freedom', in Laslett, P., Runciman, W.G. and Skinner, Q. (eds) *Philosophy, Politics and Society* (Fourth Series), Blackwell. Reprinted from *The Philosophical Review*, vol. 76 (1967), pp. 312–4.

McLean, I. (1982) *Dealing in Votes*, Martin Robertson.

McLean, I. (1986) 'Mechanisms for Democracy', in Held and Pollitt (1986).

McLean, I. (1987) *Public Choice*, Blackwell.

McLennan, G. (1984) 'Capitalist State or Democratic Polity? Recent Developments in Marxist and Pluralist Theory', in McLennan, G., Held, D. and Hall, S. (eds) *The Idea of the Modern State*, Open University Press.

Macpherson, C.B. (1962) *The Political Theory of Possessive Individualism*, Clarendon Press.

Macpherson, C.B. (1966) *The Real World of Democracy*, Oxford University Press (Clarendon Press).

Macpherson, C.B. (1977a) *The Life and Times of Liberal Democracy*, Oxford University Press.

Macpherson, C.B. (1977b) 'Do We Need a Theory of the State?', *European Journal of Sociology*, vol. 18, pp. 223–44.

McRae, K. (ed.) (1974) *Consociational Democracy: Political Accommodation in Segmented Societies*, McClelland & Stewart.

Madison, J. (1961) 'Federalist Paper 10', in *The Federalist Papers*, (first published 1787–8), Mentor.

Magee, B. (1979) *Men of Ideas*, Viking.

Mansbridge, J.J. (1980) *Beyond Adversary Democracy*, Basic Books.

Marcuse, H. (1968) *One-Dimensional Man*, Beacon Press.

Margolis, M. (1979) *Viable Democracy*, Penguin.

Maritain, J. (1945) *Christianity and Democracy*, Geoffrey Bles, The Centenary Press.

Marx, K. (1844) *Contribution to the Critique of Hegel's Philosophy of Right: Introduction*, in Bottomore (1963).

Marx, K. (1970) *The Civil War in France*, Foreign Languages Press.

Meisel, J.H. (1958) *The Myth of the Ruling Class: G. Mosca and the Elite*, University of Michigan Press.

Meisel, J.H. (ed.) (1965) *Pareto and Mosca*, Prentice Hall.

Miliband, R. (1969) *The State in Capitalist Society*, Weidenfeld & Nicolson.

Mill, J. (1955) *An Essay on Government* (ed. C.V. Shields), Bobbs-Merrill.

Mill, J.S. (1859) *Dissertations and Discussions*, Longman.

Mill, J.S. (1912) *Considerations on Representative Government*, in *Three Essays: On Liberty, Representative Government, The Subjection of Women*, Oxford University Press.

Mill, J.S. (1982) *On Liberty*, Penguin.

Miller, D. (1983) 'The Competitive Model of Democracy', in Duncan (1983).

Milne, R.S. and Mackenzie, H.C. (1958) *Marginal Seats 1955*, Hansard Society.

Mueller, D.C. (1979) *Public Choice*, Cambridge University Press.

Nehru, B.K. and Morris-Jones, W.H. (1980) *Western Democracy and the Third World*, Third World Foundation.

Nelson, W.N. (1980) *On Justifying Democracy*, Routledge & Kegan Paul.

Nie, N.H., Berba, S. and Petrocik, J.R. (1976) *The Changing American Voter*, Harvard University Press.

Niebuhr, R. and Sigmund, P.E. (1969) *The Democratic Experience: Past and Prospects*, Pall Mall.

Norman, R. (1987) *Free and Equal: A Philosophical Examination of Political Values*, Oxford University Press (Clarendon Press).

Nozick, R. (1974) *Anarchy, State and Utopia*, Blackwell.
Nursey-Bray, P. (1983) 'Consensus and Community: The Theory of African One-Party Democracy', in Duncan (1983).
Oppenheim, F. (1981) *Political Concepts: A Reconstruction*, Blackwell.
Padover, S.K. (ed.) (1946) *Thomas Jefferson on Democracy*, Mentor.
Paine, T. (1969) *Rights of Man* (first published 1791–2), Penguin Books.
Parry, G. (1969) *Political Elites*, Allen & Unwin.
Partridge, P.H. (1971) *Consent and Consensus*, Macmillan.
Pateman, C. (1970) *Participation and Democratic Theory*, Cambridge University Press.
Pateman, C. (1985) *The Problem of Political Obligation: A Critique of Liberal Theory*, Polity Press.
Paul, E.F. *et al.* (eds) (1986) *Marxism and Liberalism*, Blackwell.
Paul, J. (ed.) (1982) *Reading Nozick*, Blackwell.
Pennock, J.R. (1979) *Democratic Political Theory*, Princeton University Press.
Pennock, J.R. and Chapman, J.W. (eds) (1967) *Equality* (Nomos IX), Atherton Press.
Pennock, J.R. and Chapman, J.W. (eds) (1968) *Representation* (Nomos X), Atherton Press.
Pennock, J.R. and Chapman, J.W. (eds) (1981) *Human Rights* (Nomos XXIII), New York University Press.
Pennock, J.R. and Chapman, J.W. (eds) (1983) *Liberal Democracy* (Nomos XXV), New York University Press.
Pierson, C. (1986) *Marxist Theory and Democratic Politics*, Polity Press.
Pitkin, H.L. (1967) *The Concept of Representation*, University of California Press and Cambridge University Press.
Plamenatz, J.P. (1958) *The English Utilitarians* (2nd edn), Blackwell.
Plamenatz, J.P. (1973) *Democracy and Illusion*, Longman.
Pomper, G.M. (1975) *Voters Choice*, Dodd, Mead.
Poulantzas, N. (1980) *State, Power, Socialism*, Verso/NLB.
Pranger, R.J. (1968) *The Eclipse of Citizenship: Power and Participation in Contemporary Politics*, Holt, Rinehart & Winston.
Presthus, I.R. (1964) *Men at the Top: A Study in Community Power*, Oxford University Press.
Purcell, E.A., Jr. (1973) *The Crisis of Democratic Theory: Scientific Naturalism and the Problem of Value*, University of Kentucky Press.
Rae, D. (1981) *Equalities*, Harvard University Press.
Ranney, A. (1954) *The Doctrine of Responsible Party Government*, University of Illinois Press.
Ranney, A. and Kendall, W. (1956) *Democracy and the American Party System*, Harcourt, Brace & World.
Raphael, D.D. (ed.) (1967) *Political Theory and the Rights of Man*, Macmillan.
Rawls, J. (1972) *A Theory of Justice*, Oxford University Press.
Rawls, J. (1980) 'Kantian Constructivism in Moral Theory: The Dewey Lectures 1980', *The Journal of Philosophy*, vol. 77, pp. 515–72.
Rawls, J. (1985) 'Justice as Fairness: Political not Metaphysical', *Philosophy and Public Affairs*, vol. 14, pp. 223–51.
Rees, J. (1971) *Equality*, Pall Mall.

Reglar, S. and Young, G. (1983) 'Modern Communist Theory: Lenin and Mao Zedong', in Wintrop (1983).

Ricci, D.M. (1971) *Community Power and Democratic Theory*, Random House.

Riker, W.H. (1982) *Liberalism Against Populism*, W.H. Freeman.

Rose, R. (1974) *The Problem of Party Government*, Macmillan.

Rose, R. and McAllister, I. (1986) *Voters Begin to Choose*, Sage Publications.

Rosen, F. (1983) *Jeremy Bentham and Representative Democracy*, Oxford University Press (Clarendon Press).

Rousseau, J-J. (1968) *The Social Contract*, Penguin.

Runciman, W.G. (1969) *Social Science and Political Theory* (2nd edn), Cambridge University Press.

Ryan, A. (ed.) (1979) *The Idea of Freedom*, Oxford University Press.

Ryan, A. (1983) 'Mill and Rousseau: Utility and Rights', in Duncan (1983).

Ryan, A. (1986) Review of Heilbroner (1986) *Times Literary Supplement*, 16 May, p. 521.

Sabine, G.H. (1952) 'The Two Democratic Traditions', *Philosophical Review*, vol. 61, pp. 451–74.

Sandel, M.J. (1982) *Liberalism and the Limits of Justice*, Cambridge University Press.

Sartori, G. (1965) *Democratic Theory*, Praeger.

Sartori, G. (1987) *The Theory of Democracy Revisited* (2 vols), Chatham House. This is an updating of Sartori (1965).

Schlozman, K.L. (1986) *Organized Interests and American Democracy*, Harper & Row.

Schram, G.N. (1976) 'Reinhold Niebuhr and Contemporary Political Thought: A Review Article', *Interpretation*, vol. 6, no. 1 (Fall), pp. 65–77.

Schumpeter, J. (1976) *Capitalism, Socialism and Democracy*, Allen & Unwin.

Seliger, M. (1968) *The Liberal Politics of John Locke*, Allen & Unwin.

Shklar, J. (1969) *Men and Citizens: A Study of Rousseau's Social Theory*, Cambridge University Press.

Sigmund, P.E. (1971) *Natural Law in Political Thought*, University Press of America.

Smart, J.J.C. and Williams, B. (1973) *Utilitarianism: For and Against*, Cambridge University Press.

Spearman, D. (1957) *Democracy in England*, Rockliff.

Spitz, D. (1965) *Patterns of Anti-Democratic Thought*, Free Press.

Spitz, E. (1984) *Majority Rule*, Chatham House.

Spragens, T.A., Jr. (1973) *The Dilemma of Contemporary Political Theory: Toward a Postbehavioral Science of Politics*, Dunellan.

Stankiewicz, W.J. (ed.) (1969) *In Defence of Sovereignty*, Oxford University Press.

Steintrager, J. (1977) *Bentham*, Cornell University Press.

Svacek, V. (1976) 'The Elusive Marxism of C.B. Macpherson', *Canadian Journal of Political Science*, vol. 9, no. 3 (September), pp. 415–22.

Talmon, J.L. (1952) *The Origins of Totalitarian Democracy*, Secker & Warburg.

Tawney, R.H. (1964) *Equality* (5th edn), Allen & Unwin.

Ten, C.L. (1980) *Mill on Liberty*, Oxford University Press.

Thakur, T. (1982) 'Liberalism, Democracy and Development: Philosophical

Dilemmas in Third World Politics', *Political Studies*, vol. 30, no. 3 (September), pp. 333–49.

Thomas, D.O. (1959) 'Richard Price and Edmund Burke: The Duty to Participate in Government', *Philosophy*, vol. 30, pp. 308–22.

Thompson, D.F. (1970) *The Democratic Citizen*, Cambridge University Press.

Thompson, D.F. (1976) *John Stuart Mill and Representative Government*, Princeton University Press.

Thompson, D.F. (1983) 'Bureaucracy and Democracy', in Duncan (1983).

Thorson, T.L. (1962) *The Logic of Democracy*, Holt, Rinehart & Winston.

Tocqueville, A. de (1968) *Democracy in America* (2 vols), Fontana.

Tuck, R. (1979) *Natural Rights Theories: Their Origin and Development*, Cambridge University Press.

Tucker, D.F.B. (1980) *Marxism and Individualism*, Blackwell.

Turner, B.S. (1986) *Citizenship and Capitalism: The Debate over Reformism*, Allen & Unwin.

Usher, D. (1981) *The Economic Prerequisite to Democracy*, Blackwell.

Ware, A. (1979) *The Logic of Party Democracy*, Macmillan.

Whelan, F.G. (1983) 'Prologue: Democratic Theory and The Boundary Problem', in Pennock and Chapman (1983).

Williams, B. (1962) 'The Idea of Equality', in Laslett, P. and Runciman, W.G. (eds) *Philosophy, Politics and Society* (Second Series).

Williams, H.L. (1983) *Kant's Political Philosophy*, Blackwell.

Wintrop, N. (ed.) (1983) *Liberal Democratic Theory and Its Critics*, Croom Helm.

Wolff, R.P. (1977) *Understanding Rawls: A Reconstruction and Critique of 'A Theory of Justice'*, Princeton University Press.

Wollheim, R. (1958) 'Democracy', *Journal of the History of Ideas*, vol. 19 (April), pp. 225–42.

Author Index

Rousseau, J-J., 26, 27–8, 42, 49, 58,
    61, 73, 76, 77–8, 79, 87, 89, 90,
    96, 107, 109–10, 112, 125, 166,
    183
Runciman, W.G., 41
Ryan, A., 43, 110, 163

Sabine, G.H., 76, 78, 80
Sandel, M.J., 174
Sartori, G., 78, 102, 168
Schram, G.N., 173
Schumpeter, J., 8, 9, 162, 188
Sigmund, P.E., 13, 185
Smith, A., 70
Spitz, E., 40, 42, 181
Spragens, T.A., Jr, 179
Svacek, V., 124

Talmon, J.L., 26, 79, 80

Tawney, R.H., 15
Ten, C.L., 13, 43
Thakur, T., 185
Thompson, D.F., 42, 81, 112, 117,
    197
Thorson, T.L., 179, 186
Tocqueville, A. de, 16, 25, 29, 34,
    45
Tuck, R., 13
Tucker, D.F.B., 142, 144, 145, 174
Turner, B.S., 151

Usher, D., 162

Williams, B., 15
Williams, H.L., 174
Wolff, R.P., 174
Wollheim, R., 178, 179–80

Subject Index